POTENTIAL EXPORTS AND NONTARIFF BARRIERS TO TRADE

INDIA NATIONAL STUDY

JANUARY 2020

Contents

Tables, Figures, and Boxes   v

Acknowledgments   vii

Abbreviations   viii

Executive Summary   x

Chapter 1 Introduction   **1**
   1.1   Background   1
   1.2   Review of Literature   2
   1.3   Objectives of the Study   4
   1.4   Methodology   4
   1.5   Overview of the Diagnostic Study   6

Chapter 2 Pattern of Trade with Other SASEC Countries   **7**
   2.1.   Trade with Bangladesh   10
   2.2.   Trade with Bhutan   11
   2.3.   Trade with Maldives   11
   2.4.   Trade with Nepal   12
   2.5.   Trade with Sri Lanka   12

Chapter 3 Potential Exports Subject to Nontariff Barriers   **15**
   3.1.   Potential Exports from India to Bangladesh   15
   3.2.   Potential Exports from India to Bhutan   16
   3.3   Potential Exports from India to Maldives   18
   3.4.   Potential Exports from India to Nepal   18
   3.5.   Potential Exports from India to Sri Lanka   19
   3.6.   Potential Products and South Asia Free Trade Agreement's
       Sensitive List   21

Chapter 4 Overview of Sanitary and Phytosanitary Measures
and Technical Barriers to Trade in India   **22**
   4.1.   The Sanitary and Phytosanitary Environment   22
   4.2.   The Technical Barriers to Trade Environment   29
   4.3.   Key Issues in Domestic Legislative and Regulatory Frameworks
       for Sanitary and Phytosanitary Measures and Technical Barriers
       to Trade   33

4.4. Gaps Comparing Current National Sanitary and Phytosanitary
and Technical Barriers to Trade Legislation, Local Practices,
and International Best Practices   36
4.5   India's Evolving Position on Sanitary and Phytosanitary
and Technical Barriers to Trade Measures   40

**Chapter 5 Standards, Regulations, and Procedural Obstacles
That Impede Trade   44**
5.1. Impediments Exporting to Bangladesh   44
5.2. Impediments Exporting to Bhutan   49
5.3. Impediments Exporting to Maldives   51
5.4. Impediments Exporting to Nepal   52
5.5   Impediments Exporting to Sri Lanka   56

Chapter 6 Prioritized Recommendations for Action   62
6.1   Recommendations for National Action: India   62
6.2   Recommendations for Regional Action: SASEC Countries   65

Chapter 7 Conclusion   69

Appendixes
1   Top 10 Export Products from India to Other SASEC Countries
in 2015 at the 6-Digit HS Code Level   70
2   Identification of Potential Export Items   75
3   Availability of Food Labs and Physical Accessibility
in India, 2015–2016   96
4   Existing Sanitary and Phytosanitary and Technical Barriers
to Trade Measures by Other SASEC Countries
on Identified India Potential Exports   97
5   Stakeholders Interviewed for Sanitary and Phytosanitary
and Technical Barriers to Trade India Diagnostic Study   156

References   158

Tables, Figures, and Boxes

Tables

1	Number of Potential Exports of India to Bangladesh	15
2	Number of Potential Exports of India to Maldives	18
3	Number of Potential Exports of India to Nepal	19
4	Number of Potential Exports of India to Sri Lanka	19
5	Class I Preservatives of SASEC Countries	37
6	Class II Preservatives of SASEC Countries	38
7	Sanitary and Phytosanitary and Technical Barriers to Trade Measures Applied by Bangladesh on India's Potential Exports	45
8	Sanitary and Phytosanitary and Technical Barriers to Trade Measures Applied by Bhutan on India's Potential Exports	50
9	Sanitary and Phytosanitary Regulations and their Implementing Authorities in Maldives	52
10	Food Safety Implementing Authorities in Maldives	53
11	Sanitary and Phytosanitary and Technical Barriers to Trade Measures Applied by Nepal on India's Potential Exports	54
12	Sanitary and Phytosanitary and Technical Barriers to Trade Measures Applied by Sri Lanka on India's Potential Exports	57
A1.1	Top 10 Exports to Bangladesh in 2015	70
A1.2	Top 10 Exports to Bhutan in 2015	71
A1.3	Top 10 Exports to Maldives in 2015	72
A1.4	Top 10 Exports to Nepal in 2015	73
A1.5	Top 10 Exports to Sri Lanka in 2015	74
A2.1	Potential Export Products of India in Bangladesh Market at Harmonized System 6-Digit Level of Product Classification	75
A2.2	Potential Export Products of India in Bhutan Market at Harmonized System 6-Digit Level of Product Classification	81
A2.3	Potential Export Products of India in Maldives Market at Harmonized System 6-Digit Level of Product Classification	83
A2.4	Potential Export Products of India in Nepal Market at Harmonized System 6-Digit Level of Product Classification	89
A2.5	Potential Export Products of India in Sri Lanka Market at Harmonized System 6-Digit Level of Product Classification	92
A4.1	Sanitary and Phytosanitary and Technical Barriers to Trade Measures by Bangladesh on India's Potential Products	97
A4.2	Sanitary and Phytosanitary and Technical Barriers to Trade Measures by Bhutan on India's Potential Products	115

A4.3 Sanitary and Phytosanitary and Technical Barriers to Trade Measures
      by Nepal on India's Potential Products   119
A4.4 Sanitary and Phytosanitary and Technical Barriers to Trade Measures
      by Sri Lanka on India's Potential Products   125

Figures
1   Filters Applied to Identify Potential Export Products   6
2   India's Total Exports to SASEC and the World   8
3   India's Total Imports from SASEC and the World   8
4   India's Exports to SASEC Countries and the World   9
5   India's Imports from SASEC Countries and the World   9
6   India's Top Exports to Bangladesh   10
7   India's Top Exports to Bhutan   11
8   India's Top Exports to Maldives   12
9   India's Top Exports to Nepal
10   India's Top Exports to Sri Lanka   14
11   India's Potential Exports to Bangladesh   16
12   India's Potential Exports to Bhutan   17
13   India's Potential Exports to Maldives   17
14   India's Potential Exports to Nepal   20
15   India's Potential Exports to Sri Lanka   20
16   Potential Export Items in South Asia Free Trade Agreement's Sensitive List 21
17   Legal and Institutional Framework of Sanitary and Phytosanitary Regime
     in India   24
18   Port-Wise Distribution of Plant Quarantine Stations   28
19   Technical Barriers to Trade Regime in India   30
20   State-Wise Export Inspection Agencies   33

Boxes
1   Food Safety and Standards Authority of India Launches One-Nation,
     One-Food Safety Law   25
2   Key Elements of India's National Strategy for Standardization   43
3   Infrastructure   47

Acknowledgments

Surendar Singh, national consultant for India under the Asian Development Bank's (ADB) South Asia Subregional Economic Cooperation trade facilitation program, prepared this report, supported by the Department of Commerce, Ministry of Commerce and Industry of India. The report was designed jointly by the Trade and Investment Division of the United Nations Economic and Social Commission for Asia and the Pacific and ADB.

The project team gratefully acknowledges the strong support of Bhupinder Singh Bhalla, Additional Secretary, Department of Commerce; and Anurag Sharma, Deputy Secretary, Department of Commerce for their guidance and coordination of the many agencies and entities involved in preparing the diagnostic study. The guidance and contributions of the following are sincerely acknowledged: Anil Kumar, Advisor, Food Safety and Standards Authority of India; Shri Raj Kumar, Joint Director (Imports), Food Safety and Standards Authority of India; Pramod Siwach, Assistant Director, Export Inspection Council; Virendra Singh, Scientist, Bureau of Indian Standards; Saswati Bose, Deputy General Manager, Agricultural and Processed Food Products Export Development Authority; Pratik Navale, Research Associate, Federation of Indian Export Organisations; Nisha Taneja, Professor, Indian Council for Research on International Economic Relations; Shikhar Biswas, Deputy General Manager, Mahindra & Mahindra Ltd., Kandival-Mumbai; Nilanjan Banik, Professor, Benton University; Murali Kallummal, Professor, Centre for World Trade Organization Studies; and Somi Hazari, Director, Sudvdha Pvt Ltd. Satish K. Reddy, ADB consultant, provided valuable assistance in preparing the report and coordinating with the various offices and agencies of the Government of India.

In particular, the project team appreciates the support given by colleagues at CUTS International, including Bipul Chatterjee, Executive Director; Rahul Arora, Policy Analyst; and Sudip Kumar Paul, Research Associate for providing technical assistance in preparing this report.

Rose McKenzie, Senior Regional Cooperation Specialist, ADB, oversaw the preparation of the study, and Selim Raihan, international consultant of ADB, provided technical guidance.

Abbreviations

ADB	Asian Development Bank
AGMARK	Agricultural Marketing Standards
APEDA	Agricultural and Processed Food Products Export Development Authority
BAFRA	Bhutan Agricultural Food Regulations Act
BIS	Bureau of Indian Standards
BSTI	Bangladesh Standards and Testing Institute
CHA	customs house agent
EIC	Export Inspection Council
EU	European Union
FSSAI	Food Safety and Standards Authority of India
GAP	Good Agricultural Practices
GHP	Good Hygienic Practices
GMO	genetically modified organism
HACCP	Hazard Analysis Critical Controls Point
HS	Harmonized Commodity Description and Coding System
ICP	integrated check post
IEC	International Electrotechnical Commission
ISEC	Institute of Social and Economic Change
ISO	International Organization for Standardization
IT	information technology
MAcMap	Market Access Map (database)
MCMS	Mandatory Certification Marks Scheme
MOU	memorandum of understanding
MPEDA	Marine Products Export Development Authority
MRA	mutual recognition agreement
MSMEs	micro, small, and medium-sized enterprises
NABCB	National Accreditation Board for Certification Bodies
NABL	National Accreditation Board for Testing and Calibration Laboratories
NSW	national single window
NTB	nontariff barrier
NTM	nontariff measure
SAFTA	South Asia Free Trade Agreement
SARSO	South Asia Regional Standards Organization
SASEC	South Asia Subregional Economic Cooperation
SLSI	Sri Lanka Standards Institution
SPS	sanitary and phytosanitary
TBT	technical barrier to trade
UN	United Nations

UNCTAD	United Nations Conference on Trade and Development
US	United States
UT	union territory
WITS	World Integrated Trade Solutions
WTO	World Trade Organization
ZED	zero defect and zero effect

Executive Summary

South Asia is widely recognized as one of the least economically integrated regions in the world. Although member countries of the South Asia Subregional Economic Cooperation (SASEC) Program—Bangladesh, Bhutan, India, Maldives, Myanmar, Nepal, and Sri Lanka—have for decades, through various bilateral and regional trading arrangements, enabled a reduction in *visible* trade barriers, the *invisible* trade barriers persist in the region and negatively affect intraregional trade. Common problems and challenges in the region relate to trade facilitation and include excessive documentation, inadequate implementation of modern customs procedures, limited application of information and communication technology, lack of transparency in import–export requirements, lack of compliance with technical standards, lack of adequate border facilities, and lack of through transport arrangements, among others. South Asian legal and regulatory frameworks relevant for trade facilitation likewise require reform and modernization.

Within South Asia, India is a relatively advanced economy and plays a significant role in shaping the economic and trade environment. It has engaged in various bilateral and regional trading arrangements with most of the other SASEC member countries, which have served to bring down tariff barriers—but nontariff barriers remain. These nontariff barriers include administrative fees, labeling requirements, antidumping duties, import restrictions, countervailing measures, sanitary and phytosanitary (SPS) and technical barriers to trade (TBT) regulations, surcharges, and other specific conditions related to trade. With regard to standards, development across South Asia remains relatively immature and there are considerable asymmetries in testing procedures across South Asian countries.

The overall objective of the current national diagnostic study is to identify potential export products from India that could be traded more within South Asia, yet are subject to SPS and TBT measures applied by importing SASEC countries. It is one of six national diagnostic studies prepared for Bangladesh, Bhutan, India, Maldives, Nepal, and Sri Lanka, and will be used as an input to a SASEC regional diagnostic study on SPS and TBT measures and barriers.

With due consideration of the divergent standards of South Asian countries, the present study is an attempt to identify only those barriers to trade associated with legitimate SPS and TBT measures imposed by the importing SASEC countries on India's exported goods. India's exports to SASEC countries are highly concentrated in a few categories of products and there is much untapped potential for improvement. Additionally, India's exports to SASEC countries constitute some common products which underpin the potential fostering of regional value chains in the SASEC region. High trade complementarity in some sectors can create good opportunities to develop regional production networks which will be beneficial for all countries of the SASEC region.

The study summarizes patterns of trade between India and other SASEC countries during the period 2001–2015 and identifies India's top 10 exports to and imports from both the SASEC countries and globally for the same period, categorizing export and import products under the United Nations Harmonized Commodity Description and Coding System. Products for potential export to the other SASEC countries are also identified and compared against the South Asia Free Trade Agreement sensitive list. Data are sourced from the United Nations Comtrade International Trade Statistics database, and others, and draws directly on the findings of a questionnaire survey conducted with India's exporters to SASEC countries.

Existing legal structures and institutional frameworks related to the implementation of SPS and TBT measures in India are examined, and gaps in domestic legislation and institutional structures noted. India has already undertaken several initiatives to address these gaps, such as (i) developing a comprehensive national standardization strategy, (ii) setting up a standards portal, and (iii) developing the Ayush Mark scheme and zero defect zero effect (ZED) certification scheme. Such initiatives demonstrate India's evolving stance on SPS and TBT measures in the current global trading environment.

Findings indicate that within other SASEC countries, there are significant gaps in the institutional and regulatory architecture, which often increase the potential risk of SPS and TBT measures being applied and hampering cross-border trade. One of the main issues observed in the SASEC region is a tendency for multiple regulating agencies to produce many unwanted regulations and this lack of coordination and consistency can lead to confusion, duplication, and trade-restricting measures. The study also identified gaps in infrastructure facilities necessary to implement SPS and TBT measures. It includes a count of testing laboratories in India and other SASEC countries, and reveals a significant infrastructure deficit in the SASEC region which affects the efficiency of export and import operations.

While analyzing impediments faced by the potential Indian products for export to SASEC countries identified earlier in the study, several trade-restricting measures are identified:

(i)   Many agencies, institutions, and other bodies are involved in setting standards which can result in a lack of harmonized compliance procedures at the domestic level.

(ii)   Surveys conducted with exporters reveal that large exporters that engage agents and draw on business connections are able to meet the required standards of an importer country. Yet the same required standards when applied to smaller exporters without the advantage of agents are costly and demanding and, ultimately, negatively affect competitiveness.

(iii)   Labeling and language-restrictive requirements can impose additional burden to trade, resulting in higher costs and transaction time.

(iv)   In addition to SPS and TBT-related measures, many other types of nontariff measures become barriers to international trade and transactions, and sometimes lead to full trade diversion. For example, such measures can often include the physical inspection of goods, and often disproportionately affect smaller exporters.

Based on the diagnostic study's identification of potential export products from India to other SASEC countries, and its analysis of existing laws, policies, and regulations related to SPS and TBT measures of SASEC countries which hinder these potential exports, a series of recommendations is proposed to help resolve the application of SPS and TBT trade-restrictive measures. Recommendations are directed both for domestic areas of reforms, such as overlapping SPS and TBT laws and regulations, absence of testing infrastructure facilities, and lack of domestic regulations, and for action at a regional level, through appropriate regional platforms.

Chapter 1
Introduction

1.1   Background

India has deep-rooted cultural, ethnic, historical, linguistic, and social linkages with the member countries of the South Asia Subregional Economic Cooperation (SASEC) Program,[1] which significantly affect the economic and trade relationship between India and SASEC countries. In the SASEC region, India enjoys a distinct place, occupying approximately 75% of the region's geographic landscape and sharing land borders with most of the member countries—features that help facilitate trade.

India's trade relations continue to thrive with the member countries of SASEC countries through a series of bilateral and regional agreements. India has bilateral trade and transit agreements with Bangladesh, Bhutan, and Nepal, and a free trade agreement with Sri Lanka, which have helped India expand its economic and trade ties with SASEC countries. At a regional level, India has undertaken bold initiatives to promote intraregional trade and investment through the South Asia Preferential Trade Agreement in 1991, followed by the South Asia Free Trade Agreement (SAFTA) in 2004. However, such efforts have largely not been successful due to, among others, the agreement's shallow trade and investment provisions, the use of nontariff barriers (NTBs), suboptimal regional connectivity, and barriers at the border and beyond the border.

India's trade integration with other SASEC member countries is affected by many factors, including high tariff barriers, NTBs, ineffective trade facilitation, and suboptimal institutional coordination. Among these, sanitary and phytosanitary (SPS) measures and technical barriers to trade (TBT) are recognized as two main barriers. One of the most commonly cited reasons behind the prevalence of SPS and TBT-related impediments in SASEC countries is divergent regulatory frameworks and the absence of adequate trade-related infrastructure. India, despite being a relatively advanced economy in the SASEC region in terms of SPS and TBT regulations, still faces challenges in exporting products to SASEC countries.

Given this scenario, the present diagnostic study focuses on identifying (i) the issues related to SPS and TBT measures in SASEC countries; (ii) potential products which India could export to other SASEC countries, but which are subject to SPS or TBT measures; and

---

[1] The SASEC program brings together Bangladesh, Bhutan, India, Maldives, Myanmar, Nepal, and Sri Lanka in a project-based partnership that aims to promote regional prosperity, improve economic opportunities, and build a better quality of life for the people of the subregion. SASEC countries share a common vision of boosting intraregional trade and cooperation in South Asia, while also developing connectivity and trade with Southeast Asia through Myanmar, to the People's Republic of China (PRC), and the global market. www.sasec.asia.

(iii) SPS and TBT-related infrastructure-related impediments and their potential impact on India's exports to other SASEC countries.

1.2 Review of Literature

Most countries use SPS and TBT measures as legitimate policy objectives to regulate cross-border trade to achieve health, environmental, safety, and other socioeconomic objectives. However, it is recognized that SPS and TBT measures are sometimes used as disguised policy instruments to restrict trade and, hence, are commonly known as NTBs. Globally, NTBs exist in different forms, and one of the most commonly used NTBs is the prohibition and/or restriction of imports through import permits.[2]

A large body of literature shows that nontariff measures (NTMs) act as major barriers and inhibit the growth of intraregional trade in the South Asian region.[3] They are prevalent in different forms, such as para tariff, administrative fees, labeling requirements, antidumping duties, import restrictions, countervailing measures, SPS and TBT regulations, surcharges, and other specific conditions. One key issue is that the development of standards in the South Asian region is still not mature and huge asymmetries in the development of standards and testing procedures exist across the South Asian countries.[4] For instance, India has already formulated relatively higher standards and other South Asian countries can face severe obstacles in complying with these standards. Such differences act as a disguised barrier for the exporters of other South Asian countries (footnote 3).

An Asian Development Bank (ADB) study reveals that South Asian countries have long been imposing several kinds of NTBs on imports, with a significant share of specific NTBs (86.3%) related to SPS and TBT measures.[5] The recent findings of De (2016) support the findings of the ADB study and show how SPS and TBT measures dominate in cross-border trade between India, Bangladesh, and Nepal. In Nepal, labeling requirements were found to be a major barrier, while in India and Bangladesh, marking requirements and inspection requirements were the key NTBs barriers affecting trade flow.[6]

Maldives imposes non-automatic licensing, quotas, prohibitions due to human health, safety and security, environmental concerns, and religious reasons as quality control measures (footnote 1). There are specific requirements of SPS certificates for the import of live animals and live plants. Divergent labeling standards are also major barriers for India's exporters in the Maldives market. Similarly, Sri Lanka also imposes NTBs, including licensing, and requires prior authorization for import of genetically modified food.

It is important to note that the nature and underlying motives of imposing NTBs are different due to the divergent regulatory and institutional mechanisms in each country

---

[2] Weerahewa (2009).
[3] Raihan (2012).
[4] Nanda (2012).
[5] Asian Development Bank (2008).
[6] De (2016).

of South Asia. For example, Bangladesh uses mandatory requirements of non-automatic licensing and prohibitions as quality control measures on imported goods. To import products classified under the restricted category, the importer has to obtain a letter of credit authorization form, and this process is cumbersome. Other types of NTBs in Bangladesh include technical measures, such as standards and certification for processed food items, and labeling and packaging requirements (footnote 1).

Trade in agricultural products in South Asia faces manifold challenges in standards, testing, certification procedures, and complicated clearance procedures. In India, there are strict biosecurity and SPS requirements. Imports of agricultural products, such as livestock and food products, require SPS certificates and an import permit. Obtaining such certification is time-consuming and laden with regulatory complexities (footnote 2).

An examination of country-specific NTBs in India and Nepal finds a diverse range of barriers in each country that restrict cross-border trade.[7] Nepalese export of agricultural products to India requires testing and certification at land custom stations. It was noted that Indian testing laboratories are located in distant locations, which increases the challenge to obtain testing certificates for clearance of consignments. In addition, specific products are subject to tariff quota limits, including imports of vegetable fats, acrylic yarn, copper products, and zinc oxide. Nepal's exporters in India also face barriers such as transit fees, special additional duties, and state-specific taxes. Exports from India to Nepal face obstacles and restricted market access, the majority of which occur at the border, such as port hassles and delays, congestion, and unavailability of railway wagons.

A study by the Institute of Social Economic Change reveals that India's exports to Sri Lanka face obstacles in obtaining an objective certificate from food laboratories.[8] The process for obtaining the certificate is complicated and time-consuming. For instance, in the export of mango pulp to Sri Lanka, India's exporters are required to obtain a Health Certificate from Sri Lanka's Ministry of Health and conduct routine analysis on the export product. Such avoidable barriers routinely affect the costs of trade across South Asia (footnote 7). Sri Lanka's exports to India face similar avoidable hurdles with Indian officials demanding multiple samples from the same product and batch due to different packaging sizes of the goods. The cost associated with certification is very high and can be set arbitrarily: unnecessary procedures add costs to the products, increase the price of imports, and render them less competitive.

A lack of harmonized labeling requirements is recognized as a key concern in South Asia. For example, the Food Safety and Standards Authority of India (FSSAI) prefers stickers over labels on imported food products from other countries, which often creates the need to relabel entire consignments.[9] The complexity and rigidity involved in India's labeling regulations significantly undermine the competitiveness of South Asian products exported to India. Relabeling often incurs expenses for repackaging, warehousing, and making the India-specific labels. Such requirements can be onerous and expensive for

---

[7]   Ojha (2013).
[8]   Institute for Social and Economic Change (2015).
[9]   Prasai (2015).

small importers who must bear the extra costs resulting from the complex regulations of FSSAI (footnote 8).

1.3   Objectives of the Study

The main objectives of this diagnostic study include:

(i)   identification of specific products that have potential for export from India to other SASEC countries where India is not able to export, or exports in less quantity due to SPS and TBT measures imposed by the importing SASEC countries;

(ii)   identification of current SPS and TBT infrastructure constraints in India and recommendations for necessary future investments; and

(iii)   identification of priority areas for capacity building in India, particularly in the area of standards and regulations.

1.4   Methodology

The diagnostic study draws on both primary and secondary data. The primary data analysis is based on stakeholder consultations and key informant interviews, which were conducted to develop an understanding of ground-level realities with exporters, importers, clearing agents, and government officials sharing their experiences while dealing with testing and standards-related institutions in the region. The study used structured questionnaires to record the responses of various stakeholders.

The study also uses trade data for 5 years (2011–2015) at a 6-digit level of product classification, to calculate potential exports of India to other SASEC countries. The main source of data is United Nations (UN) Commodity Trade Statistics (Comtrade),[10] downloaded using the world integrated solutions interface. To prepare the list of potential products, data on the following variables were used:

(i)   value and quantity of exports of India to the world,

(ii)   value and quantity of imports of other SASEC countries from the world (the study uses mirror data if reported data are unavailable), and

(iii)   value of India's exports to other SASEC countries.

Applying the preceding variables to the data, India's potential export products in the markets of five SASEC countries were identified by following the two-step procedure described below:

---

[10]   UN Comtrade. *World Integrated Trade Solutions.* 2016.

Step 1: Construction of Relevant Data

Construct the following average data series from raw data on exports and imports, based on the world integrated solutions interface methodology:

(i)   average exports of India to the world,
(ii)   average unit value of exports of India,
(iii)   average imports of other SASEC countries from India,
(iv)   average imports of other SASEC countries from the world,
(v)   average unit value of imports of other SASEC countries,
(vi)   average import share of other SASEC countries, and
(vii)   average export share of India.

The term "average" refers to the time average of product-wise data on exports and imports. The average unit value of exports and imports is calculated using 5 years' data on unit value of exports and imports of exporter (India) and importer (other SASEC country). For each year, the unit value is calculated by using the following formula:

$$\text{Unit value of export or import} = \frac{\text{Value of export or import}}{\text{Quantity of export or import}}$$

Further, the average value of export share and import share is calculated by taking the time average of 5 years' data on export and import shares. For each year, the export and import share is calculated by using the following formulas:

$$\text{Product-wise export share} = \frac{\text{Export value of India to other SASEC countries in a particular product}}{\text{Total exports of India in that particular product}}$$

$$\text{Product-wise import share} = \frac{\text{Import value of other SASEC countries from India in a particular product}}{\text{Total global import of other SASEC countries from world in that particular product}}$$

Step 2: Selection of Potential Export Products

The study consistently applied the following filters and rules in identifying potential export products of India to other SASEC countries:

Figure 1: Filters Applied to Identify Potential Export Products

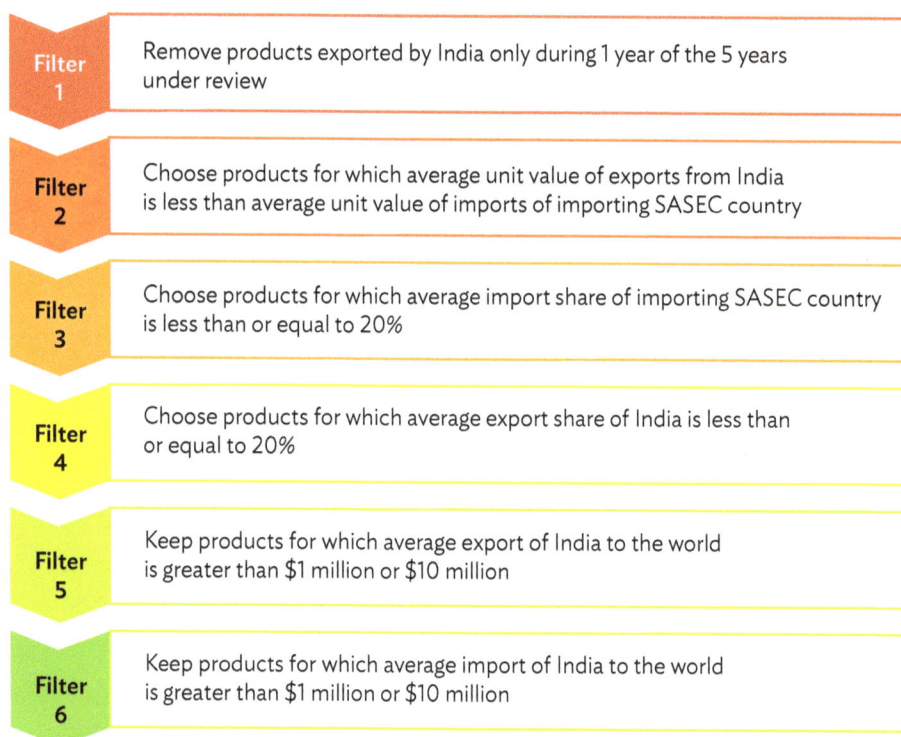

Filter	Description
Filter 1	Remove products exported by India only during 1 year of the 5 years under review
Filter 2	Choose products for which average unit value of exports from India is less than average unit value of imports of importing SASEC country
Filter 3	Choose products for which average import share of importing SASEC country is less than or equal to 20%
Filter 4	Choose products for which average export share of India is less than or equal to 20%
Filter 5	Keep products for which average export of India to the world is greater than $1 million or $10 million
Filter 6	Keep products for which average import of India to the world is greater than $1 million or $10 million

SASEC = South Asia Subregional Economic Cooperation.
Source: Asian Development Bank.

1.5 Overview of the Diagnostic Study

The diagnostic study is divided into seven chapters. Chapter 1 includes a review of available literature on nontariff measures (NTMs) applied by other SASEC countries to India's exports, and explains the methodology used in the analysis. Chapter 2 examines the pattern of India's trade with other SASEC countries and provides a comprehensive discussion on the top 10 exports of India to other SASEC countries in 2015. The potential exports of India are detailed in Chapter 3 at the HS 6-digit level of product classification on the basis of the last 5 years' import and export data. Chapter 4 provides an overview of SPS and TBT norms in India; including their legal structure, institutional framework, and infrastructure facilities. It also explains the gaps in current SPS and TBT rules and regulations in India through comparison with the norms of international best practices. In Chapter 5, SPS and TBT-related impediments to potential exports of India to other SASEC countries are presented. Prioritized recommendations for necessary future actions to address the issues presented in the diagnostic study are laid out in Chapter 6, and Chapter 7 concludes the report.

Chapter 2
Pattern of Trade
with Other SASEC Countries

The economic and trade relationship between India and the other SASEC countries is shaped by historical, cultural, linguistic, and geographical proximity. These factors have been natural facilitators of trade growth between India and the SASEC region even during times of political difference and border-related dispute. In terms of value, India's exports to SASEC countries have increased remarkably during 2001-2015: in 2001, India's total exports to the SASEC region totaled $1.9 billion which increased to $14.7 billion in 2015 (Figure 2). On the other hand, India's global exports were $43.9 billion in 2001 and reached to $264.4 billion in 2015.

It is noteworthy that India's global exports grew rapidly during 2001-2011 but declined subsequently. One of the key reasons for this sharp deceleration was the global trade slowdown, which led to the fall of global aggregate demand, particularly in export markets such as the United States (US) and the European Union. However, India's total exports to the SASEC region grew at a relatively modest pace during this period, which indicates deepening trade ties with the SASEC region.

India's imports from the SASEC region and the world increased significantly during 2001–2015. In terms of value, India's imports from SASEC countries were $0.5 billion in 2001 and increased to $2.2 billion in 2015. At the same time, India's imports from the world stood at $50.7 billion in 2001 and had increased to $390.7 billion by 2015 (Figure 3). However, it is worth noting that India's imports from the world experienced a downward trend beginning in 2011 while its imports from SASEC countries increased marginally.

Figure 4 demonstrates that India's exports to SASEC countries increased during 2001–2015. In 2001, India's export share to SASEC countries was 4.35%, increasing to 5.58% in 2015. However, in terms of growth, there are significant differences across countries: India's exports to two landlocked least-developed countries, Bhutan and Nepal, increased at a much faster pace than to the other SASEC countries—Bangladesh, Maldives, and Sri Lanka.

India's imports from SASEC countries also expanded during 2001-2015 despite domestic, political, and border-related friction. Imports continue to increase from SASEC countries and have helped expand their economic and trade relationships with India (Figure 5). In 2001, India's share of imports from SASEC countries was 0.99%, which reduced to 0.56% in 2015.

In the overall export and import scenario, India's share of exports to SASEC increased during 2001-2015, yet its import share decreased. This means that India was able to

Figure 2: India's Total Exports to SASEC and the World
($ billion)

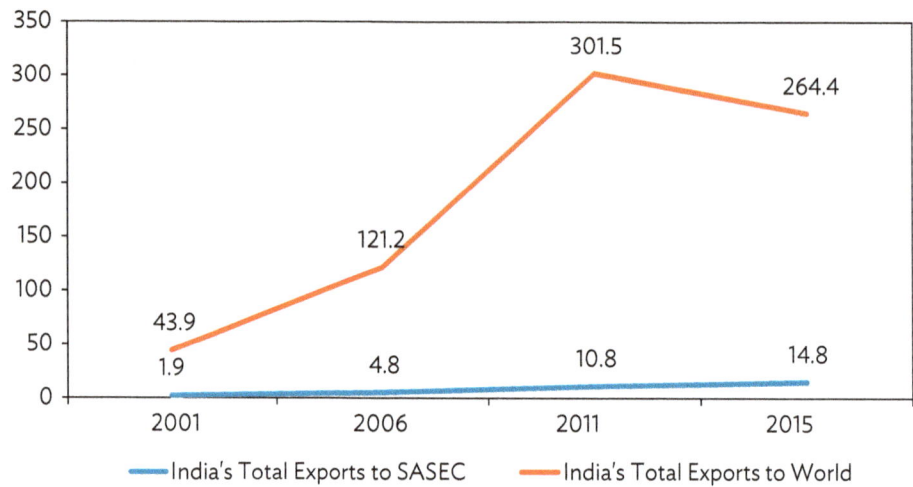

SASEC = South Asia Subregional Economic Cooperation.

Source: UN Comtrade. World Integration Trade Solutions. URL https://wits.worldbank.org/ (accessed April 2017).

Figure 3: India's Total Imports from SASEC and the World
($ billion)

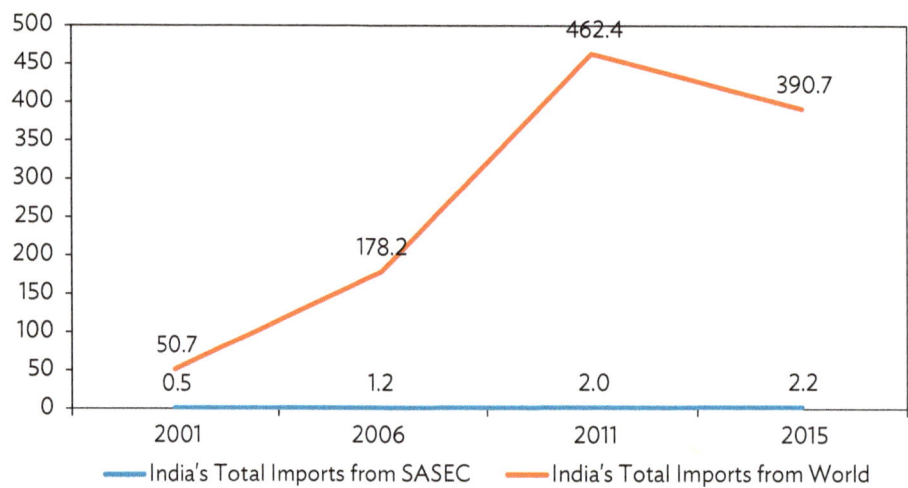

SASEC = South Asia Subregional Economic Cooperation.

Source: UN Comtrade. World Integration Trade Solutions. URL https://wits.worldbank.org/ (accessed April 2017).

Figure 4: India's Exports to SASEC Countries and the World

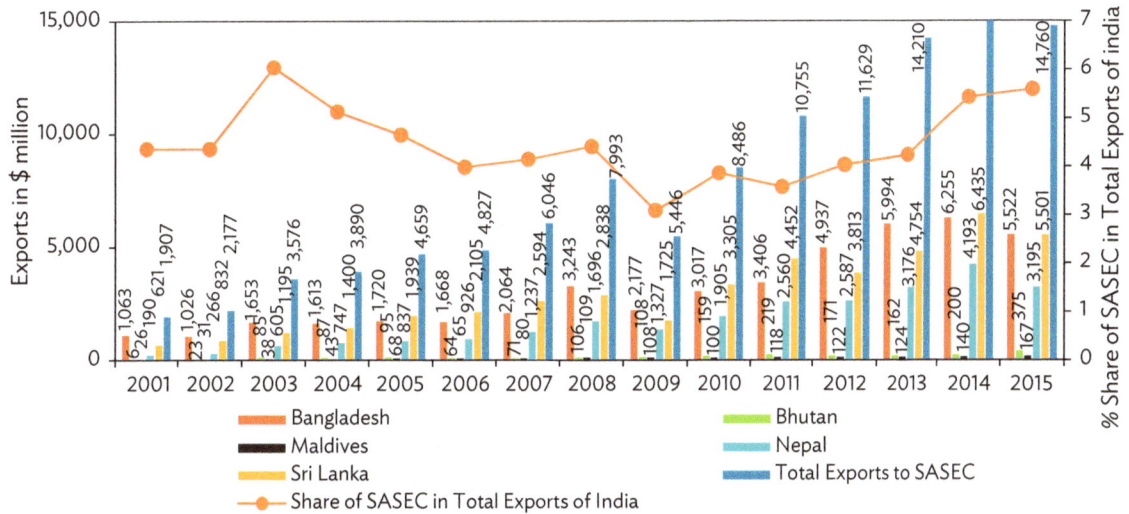

Exports in $ million / % Share of SASEC in Total Exports of india

Legend:
- Bangladesh
- Bhutan
- Maldives
- Nepal
- Sri Lanka
- Total Exports to SASEC
- Share of SASEC in Total Exports of India

SASEC = South Asia Subregional Economic Cooperation.

Source: UN Comtrade. World Integration Trade Solutions. URL https://wits.worldbank.org/ (accessed April 2017).

Figure 5: India's Imports from SASEC Countries and the World

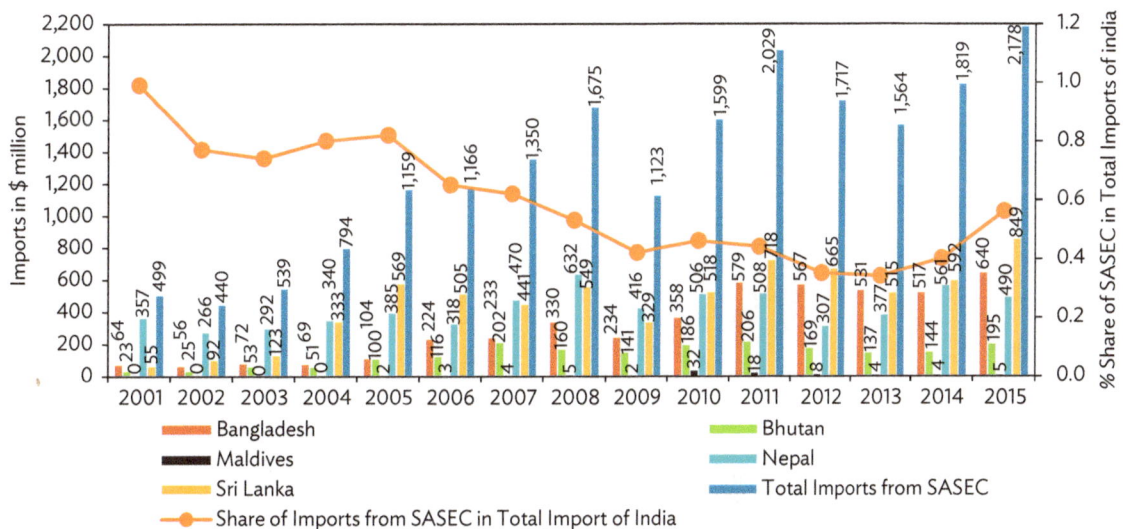

Imports in $ million / % Share of SASEC in Total Imports of india

Legend:
- Bangladesh
- Bhutan
- Maldives
- Nepal
- Sri Lanka
- Total Imports from SASEC
- Share of Imports from SASEC in Total Import of India

SASEC = South Asia Subregional Economic Cooperation.

Source: UN Comtrade. World Integration Trade Solutions. URL https://wits.worldbank.org/ (accessed April 2017).

expand its forward linkages in the supply of key inputs to SASEC countries, but its backward linkages weakened during this time.

The current trend of India's export and import to and from SASEC countries offers two crucial insights. First, India's trade with SASEC countries is increasing despite less than optimally effective trade facilitation and border-related disputes. Second, bilateral trade between India and SASEC countries remains intact despite the current global trade slowdown.

2.1. Trade with Bangladesh

Among SASEC countries, Bangladesh is one of India's most important trading partners. India's total exports of its top 10 products (at HS 6-digit level) to Bangladesh stood at $1.7 billion in 2015. The share of India's top 10 exports in total exports to Bangladesh was 32.05% (Figure 6). India's exports to Bangladesh are dominated by raw materials and capital-intensive items. The top export from India to Bangladesh is cotton which constitutes 20.8% of the total exports (Table A1.1).

Figure 6: India's Top Exports to Bangladesh,
Harmonized System Code, %

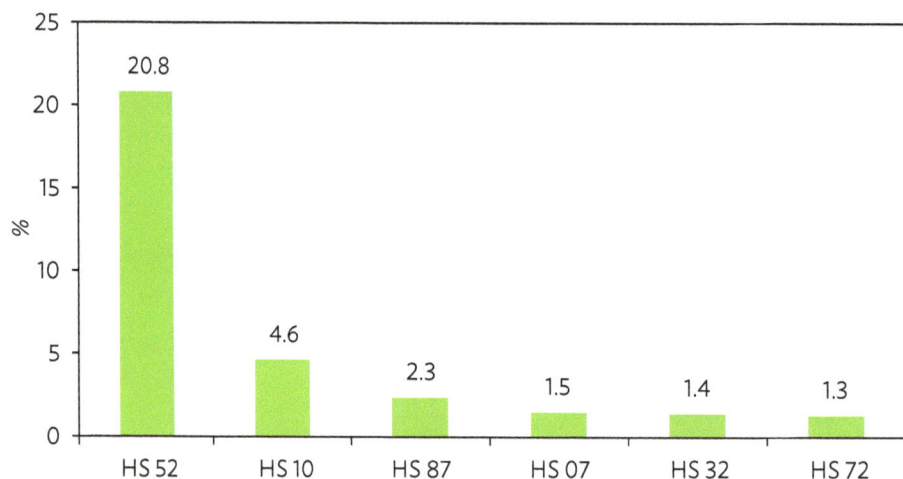

Harmonized Commodity Description and Coding System; HS 52 = cotton; HS 10 = cereals; HS 87 = vehicles other than railway or tramway rolling stock, and parts and accessories thereof; HS 07 = edible vegetables and certain roots and tubers; HS 32 = tanning or dyeing extracts, tannins and their derivatives, dyes, pigments, and other coloring matter, paints and varnishes, putty and other mastics, inks; HS 72 = base metals and articles of base metal.

Source: UN Comtrade. World Integration Trade Solutions. URL https://wits.worldbank.org/ (accessed May 2017).

2.2. Trade with Bhutan

Bhutan is a landlocked, least-developed country in the SASEC region and is highly dependent on India for imports. India's top 10 exports (at HS 6-digit level) to Bhutan accounted for $153.27 million in 2015. The share of India's top 10 export products was 45.98%. India's main exports to Bhutan are in primary and heavy machinery products (Figure 7). In 2015, the top category of exports from India to Bhutan was mineral fuels, the share of which was 21.1% of India's total exports to Bhutan. The second most exported category was boilers, machinery, and mechanical items (Table A1.2).

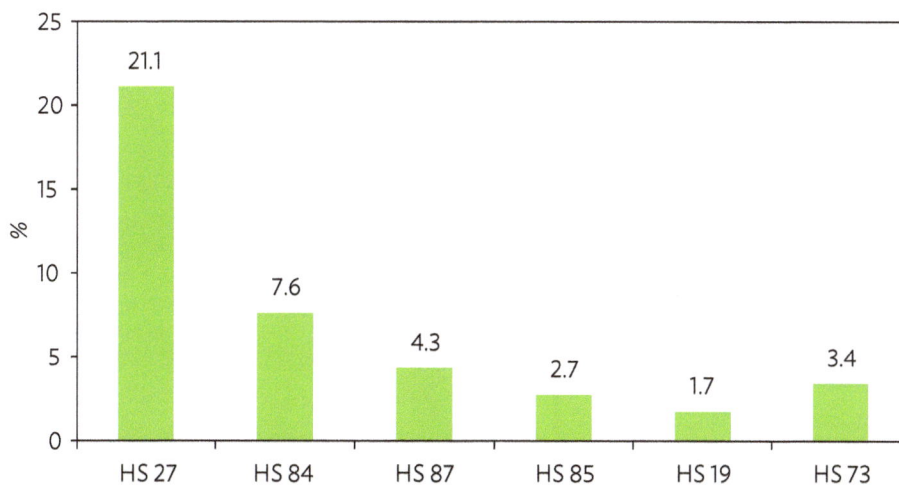

Figure 7: India's Top Exports to Bhutan,
Harmonized System Code, %

HS = Harmonized Commodity Description and Coding System; HS 27 = mineral fuels, mineral oils, and products of their distillation, bituminous substances, mineral waxes; HS 84 = machinery and mechanical appliances, electrical equipment, parts thereof, sound recorders and reproducers, television image and sound recorders and reproducers, and parts and accessories of such articles; HS 87 = vehicles other than railway or tramway rolling stock, and parts and accessories thereof; HS 85 = electrical machinery and equipment and parts thereof, sound recorders and reproducers, television image and sound recorders and reproducers, and parts and accessories of such articles; HS 19= preparations of cereals, flour, starch or milk, pastry cooks' products; HS 73 = articles of iron or steel.

Source: UN Comtrade. World Integration Trade Solutions. URL https://wits.worldbank.org/ (accessed April 2017).

2.3. Trade with Maldives

India has made remarkable progress in expanding trade ties with Maldives and continues to be a supplier of many essential items. India's top 10 exports (at HS 6-digit level) to Maldives accounted for $68.61 million in 2015. Furthermore, the share of India's top 10 exports in total exports to Maldives was 41.13%. India's top export categories to Maldives include many primary products (Figure 8): in 2015, salt, sulfur, earths, and stones were the top exported products and their share in India's total export to Maldives was 15.8%. The second most exported product was cereals with a share of 7.2% (Table A1.3).

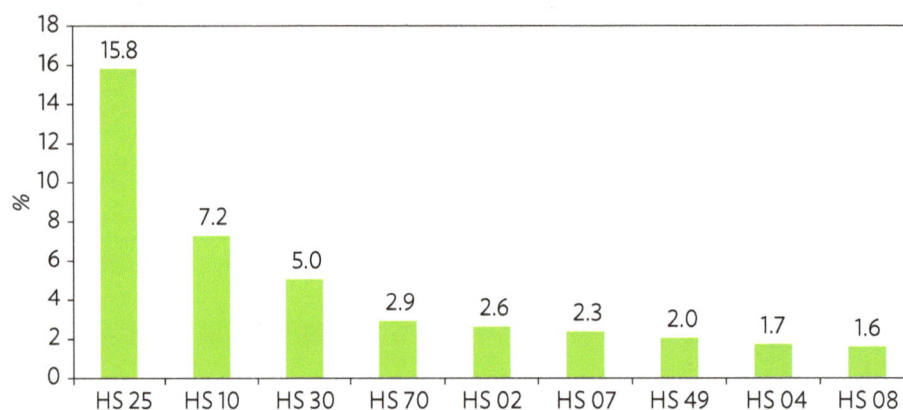

Figure 8: India's Top Exports to Maldives
Harmonized System Code, %

HS = Harmonized Commodity Description and Coding System; HS 25 = salt, sulfur, earths, and stone, plastering materials, lime and cement; HS 10 = cereals; HS 30 = pharmaceutical products; HS 70 = glass and glassware; HS 02 = meat and edible meat offal; HS 07 = edible vegetables and certain roots and tubers; HS 49 = printed books, newspapers, pictures, and other products of the printing industry, manuscripts, typescripts, and plans; HS 08 = edible fruit and nuts, peel of citrus fruit or melons.

Source: UN Comtrade. World Integration Trade Solutions. URL https://wits.worldbank.org/ (accessed May 2017).

2.4. Trade with Nepal

Like Bhutan, Nepal is a landlocked country that relies on India for in-transit trade. Despite some fluctuations, India's exports to Nepal are continuously expanding and India has been an exporter of key essential items to Nepal. In 2015, India's top 10 exports (at HS 6-digit level) to Nepal stood at $1.22 billion, including both primary and capital-intensive products. The share of India's top 10 exports in total exports to Nepal was 38.26%. The most exported product was mineral fuels and mineral oil which constituted 21.03% of India's total exports to Nepal in 2015 (Figure 9). The second largest export was in cereals items with percentage share of 5.50% (Table A1.4 in Appendix 1).

2.5. Trade with Sri Lanka

Home to a major transshipment hub for the South Asian region, Sri Lanka plays a pivotal role for South Asia in global overseas trade with the rest of the world. India's total exports to Sri Lanka were $2.88 billion in 2015 which included both primary and heavy machinery items.

Figure 9: India's Top Exports to Nepal,
Harmonized System Code, %

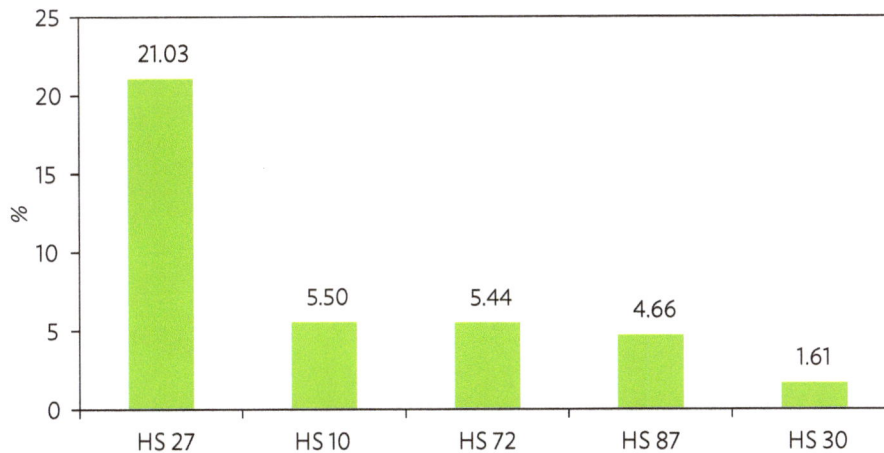

HS = Harmonized Commodity Description and Coding System; HS 27 = mineral fuels, mineral oils, and products of their distillation, bituminous substances, mineral waxes; HS 10 = cereals; HS 72 = base metals and articles of base metal; HS 87 = vehicles other than railway or tramway rolling stock, and parts and accessories thereof; HS 30 = pharmaceutical products.
Source: UN Comtrade. World Integration Trade Solutions. URL https://wits.worldbank.org/ (accessed May 2017).

The share of India's top 10 export products (at HS 6-digit level) to Sri Lanka was 52.45%. India's top export products were aircraft, spacecraft, and parts thereof in 2015 with a share of 19.14% in total exports to Sri Lanka (Figure 10). The second most exported products were mineral fuels and mineral oil which had a share of 14.32% (Table A1.5 in Appendix 1).

The current composition of India's exports to SASEC countries provides a reasonable understanding of the nature of the overall trade relationship and indicates possible areas where trade and investment integration could be enhanced. From the current pattern of exports, it is apparent that India's trade with SASEC countries is concentrated in its top 10 products, which include both primary and capital-intensive goods. Exports to Bangladesh, Bhutan, Maldives, and Nepal constitute primary products; while exports to Sri Lanka include capital-intensive items. Given that India's exports are densely concentrated in a few product categories, there is significant scope to diversify exports in other product categories.

Furthermore, it is equally important to note that India's exports to SASEC countries include some common products which underpin the potential of fostering bilateral and regional value chains in the region. Analysis carried out in 2015 identified a large number of products in which India could take the lead—along with the least developing countries (Bangladesh, Bhutan, Maldives, and Nepal)—to foster value chains.[11] Such products could be processed

[11]   Banga (2016).

Figure 10: India's Top Exports to Sri Lanka,
Harmonized System Code, %

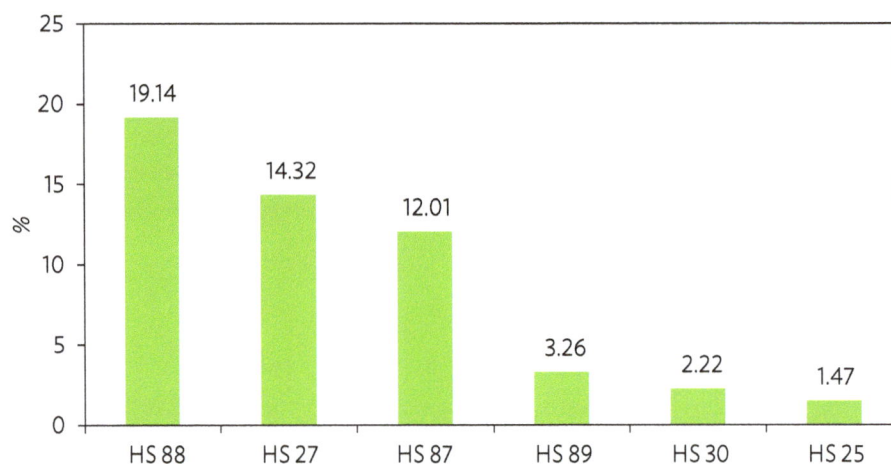

HS = Harmonized Commodity Description and Coding System; HS 88 = aircraft, spacecraft, and parts thereof; HS 27 = mineral fuels, mineral oils, and products of their distillation, bituminous substances, mineral waxes; HS 87 = vehicles other than railway or tramway rolling stock, and parts and accessories thereof; HS 30 = pharmaceutical products; HS 25 = salt, sulfur, earths, and stones, plastering materials, lime and cement.

Source: UN Comtrade. World Integration Trade Solutions. URL https://wits.worldbank.org/ (accessed May 2017).

fish, cashew nuts, appliances, dyes, leather articles, footwear, carpets, women's dresses, textiles, furnishing articles, jewelry, machinery, turbines, transformers, and tractors.

One reason for the low volume of India's exports to SASEC countries is the significant mismatch in import baskets of SASEC countries. India's exports are largely shaped by its key markets such as the US, the European Union, United Arab Emirates, and selected Association of Southeast Asian Nations countries. India has paid less attention to smaller markets than bigger ones, which could be one of the factors behind the insignificant volume of trade. In addition, the high cost of doing trade in the SASEC region remains a key concern: suboptimal trade and transport infrastructure at border points escalates the cost of export and import which, in turn, affects potential intraregional trade opportunities.

Chapter 3
Potential Exports Subject to Nontariff Barriers

This chapter presents potential exports of India to the other five SASEC countries, identified using the methodology described in Chapter 1. These potential exports were identified at the 6-digit level of product classification (Appendix 2), although for interpretation and analysis, the diagnostic study analysis grouped potential products into their corresponding 2-digit category. The following five subsections detail the potential exports by country.

3.1. Potential Exports from India to Bangladesh

Table 1 shows the number of potential export items at the HS 6-digit level of product classification, with the values representing the number of potential products at two different levels of trade volume. The study selected 108 potential exports of India to the Bangladesh market for which the value of India's exports to the world and Bangladesh imports from the world are greater than $10 million (Table A2.1 in Appendix 2).

Table 1: Number of Potential Exports of India to Bangladesh

Filter	Number of Potential Products
If average value of India's exports and average value of Bangladesh's imports are greater than $1 million	580
If average value of India's exports and average value of Bangladesh's imports are greater than $10 million	108

Source: Asian Development Bank.

After aggregating these 108 products using 2-digit HS product codes (Figure 11), and following the classification given by UN Comtrade, India shows the highest export potential in machinery and electrical products (HS codes 84–85), followed by textiles and clothing (HS codes 50–63), chemicals (HS codes 28–38), plastic and related products (HS codes 39–40), and base metal articles (HS codes 72–83) in the Bangladesh market. Product-wise data show that India has the highest export potential in machinery and mechanical appliances

(HS codes 84–85), followed by plastic products (HS code 39), wood products (HS code 48), man-made staple fibers (HS code 55), medical and surgical instruments (HS code 90).

Figure 11: India's Potential Exports to Bangladesh

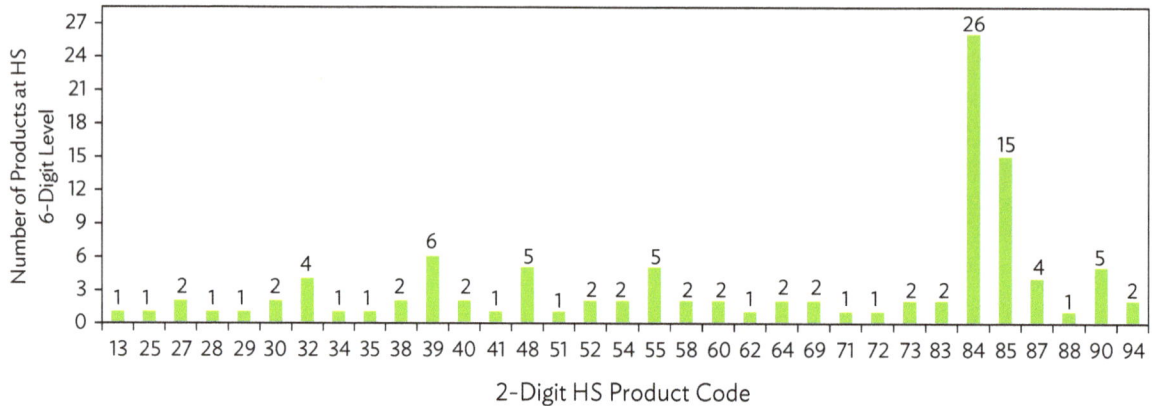

HS = harmonized system.
Source: Asian Development Bank.

The analysis indicates that in 10 products at 6-digit level, India's export share in Bangladesh's total imports is the highest relative to the export share of other countries to Bangladesh. Five of these products belong to the broader product category of machinery and mechanical appliances (HS codes 84–85). It is also noted that India's unit price of exports to the world is less than Bangladesh's unit price of imports from the world (Table A2.1 in Appendix 2). Given this, India appears to have the potential for exports in selected items and could export to Bangladesh at competitive prices. This would benefit both producers in India and consumers in Bangladesh and would create greater trade and investment opportunities.

3.2. Potential Exports from India to Bhutan

The analysis identifies 35 potential products at the HS 6-digit level of product classification in which India has export potential in Bhutan's market (Table A2.2 in Appendix 2). For these products, the volume of India's exports and Bhutan's imports in value is not much higher. This is proved using the filters of $1 million and $10 million: only three products emerge using the $1 million filter, and zero products using the $10 million filter. Hence, for the purpose of analysis, no restriction on value of trade is assumed and the 35 products were deemed potential export items.

Figure 12 shows the 35 potential products classified into their respective 2-digit HS product codes. Following UN product classification, India has the highest export potential in machinery and electrical equipment (HS codes 84–85), followed by medical and surgical instruments (HS code 90), and plastics and related products (HS codes 39–40). For these products, India's unit price of exports to the world is less than Bhutan's unit price of imports from the world. It was also found that India's export share in Bhutan's total imports is highest in 21 products out of 35 potential items, relative to export share of other exporting countries. For the rest of the products, India's share puts it among the first four top exporters to Bhutan.

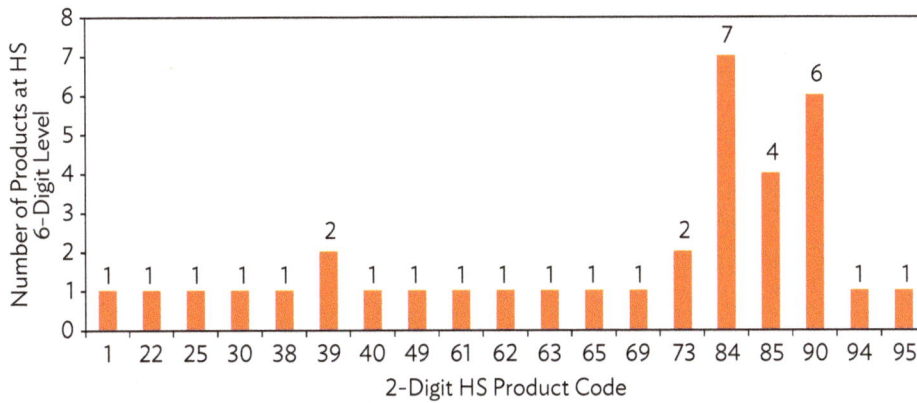

Figure 12: India's Potential Exports to Bhutan

HS = harmonized system.
Source: Asian Development Bank.

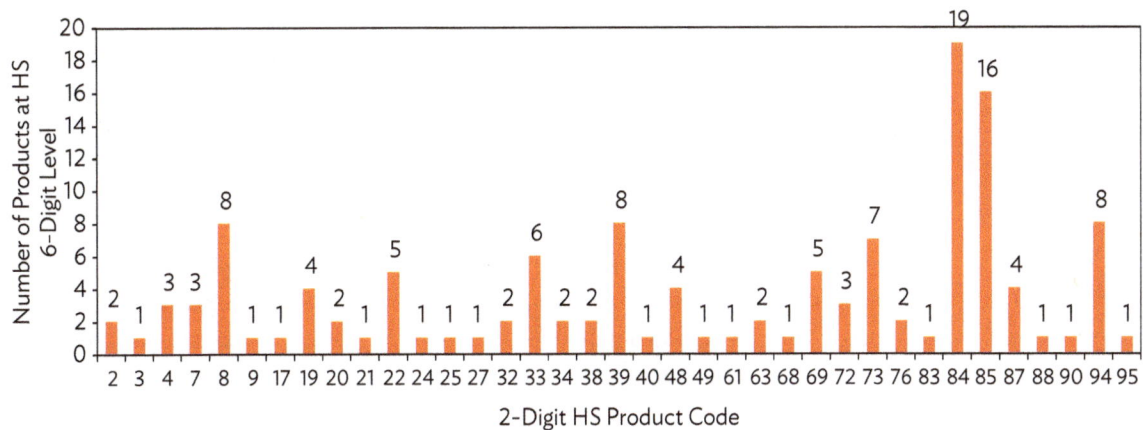

Figure 13: India's Potential Exports to Maldives

HS = harmonized system.
Source: Asian Development Bank.

3.3   Potential Exports from India to Maldives

Table 2 shows the number of potential export items from India to the Maldives market at two levels of trade volume. The study found 132 such products under the $1 million category and four products under the $10 million category. For the purpose of analysis, the study assumes 132 potential products at the HS 6-digit level of product classification in which India has export potential in Maldives' market (Table A2.3 in Appendix 2).

Table 2: Number of Potential Exports of India to Maldives

Filter	Number of Potential Products
If average value of India's exports and average value of Maldives' imports are greater than $1 million	132
If average value of India's exports and average value of Maldives' imports are greater than $10 million	4

Source: Asian Development Bank.

Figure 13 shows the classification of these 132 potential products into their respective 2-digit HS product codes. Following UN product classification, India has the highest export potential in machinery and electrical equipment (HS codes 84–85), followed by food products (HS codes 16–24), base metal articles (HS codes 72–83), vegetable products (HS codes 6–15), chemicals (HS codes 28–38), plastics and related products (HS codes 39–40), and wooden furniture (HS code 94). The lower unit price of exports of India in comparison to the unit price of imports of Maldives from the world indicates India's potential for these products (Table A2.3 in Appendix 2).

3.4.   Potential Exports from India to Nepal

The study identifies 63 potential products of India in Nepal's market using the HS 6-digit level of product classification under $1 million category, and seven such products under $10 million category (Table 3). For the purpose of analysis, the study assumes 63 potential export items for which India has export potential in Nepal's market (Table A2.4 in Appendix 2).

Figure 14 shows 63 potential products classified into their respective 2-digit HS product codes. Following the UN product classification, India has highest export potential in machinery and electrical equipment (HS codes 84–85), followed by base metals articles (HS codes 72–83), plastic and related products (HS codes 39–40), chemicals and allied products (HS codes 28–38), medical instruments (HS code 90), metal and wooden furniture items (HS codes 94), and food products (HS codes 16–24), among others. For these potential products, India's unit price of exports to the world is less than Nepal's unit price of imports from the world, thereby indicating the existing potential of India's exports to Nepal.

Table 3: Number of Potential Exports of India to Nepal

Filter	Number of Potential Products
If average value of India's exports and average value of Nepal's imports are greater than $1 million	63
If average value of India's exports and average value of Nepal's imports are greater than $10 million	7

Source: Asian Development Bank.

By looking product-wise at India's existing share of exports to Nepal within Nepal's total imports (Table A2.4 in Appendix 2), India's huge potential to increase exports to Nepal is clearly seen. From the analysis, it was found that in 18 such products at 6-digit level, India's export share to Nepal is already the highest relative to the export share of other countries to Nepal.

3.5. Potential Exports from India to Sri Lanka

For Sri Lanka, the number of potential export items is 395 using the $1 million filter, and 66 using the $10 million filter (Table 4). However. for the purpose of analysis, the study considers only 66 potential products at the HS 6-digit level of product classification in which India has export potential in Sri Lanka's market (Table A2.5 in Appendix 2).

Figure 14 shows the classification of 66 potential products into their respective 2-digit HS product codes. Following UN product classification, India has the highest export potential in machinery and electrical equipment (HS codes 84–85), followed by plastic and related products (HS codes 39–40), base metals materials (HS codes 72–83), food products (HS codes 16–24), chemicals (HS codes 28–38), wood-related products

Table 4: Number of Potential Exports of India to Sri Lanka

Filter	Number of Potential Products
If average value of India's exports and average value of Sri Lanka's imports are greater than $1 million	395
If average value of India's exports and average value of Sri Lanka's imports are greater than $10 million	66

Source: Asian Development Bank.

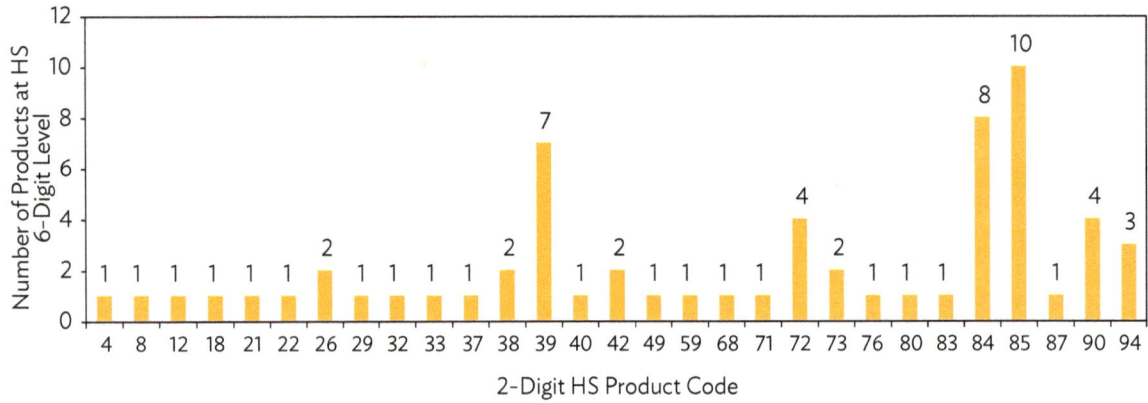

Figure 14: India's Potential Exports to Nepal

HS = harmonized system.
Source: Asian Development Bank.

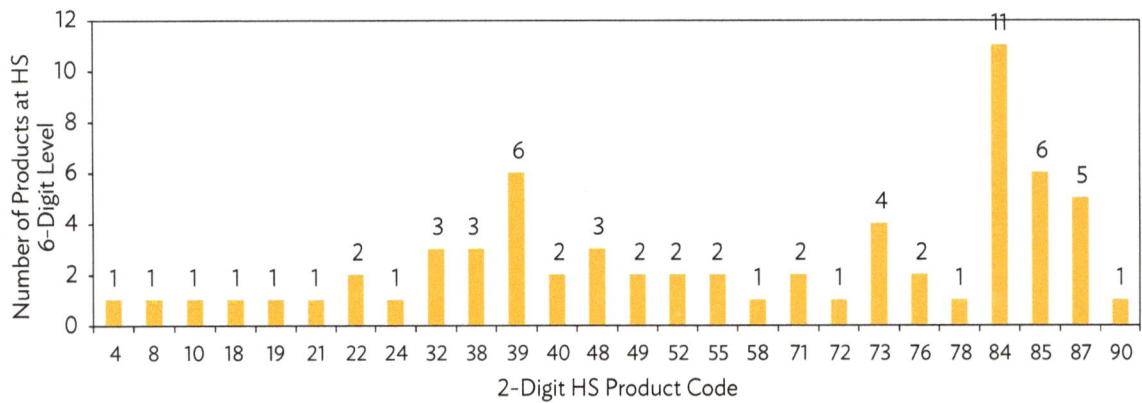

Figure 15: India's Potential Exports to Sri Lanka

HS = harmonized system.
Source: Asian Development Bank.

(HS codes 44–49), textiles and clothing products (HS codes 50–63), and vehicles other than railways and parts and accessories thereof (HS code 87). Analysis of the product share of India's exports in Sri Lanka's total imports (Table A2.5 in Appendix 2) clearly indicates that India has tremendous potential to increase its exports to Sri Lanka as the unit price of India's exports in these products to the world is less than Sri Lanka's unit price of imports from the world.

In summary, India's export potential to other SASEC countries lies mainly in machinery and electrical products (HS codes 84–85). For the identified potential products, the existing contribution of India's exports as part of the total imports of other SASEC countries from all countries of the world is still not significant and, therefore, provides scope for further improvement.

Many policy barriers, including tariff and nontariff trade barriers, can be considered one of the primary reasons for India's low export share of these products to SASEC countries. In addition, India's lack of production capacity could be a contributing factor to the very limited export share. This diagnostic study seeks to determine the extent to which SPS and TBT measures also act as major impediments to the growth of regional trade in the SASEC region (footnotes 2 and 4).

3.6. Potential Products and South Asia Free Trade Agreement's Sensitive List

Analysis of the potential exports from India to SASEC countries, reveals that a relatively high number fall under SAFTA's sensitive list (Figure 16): out of 108 potential export items of India to Bangladesh, 39 products are in the sensitive list. In the case of Bhutan, only 1 of the 35 potential export items of India is in the sensitive list. Of 63 potential export items of India to Maldives, 19 are in the sensitive list. Of India's 132 potential export items to Nepal, 30 are in the potential list; and of India's 66 exports items to Sri Lanka, 17 are in the sensitive list. To stimulate the growth of intraregional trade, elimination of these potential export products from the sensitive list is critical.

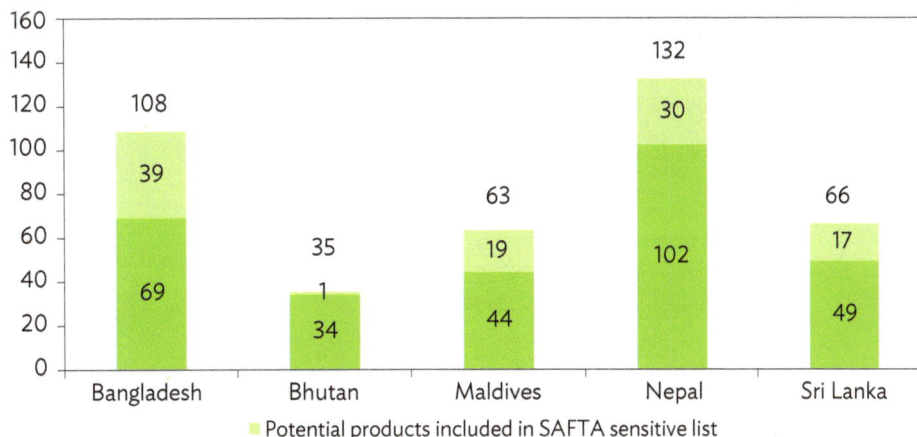

Figure 16: Potential Export Items in South Asia Free Trade Agreement's Sensitive List

SAFTA = South Asia Free Trade Agreement.

Source: South Asian Association for Regional Cooperation.

Chapter 4
Overview of Sanitary and Phytosanitary Measures and Technical Barriers to Trade in India

4.1. The Sanitary and Phytosanitary Environment

The SPS regime in India has evolved based on the World Trade Organization (WTO) Agreement on the Application of SPS Measures (SPS Agreement),[12] which allows countries to design and formulate their own national SPS regulations, although mandating that these regulations be based on "sound scientific principles" and "backed by scientific evidence and justification." SPS measures must be aligned with international guidelines and risk assessment procedures of the SPS Agreement.[13] However, the SPS Agreement also allows countries to use "policy measures" to protect public health within their geographical boundaries as long as they are not protectionist and do not hinder trade.[14]

A range of laws, institutions, and agencies in India deal with the SPS regime and provide a broader framework to design, formulate, and implement SPS regulations. Different ministries and departments of central and state governments are involved in the formulation and execution of policies, with specific organizations and agencies playing an active role in implementation of SPS regulations.

4.1.1. Legal Framework

The central and state governments are primarily responsible for formulating and enforcing legislation for the SPS regime with the overarching goal to "regulate sanitary requirements" and lay down the "minimum requirement" to achieve the objectives of SPS laws. The Government of India enacted the **Food Safety and Standards Act of 2006** to consolidate a diverse range of food laws, including the following:

(i)   Prevention of Food Adulteration Act of 1954;
(ii)   Essential Commodities Act, 1955;
(iii) Fruit Products Order of 1955;
(iv)   Meat Food Products Order of 1973;
(v)   Vegetable Oil Products (Control) Order of 1947;
(vi)   Edible Oils Packaging (Regulation) Order of 1988;

---

[12]   WTO webpage on the SPS Agreement: https://www.wto.org/english/tratop_e/sps_e/spsagr_e.htm.
[13]   Kaul (2016).
[14]   SPS measures and TBT summary. Center for International Development. Harvard University. http://www.cid.harvard.edu/cidtrade/issues/spstbt.html.

(vii)   Solvent Extracted Oil, De-Oiled Meal, and Edible Flour (Control) Order of 1967; and

(viii)   Milk and Milk Products Order of 1992.

Additional key legislation includes

(i)   Essential Commodities Act, 1954;

(ii)   Prevention of Food Adulteration Act, 1954;

(iii)   Livestock Importation Act, 1898 (amended); and

(iv)   Plant Quarantine (Regulation of Import into India) Order 2003.[15]

Product-specific acts are also applied: for example, imports of plants and plant materials are governed by the Destructive Insects and Pests Act (1914), Plant Quarantine (Regulation of Import into India) Order 2003, and other acts. Similarly, imports of animals with relevant health and related issues are regulated by Animal Quarantine under the Department of Animal Husbandry, Dairying, and Fisheries.

4.1.2.   Institutional Framework

The Government of India has developed a strong institutional framework under different legal acts to regulate domestic, exported, and imported products. The Department of Commerce, under the Ministry of Commerce and Industry, has set up three enquiry points to deal with all queries relating to SPS notification and regulations issued by WTO members. These inquiry points are

(i)   Department of Agriculture and Cooperation for plant health or phytosanitary issues;

(ii)   Department of Animal Husbandry, Dairying, and Fisheries for animal health and related issues; and

(iii)   Department of Health for food safety-related issues and plant protection.

The three departments coordinate with each other and with other relevant ministries, departments, regulatory bodies, and/or trade bodies to prepare responses to queries raised by WTO members.

Food Safety and Standards Authority of India

In 2008, the Government of India established the **Food Safety and Standards Authority of India** (FSSAI) under the government's Ministry of Health and Family Welfare, with the aim of developing "scientific standards" for food products and "regulating their manufacturing, storage, distribution, sale, and import to ensure availability of safe and wholesome food for human consumption."[16] It is a single reference point for all queries related to safety and other standards for food products. FSSAI lays down regulations and guidelines for food products and has developed an appropriate system of implementing

---

15   Center for WTO Studies. 2012. Trade Policies and Institutions. http://wtocentre.iift.ac.in/FA/INDIA. pdf.

16   Food Safety and Standards Act, 2006, No. 34 of 2006. Ministry of Health and Family Welfare, Government of India. https://fssai.gov.in/cms/food-safety-and-standards-act-2006.php.

Figure 17: Legal and Institutional Framework of Sanitary and Phytosanitary Regime in India

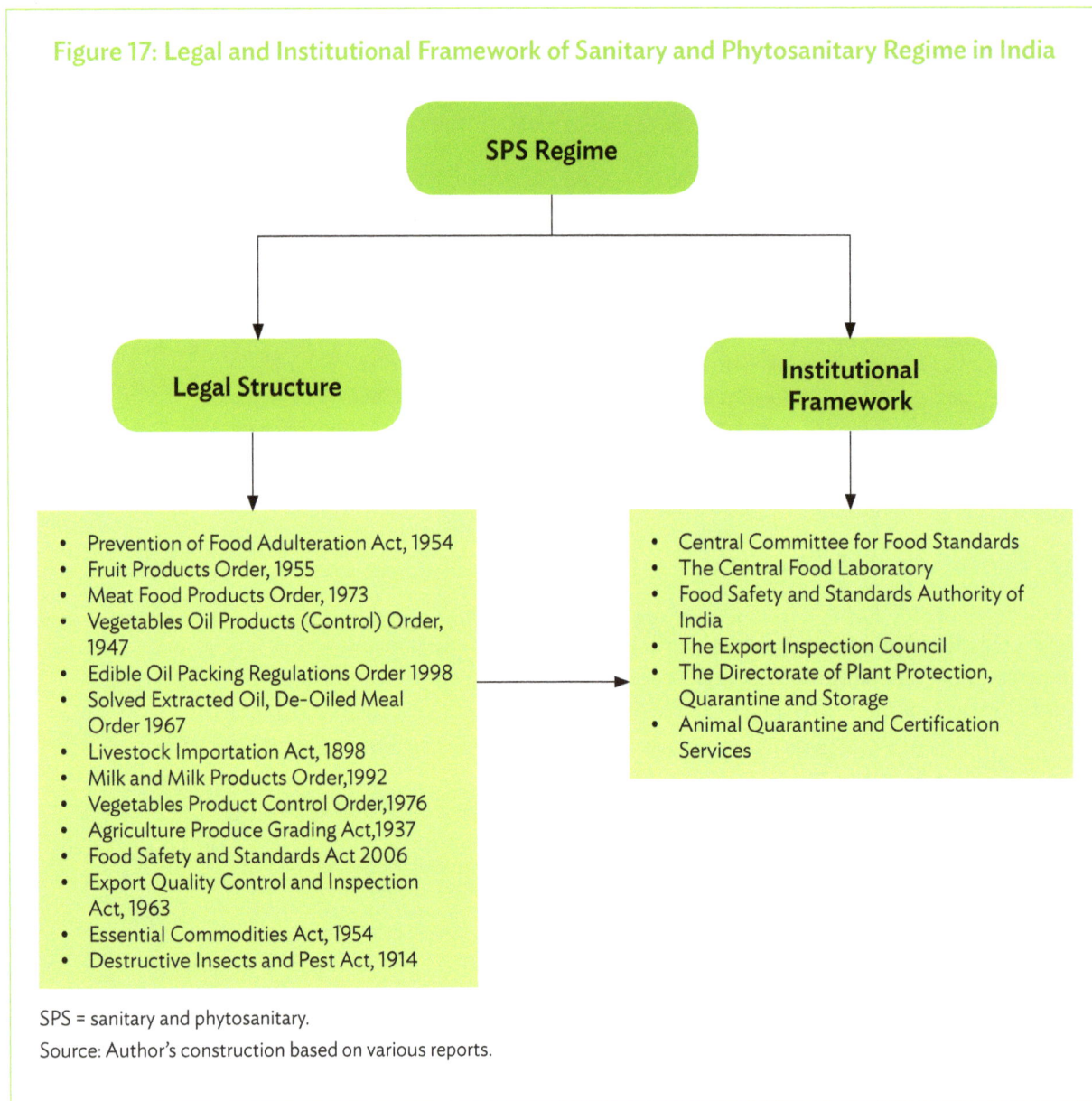

```
                        ┌─────────────────┐
                        │   SPS Regime    │
                        └─────────────────┘
                                 │
              ┌──────────────────┴──────────────────┐
              ▼                                      ▼
    ┌──────────────────┐              ┌──────────────────────┐
    │  Legal Structure │              │    Institutional     │
    │                  │              │     Framework        │
    └──────────────────┘              └──────────────────────┘
```

Legal Structure

- Prevention of Food Adulteration Act, 1954
- Fruit Products Order, 1955
- Meat Food Products Order, 1973
- Vegetables Oil Products (Control) Order, 1947
- Edible Oil Packing Regulations Order 1998
- Solved Extracted Oil, De-Oiled Meal Order 1967
- Livestock Importation Act, 1898
- Milk and Milk Products Order,1992
- Vegetables Product Control Order,1976
- Agriculture Produce Grading Act,1937
- Food Safety and Standards Act 2006
- Export Quality Control and Inspection Act, 1963
- Essential Commodities Act, 1954
- Destructive Insects and Pest Act, 1914

Institutional Framework

- Central Committee for Food Standards
- The Central Food Laboratory
- Food Safety and Standards Authority of India
- The Export Inspection Council
- The Directorate of Plant Protection, Quarantine and Storage
- Animal Quarantine and Certification Services

SPS = sanitary and phytosanitary.

Source: Author's construction based on various reports.

various safety standards. It has also created a mechanism to accredit certified bodies and laboratories engaged in certification of food safety management for exporters, importers, and domestic food businesses.

Furthermore, FSSAI is making considerable efforts to upgrade existing regulations to match international best practice. In 2016, it made two major amendments in import regulations of food products and completely overhauled the process of clearance for imported food items. The introduction of a risk-based framework means that the regulator now only needs to review the risk associated with imported food items and ask for inspection based on a risk-based sampling approach.

New import regulations allow an authorized officer to issue a no objection certificate, without laboratory testing, for food items that have a shelf life of less than 7 days.[17] The laboratory analysis is shared with the customs authority, together with the no objection certificate, if the product meets the standards. However, if the product fails to meet necessary standards, the authorized officer immediately requests the importer and customs house agent to submit a detailed compliance report within 24 hours. After this, FSSAI issues an alert to all authorized officers at ports to monitor the entry of such products.

Box 1: Food Safety and Standards Authority of India Launches One-Nation, One-Food Safety Law

Food Safety and Standards Authority of India introduced a "one nation, one food safety law" in 2017 to regulate food products with standard practice and procedures across the country. This landmark development in the food regulatory landscape of India will reduce inconsistency in food laws across states, promoting a "standard practice for the implementation, compliance, and surveillance of food safety regulations which, in turn, will ensure smoother operations for food companies."

The one nation, one food safety law will bring greater transparency and eliminate "discrepancies in food safety regulations across states, and standardize surveillance, sampling, and inspection." Under the new regime, inspection and sampling will be monitored, and cloud-based electronic storage of information will increase transparency. The number of unnecessary interventions by multiple regulators for the import of food products will be reduced.

Source: FSSAI plans "one nation, one food safety law." *Livemint*. www.livemint.com/Companies/ m0PSH2b0htUADu GMJ4 K1YL/FSSAI-plans-one-nation-one-food-safety-law.html.

In 2017, FSSAI expanded the scope of new regulations and standards to include a wide range of food products, including amendments in product standards and food additives, as well as unified regulations for organic products. The latter include changes in usage of different types of contaminants, toxins, and residues in food products.

Other new notifications introduce major change: for example, products with a shelf life of less than 60% or 3 months before expiry (whichever is less) shall not be cleared. In addition, the importer is required to provide the certificate of sanitary export from authorized agencies in exporting countries for the categories of food as specified by FSSAI from time to time.[18]

---

[17] Food Import Regulations. 2016. http://agriexchange.apeda.gov.in/IR_Standards/Import_Regulation/ 2016%20 Food%20Import%20RegulationsNew%20DelhiIndia1292016.pdf.

[18] FSSAI. Import Regulation 2017, https://www.fssai.gov.in/dam/jcr:e22fae42-974e-4c9b-bc52-a56a2 ea9bc8a/ Compendium_Food_Import_Regulations_26_04_2018.pdf.

Directorate of Plant Protection Quarantine and Storage

The **Directorate of Plant Protection Quarantine and Storage** is an apex body under the Department of Agriculture, Cooperation, and Farmers Welfare. Under the Plant Quarantine Order 2003, it regulates trade in plants and plant products, certifying whether plants and plant products exported from or imported into India are in line with the SPS regime and safe for consumption. The regulations for dealing with plant protection are governed under the

(i)   Destructive Insect and Pests Act, 1914;
(ii)   Insecticide Act, 1968;
(iii)   Plant Fruits and Seeds Regulation, 1989;
(iv)   Plant Quarantine Order 2003 (Import Regulations); and
(v)   Seeds Act, 1966; and Foreign Trade (Development and Regulation) Act, 1992.

The importance of plant quarantine has increased significantly due to the globalization and liberalization of world trade in plants and plant products, particularly in the light of the WTO SPS Agreement.

Animal Quarantine and Certification Services

The **Animal Quarantine and Certification Services** under the Livestock Importation Act, 1898, and its subsequent amendments, serves as a nodal agency under the Department of Animal Husbandry, Dairying, and Fisheries, and regulates trade of livestock and livestock products under the guidelines of SPS standards. The Animal Quarantine and Certification Services was established to prevent the entry of dangerous exotic diseases into the country through imported livestock and livestock products. The import of livestock and livestock products is subject to the Sanitary Import Permit and accompanies veterinary health certificates issued by the department. The Sanitary Import Permit is valid for 1-12 months, depending on the nature of the product.

4.1.3.   Infrastructure Facilities

The state of infrastructure facilities in India directly affects the capacity of institutions to implement SPS regulations. The availability and accessibility of laboratories located in sea and land ports is critical not only for efficient clearance of food cargoes, but also in affecting the ability of domestic firms to participate in global and regional food supply chains. Lack of efficient clearance of goods increases the cost of trading across borders. India generally lags in both soft and hard infrastructure facilities, particularly at land ports (footnote 5).

FSSAI has 121 **National Accreditation Board for Testing and Calibration Laboratories** (NABL)-accredited food testing laboratories, and 16 referral laboratories. In addition, there are 72 state food laboratories to test the quality of food products sold in the domestic market. The NABL-accredited laboratories are responsible for testing of imported food products, while referral laboratories conduct laboratory tests for food items and other articles whenever a second test is required.

However, the physical locations of FSSAI and its NABL-accredited laboratories appears highly skewed. The geographic spread of NABL-accredited labs is uneven and clearly shows the asymmetries in India's laboratory testing infrastructure: while there are 121 NABL laboratories in India, nearly 17% of these are found in Maharashtra alone, and another 45% are spread between only five states—Delhi, Uttar Pradesh, Gujarat, Karnataka, and Tamil Nadu. Overall, while laboratories are concentrated in the northern, western, and southern regions, there are no NABL-accredited laboratories in Assam, Bihar, Chhattisgarh, Jharkhand, Manipur, Meghalaya, Mizoram, Nagaland, Sikkim, Tripura, and Andaman Nicobar Islands. Furthermore, there is no food laboratory to handle agricultural produce in the northeastern region. And finally, accessibility of food laboratories per 0.04 per square kilometer is only 0.002128 (Appendix 4), which clearly indicates a critical insufficiency of laboratories and a testing-capacity deficit in India.

There is, however, tremendous potential for SPS-related trade exports from the northeastern region due to the good agroclimatic conditions. Products such as spices, organic or inorganic products, ginger, and pepper can be grown and easily exported, but the region lacks adequate testing and certification laboratories, which creates trade inefficiencies and barriers. At present, products are sent to Kolkata for testing, which is time-consuming and costly. The need for NABL-accredited laboratories in the northeastern region is clear.

The absence of food laboratories at land ports puts an additional burden on local producers, exporters, and importers to send their consignments to other states for testing. For instance, FSSAI does not have laboratory testing facilities at the Petrapole Integrated Check Post, so imported food samples must be sent to Kolkata for testing and examination. Similar infrastructure-related constraints at Chennai Port result in food samples usually being referred to the Central Food Testing and Research Institute, Mysore, for testing, including tests for residual pesticides. The Central Food Testing and Research Institute takes more than 2 weeks to issue a laboratory test report, and the importer must hold the consignment for a long period in a warehouse, necessitating payment of "demurrage charges". The procedure to obtain the testing certificate is laden with regulatory and procedural hurdles: this results in increased trade costs and, in turn, hinders potential opportunities for improved cross-border trade with Sri Lanka.

Given such infrastructure constraints, FSSAI is working to upgrade the existing food testing infrastructure across the country under a $67 million initiative to strengthen necessary infrastructure at state level, as well as referral laboratories. This initiative will set up 45 state or union territory food testing laboratories and 14 referral food testing laboratories to enable NABL accreditation for exporters. In addition, 62 mobile testing laboratories and 1,500 school laboratories will be established across all states and union territories.[19]

The Directorate of Plant Protection, Quarantine, and Storage has 52 plant quarantine stations at different international airports, seaports, and land ports to enforce plant quarantine regulations. There are 60 inland container depots or container freight stations,

---

[19]   FSSAI Rolls Out Scheme to Upgrade Food Testing Labs. 2017. *The Hindu.* 3 November. http://www.thehindu businessline.com/news/fssai-rolls-out-scheme-to-upgrade-food-testing-labs/article9301301.ece.

and 11 foreign post offices that are notified for the entry of plants or plant materials under the Plant Quarantine Order, 2003. In addition, there are 42 post-entry quarantine facilities for relevant products.

The geographical mapping of plant quarantine stations shows a similar trend to the distribution of food testing laboratories, with more of these facilities located in the northern, western, and southern regions than the eastern region. Of the total 52 plant quarantine stations, nearly 79% are in the northern, western, and southern regions; and the remaining 21% are in the eastern region. States such as Meghalaya, Mizoram, and Sikkim do not have plant quarantine stations. The lack of plant quarantine stations poses severe challenges for local producers, exporters, and importers.

The Directorate of Plant Protection, Quarantine, and Storage has plans to establish plant quarantine and testing laboratories at Agartala, Manipur Mizoram, and Meghalaya, although relevant assessments are required before these plans can be implemented.

Port distribution of plant quarantine stations is likewise highly uneven. Of the 52 plant quarantine stations, 28 are in land frontiers, 10 in seaports, 12 in airports, and only 3 are located in inland container depots.

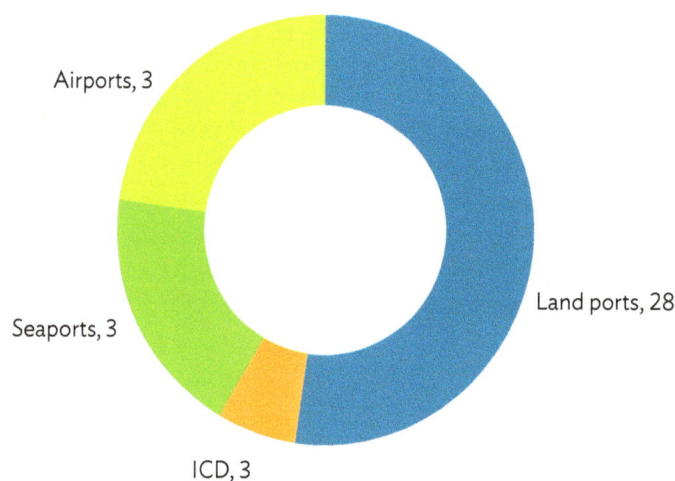

Figure 18: Port-Wise Distribution of Plant Quarantine Stations

Airports, 3

Land ports, 28

Seaports, 3

ICD, 3

ICD = inland container depot.

Source: Directorate of Plant Protection, Quarantine, and Storage http://ppqs.gov.in/contactus/plant -quarantine-stations-pqs (accessed 31 May 2016).

4.2. The Technical Barriers to Trade Environment

India's TBT-related laws and regulations have been developed according to the WTO Agreement on Technical Barriers to Trade (TBT Agreement),[20] which clearly mandates that "technical regulations, standards, and conformity assessment procedures are transparent, nondiscriminatory, and do not create unnecessary obstacles to trade." At the same time, it permits all member countries to use policy instruments to achieve their legitimate policy objectives, such as protection of the environment, protection of human health, and safety (footnote 17). The TBT laws and regulations in India are governed and enforced by different ministries and departments of central and state governments that are primarily responsible for the formulation and execution of policies.

4.2.1. Legal Framework

In 2016, the Government of India comprehensively overhauled the outdated **Bureau of Indian Standards Act 1986** and introduced the new **Bureau of Indian Standards Act 2016**. With this, it also changed the name of the Bureau of Indian Standards to the National Standards Body of India. The new act reflected the evolving modern business environment, bringing more products and services under the umbrella of a mandatory standard regime. It introduced a compulsory certification regime for any goods and services that are classed as critical for public interest or for the protection of human health, safety of the environment, and prevention of unethical practices. It also includes an enabling provision for hallmarks of gems, jewelry, and other related articles.

The Bureau of Indian Standards Act 2016 entails "multiple simplified conformity assessment schemes, including self-declaration of conformity", which provides many simplified options to manufacturers to adhere to the necessary standards and obtain certificates of conformity. Additionally, it has a provision that allows designation to any authority or agency, in addition to the National Standards Body of India, to check the conformity of products and services to a standard, and issue certificates of conformity. Moreover, the Act contains provisions for repair or recall, including product liability of products bearing the standard mark but not complying with the relevant Indian standard.

India's legal framework has many additional laws that deal with TBT measures, which serve as the sole parameter to design, formulate, and implement TBT regulations. Key relevant legislation includes the following:

(i)   Prevention of Food Adulteration Act, 1954;
(ii)   Plant Quarantine (Regulation of Import into India) Order, 2003;
(iii)   Meat Food Product Order, 1973;
(iv)   Milk and Milk Product Order, 1992;
(v)   Bureau of Indian Standards (BIS) Act, 1986 and BIS Rules, 1987;
(vi)   Standards of Weight and Measures Act, 1976;

---

[20]   World Trade Organization. Agreement of Technical Barriers to Trade: www.wto.org/english/docs_e/ legal_e/17-tbt.pdf.

(vii)   Livestock Importation Act, 1898;
(viii)   Agricultural Marketing Standards (AGMARK) Act, 1937;
(ix)   The Infant Milk Substitutes, Feeding Bottles and Infant Foods Act, 2002;
(x)   Export (Quality Control and Inspection) Act, 1963;
(xi)   Essential Commodities Act, 1955;
(xii)   Indian Explosives Act, 1884; and
(xiii)   Energy Conservation Act, 2001.

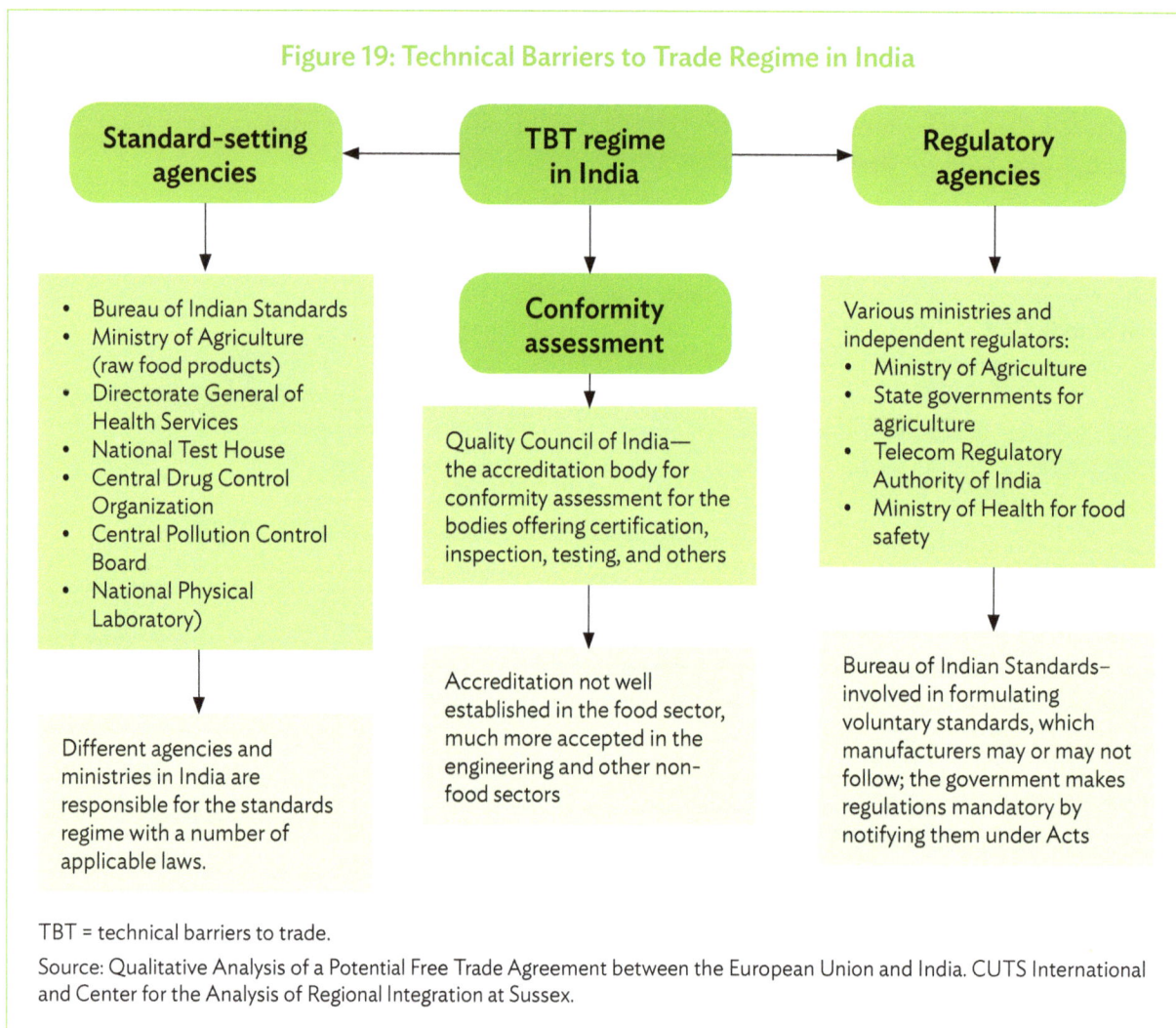

Figure 19: Technical Barriers to Trade Regime in India

Standard-setting agencies	TBT regime in India	Regulatory agencies
• Bureau of Indian Standards • Ministry of Agriculture (raw food products) • Directorate General of Health Services • National Test House • Central Drug Control Organization • Central Pollution Control Board • National Physical Laboratory)	**Conformity assessment**	Various ministries and independent regulators: • Ministry of Agriculture • State governments for agriculture • Telecom Regulatory Authority of India • Ministry of Health for food safety
Different agencies and ministries in India are responsible for the standards regime with a number of applicable laws.	Quality Council of India—the accreditation body for conformity assessment for the bodies offering certification, inspection, testing, and others Accreditation not well established in the food sector, much more accepted in the engineering and other non-food sectors	Bureau of Indian Standards–involved in formulating voluntary standards, which manufacturers may or may not follow; the government makes regulations mandatory by notifying them under Acts

TBT = technical barriers to trade.
Source: Qualitative Analysis of a Potential Free Trade Agreement between the European Union and India. CUTS International and Center for the Analysis of Regional Integration at Sussex.

4.2.2.   Institutional Framework

Bureau of Indian Standards

The Department of Commerce is the leading body in India responsible for all issues related to TBT measures in the WTO. However, the **Bureau of Indian Standards** (BIS) is the apex body responsible in formulating and implementing standards under the BIS Act

1986 and BIS Rules 1987: currently, 165 products fall under mandatory standards. There are over 19,226 standards in 14 sectors and many of these standards are currently being harmonized with global standards. A key role of BIS is to set parameters for certification of product and quality systems, international cooperation, testing, enforcement of standards, and generating awareness among consumers. The Department of Commerce designated BIS as the TBT WTO enquiry point for disseminating information on standards, technical regulations, and certifications.

BIS functions through sector coordination committees for power, steel, automotive, food processing, textiles, and information technology, which promote harmonization of standards at the national level. A member of both the International Organization for Standardization (ISO) and International Electrotechnical Commission (IEC), it heavily emphasizes harmonizing national standards with regional and global standards, and global standards are frequently accepted as national standards in India. Sometimes, national standards are streamlined and harmonized with international standards in the areas of India's export interest.

Furthermore, BIS has signed bilateral agreements with the national standards bodies of Afghanistan, Bhutan, Brazil, France, Germany, Israel, Mauritius, Nigeria, South Africa, the United Arab Emirates, and the US. BIS has also inked 21 memorandums of understanding (MOUs) in the area of "standardization and conformity assessment." It has signed mutual recognition agreements (MRAs) with the Sri Lanka Standards Institution (SLSI); the Pakistan Standards and Quality Control Authority; the Bangladesh Standards and Testing Institute (2015); and the Bhutan Standards Bureau (2015). BIS actively engages in regional forums, such as the South Asia Regional Standards Organization (SARSO) and the Pacific Asia Standards Congress.

Export Inspection Council

The **Export Inspection Council** (EIC) has been established under the Export Quality Control and Inspection Act, 1963, Government of India and is responsible for preshipment inspection and certification of all consignments for export. It provides quality control certificates based on Food Safety Management Systems at par with international standards on Hazard Analysis Critical Controls Point (HACCP) to ensure the quality of food processing. The EIC provides a range of quality-related certificates that include authenticity of origin, health certificates, phytosanitary certificates, and preshipment certificates.

The EIC has likewise signed many international recognition arrangements in efforts to improve effective market access for India's exports to international markets. The EIC and SLSI, for example, have entered into recognition of the export certification system: currently, SLSI accepts the EIC inspection certificate for 85 commodities, including milk products, fruits and vegetable products, household electrical appliances and switches, steel and steel products, electrical cables and cement, and others. Similarly, the Bhutan Food Regulatory Authority (BAFRA) has signed an MOU with EIC for the recognition of inspection certificates on dry fish and frozen chicken. The certificate issued by the EIC will be accepted by BAFRA without any laboratory test.

India has many other institutions responsible for developing standards in their respective areas, such as:

(i)   Petroleum and Explosives Safety Organization,
(ii)   Directorate of Standardization,
(iii)   Central Electricity Authority,
(iv)   Food Corporation of India,
(v)   Directorate of Marketing and Inspection,
(vi)   Central Pollution Control Board,
(vii)   Oil Industry Safety Directorate,
(viii)   Atomic Energy Regulatory Board,
(ix)   Petroleum and Natural Gas Regulatory Board, and
(x)   Directorate General of Mines Safety.

Several bodies, ministries, and agencies are involved in the implementation of TBT regulations in India, including:

(i)   Directorate General of Health Services,
(ii)   Ministry of Food Processing Industry,
(iii)   Department of Consumer Affairs,
(iv)   Directorate of Marketing and Inspection,
(v)   Department of Agriculture and Cooperation,
(vi)   Department of Animal Husbandry and Dairying,
(vii)   Department of Legal Metrology,
(viii)   Bureau of Energy Efficiency,
(ix)   Chief Controller of Explosives,
(x)   Directorate General of Mines Safety,
(xi)   Department of Road Transport and Highways, and
(xii)   Central Pollution Control Board.

4.2.3.   Infrastructure Facilities

BIS has 194 recognized and 47 specialized laboratories spread across India. Yet there are significant disparities in these facilities: of the 194 recognized labs, nearly 72% are in Uttar Pradesh, Delhi, Maharashtra, Karnataka, Tamil Nadu, Haryana, and Gujarat, with the remaining 38% of facilities scattered throughout all other states. BIS-recognized laboratories are absent from states such as Chhattisgarh, Jharkhand, Manipur, Meghalaya, Mizoram, Nagaland, Sikkim, and Tripura, creating a clear laboratory infrastructure gap.

EIC has 26 laboratories located throughout India that provide quality inspection certificates for all exported products. However, the state-wise distribution of laboratories is again skewed: states such as Andhra Pradesh, Maharashtra, Tamil Nadu, and Kerala have 80% of the laboratories, while other states have only 20%. Furthermore, there is a shortage of export inspection agencies in some states: most states in the northeast part of India do not have export inspection agencies and rely primarily on agencies of other states for testing certificates.

Figure 20: State-Wise Export Inspection Agencies

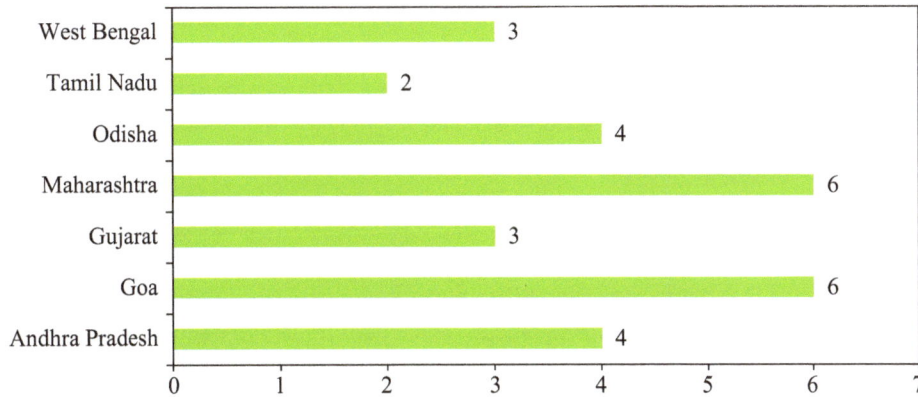

West Bengal	3
Tamil Nadu	2
Odisha	4
Maharashtra	6
Gujarat	3
Goa	6
Andhra Pradesh	4

Source: Export Inspection Agency, Government of India, https://eicindia.gov.in/Approved-Units/Approved-Units/Lab_List.aspx (accessed 30 May 2017).

4.3. Key Issues in Domestic Legislative and Regulatory Frameworks for Sanitary and Phytosanitary Measures and Technical Barriers to Trade

Despite significant efforts to overhaul its domestic legislative and regulatory framework of SPS and TBT institutions, India still faces multidimensional challenges, including, for example, the absence of a robust legislative framework and technical regulations, complex and overlapping regulations, lack of coherence with international standards, and enforcement-related issues.

4.3.1. Lack of Legislative Framework and Technical Regulations

India has a significant deficit in technical regulations in sectors such as telecommunications, electronics, information technology products, toys, chemicals, lead in paints, and others. While most developed and developing countries have already established technical regulations in these sectors to protect consumers and provide safeguards to domestic industries against imports, many of these sectors still require regulation in India. For example, India lacks regulations for telecommunications products, and lags behind many other countries in this area. The Telecom Engineering Center has established standards, but to date no legislative framework under which these standards can be followed, even in cases where the BIS Act could be used for this purpose. Telecom Engineering Center standards must be transformed into BIS standards before the standards can be followed, making the whole process more complex.

4.3.2.   Complex Multi-agency Regulatory Mandates

The current SPS and TBT regulatory framework is complex due to the large number of regulatory bodies under various ministries. Although FSSAI is now established as a single point for regulating the domestic food sector and imports, critical areas are not yet fully regulated. FSSAI cannot regulate the primary production of food products, which could have far-reaching implications for food safety, and similarly there are issues related to meat products and dairy products which are regulated by both FSSAI and Department of Animal Husbandry.

BIS is an apex organization in India and actively participates in the SARSO Committee for Harmonization of Standards. However, BIS is a standard-setting body and has no mandate to regulate standards, which creates significant challenges for BIS to negotiate standards at a regional or bilateral level without consulting domestic regulators in respective sectors. Any commitment BIS makes in SARSO without adequate consultation with domestic regulators could become a source of conflict which, in turn, could affect regional negotiations.

India's EIC is a regulatory body for exported products and primarily deals in international trade, being mandated to conduct compulsory inspections of 958 notified exported products under the EIC Act. The increasing importance of trade has persuaded the Government of India to set up more institutions to meet specific requirements of selected products or sectors, such as the Agricultural and Processed Food Products Export Development Authority (APEDA); AGMARK; Marine Products Export Development Authority (MPEDA); the Chemical and Allied Export Promotion Council of India; and the Chemicals, Cosmetics, and Dyes Export Promotion Council to promote trade in selected products. Over time, the rapid growth in these areas has increased the importance of quality and safety standards in exported products, and these bodies are also involved in the regulatory landscape of these exported products. For example, the APEDA is an apex institution established under the APEDA Act with a mandate of setting standards for selected agricultural and processed food products; but it has not yet developed its own standards for export products and, instead, uses AGMARK standards for these products. At the same time, these products also come under the purview of EIC.

In like manner, several products sold under BIS mandatory certification are also covered under the FSSAI Act 2006. Under regulation restrictions relating to conditions for sale, Food Safety and Standards (Prohibition and Restrictions on Sales) Regulations, 2011, Clause 4 states that "No person shall manufacture, sell, store or exhibit for sale, an infant milk food, infant formula and milk cereal-based weaning food, processed cereal-based weaning food and follow-up formula except under Bureau of Indian Standards Certification Mark." Therefore, the following food requires mandatory BIS certification: (i) infant milk food, (ii) milk cereal-based weaning food, and (iii) processed cereal-based weaning food.[21]

Similarly, a notable study by Hanzhou Yang identified that producers dealing with powered evaporated and condensed milks should meet the necessary conditions stipulated by

---

[21]   FSSAI Proposes Review of Provisions for Mandatory Certification under BIS, Food Safety Helpline, https://foodsafetyhelpline.com/2018/01/fssai-proposes-review-provisions-mandatory-certification-bis/.

both FSSAI and BIS.[22] Both have divergent "hygiene, additives, and limits of containments standards" to assess the quality of products.[23] Likewise, fruits and vegetables can come under the purview of FSSAI, BIS, and AGMARK.

The multi-agency regulatory framework coupled with overlapping functions and responsibilities leads to (i) a convoluted trade environment, and (ii) a dilemma when entering into MRAs as there is ambiguity in defining the role of the institution involved.

4.3.3.   Alignment of National and International Standards

Although India is making considerable efforts to align its standards with international standards, it has yet to integrate domestic standards with global standards. FSSAI has aligned its food standards with Codex standards, although gaps remain. For instance, the requirement of Good Agricultural Practices, Good Hygienic Practices (GHP), and HACCP are not fully regulated in India. This is demonstrated in the lack of compliance of seafood and dairy products with HACCP and GHP requirements.

4.3.4.   Enforcement of Standards

Despite many technical regulations being in force for several decades, the practical level of enforcement can fall short of the goal in India. Lack of uniformity in interpretation of legal text provisions and their implementation, together with the varying levels of competence of regulatory bodies are key factors behind suboptimal performance. Several factors negatively impact the effective enforcement of regulations in India, including a weak enforcement infrastructure at both state and central levels, inadequate testing agencies, shortage of inspectors, lack of skilled personnel, nonuniformity of enforcement, and nonavailability of information.

The enforcement of regulations in India has some fundamental flaws inherent to its structure: for instance, it relies excessively on its own inspection machinery (government laboratories and other agencies) to verify compliance. This effectively pushes the onus of compliance with regulations onto the industry, and that regulatory compliance should be fulfilled before any inspection takes place. However, this does not happen in practice, and there is need to create a system where the industry meets with compliance without any regulatory inspection.

Furthermore, India's exports face SPS-related barriers in international markets due to the lack of a domestic monitoring system. India has not yet drafted appropriate guidance documents for domestic and export manufacturing units and products, including additives, contaminants, packaging, storage, and transportation. The current infrastructure for regular monitoring (additives, contaminants, and residue limits) is very weak for both domestic and imported products.

---

[22]   Food Safety in India: Status and Challenges. https://tarina.tci.cornell.edu/wp-content/uploads/ 2017/ 05/TCI-TARINA-Policy-Brief-No.5.pdf.

[23]   Ibid.

4.3.5.   Lack of Information

India's SPS and TBT regulatory bodies continue to struggle with the lack of information on food regulations of other countries and their agreements, quarantine procedures, HAPPC, and other related procedures. The availability of such information is critical not only for exports, but also for imports; for identifying strategic changes needed in the national, regional, and global regulatory environments; and for keeping Indian industry updated and fully informed.

The overall policy regime dealing with production, marketing, and imports of agriculture products is controlled centrally, meaning that the basic agriculture production of states must be aligned with national standards and inspection procedures. Recently, India's rice exports to the US and European Union were affected due to excessive use of tricyclazole and isoprothiolane pesticides.[24] The Ministry of Agriculture and Farmers Welfare subsequently issued an alert to states such as Andhra Pradesh, Karnataka, Kerala, Tamil Nadu, and Telangana to monitor farmers' use of pesticides that enter into the food supply chain. This demonstrates (i) a need to promote dynamic communication between the central authorities and the states in sharing of information; and (ii) a need to create awareness among farmers on ramifications of excessive use of pesticides.

4.4. Gaps Comparing Current National Sanitary and Phytosanitary and Technical Barriers to Trade Legislation, Local Practices, and International Best Practices

Many SASEC countries—with the exception of India—developed standards several decades ago, but did not update them to reflect scientific and technological advancement. Today however, given the very different stages of growth and development of the SASEC countries, India is relatively advanced in developing standards. Several SASEC countries have significant SPS and TBT-related gaps in institutions and regulatory architectures, which hamper cross-border trade. One of the key problems faced in the SASEC region is that of multiple regulating agencies that have produced numerous outdated and/or unnecessary regulations.

The overarching problem of a multiplicity of standards and regulations relating to SPS and TBT frameworks within India also exists in other countries. This multiplicity of standards within the domestic environment of an importing country acts as a barrier, largely because the legitimate expectations of both exporters and importers are heavily compromised by divergent regulatory frameworks. Ultimately, this negatively impacts the entire cross-border trade ecosystem in the SASEC region. Divergent rules and regulations are also the source of many regulatory and technical impediments to the growth of intraregional trade in the

---

[24]   Reduce pesticide residue in rice, States told. http://www.thehindu.com/news/national/ karnataka/ reduce-pesticide-residue-in-rice-states-told/article21823605.ece.

region. This subsection examines some of the legislative and regulatory gaps within the region in comparison to international best practice.

(i)   **Gaps in food standards across the SASEC countries.** Among SASEC countries, India and Sri Lanka have well developed comprehensive food regulations covering information on food additives, containments, toxins, maximum residue limit, preservatives, antioxidants, processing aids, colors, sweeteners, flavors, and emulsifying and stabilizing agents. Bangladesh and Nepal have limited information, while Bhutan and Maldives have almost no information on the same components. There are likewise significant gaps in food standards across the SASEC countries: for example, FSSAI have established specific standards for instant noodles in India, while other SASEC countries have no standards for the same product; and while frozen food is well-regulated in India and Sri Lanka under their respective food acts, they are not regulated in Bangladesh, Bhutan, Maldives, and Nepal.

(ii)   **Food preservatives** are categorized as class I preservatives or class II. Tables 5 and 6 analyze preservatives used in food products across SASEC countries. Most class I preservatives are common across India, Bangladesh, Nepal, and Sri Lanka; while Bhutan and Maldives have no information on class I preservatives. India classifies edible vegetable oil as class I, while Bangladesh and Nepal consider wood smoke under this class of preservatives. Bangladesh, Nepal, and Sri Lanka recognize hops and portable alcohol as class I preservatives.

Table 5: Class I Preservatives of SASEC Countries

Class I Preservatives	India	Bangladesh	Bhutan	Maldives	Nepal	Sri Lanka
Not restricted Unless Otherwise provided in the rules	Common salt Sugar Dextrose Glucose Syrup Spices Vinegar Honey Edible vegetable oils	Common salt Sugar Dextrose Glucose Syrup Spices Vinegar Honey Wood smoke Hops Commercial salt Alcohol or potable spirit	Not applicable	Not applicable	Common salt Sugar Dextrose Glucose Syrup Spices Vinegar Honey Wood smoke Hops Alcohol	Common salt Any soluble carbohydrate sweetening matter Spices Vinegar Honey Potable spirits or wines

Source: Food Regulations of South Asia Subregional Economic Cooperation countries.

The use of class II preservatives is limited in food products: only one class II preservative can be used in any one food product. India, Bangladesh, Nepal, and Sri Lanka allow the use of selected types of class II preservatives in their food products, and commonly used class II preservatives in these countries are benzoic acid, including salts; sulfurous acid including salts; nitrates; and nitrites of sodium or potassium. Sorbic acid and its salt are also included in India, Bangladesh, and Sri Lanka, but not in Nepal. India and Sri Lanka permit nisin and propionic acid in their food regulations. On the other hand, food regulations in Bhutan and Maldives do not provide any specific information on class II preservatives. Table 6 lays out the different types of class II preservatives allowed in SASEC countries' food regulations, with the exception of Bhutan and Maldives

Table 6: Class II Preservatives of SASEC Countries

India	Bangladesh	Bhutan	Maldives	Nepal	Sri Lanka
1. Benzoic acid, including salts thereof 2. Sulfurous acid, including salts thereof 3. Nitrates or nitrites of sodium or potassium in respect of food, such as ham and pickled meat 4. Sorbic acid, including its sodium, potassium and calcium salts, propionates of calcium or sodium, lactic acid, and acid calcium phosphate 5. Nisin 6. Sodium and calcium propionate 7. Methyl or propyl parahydroxy-benzoate 8. Propionic acid, including esters or salt thereof 9. Sodium diacetate 10. Sodium, potassium and calcium salts of lactic acid	1. Benzoic acid, including salts thereof 2. Sulfurous acid, including salts thereof 3. Nitrites of sodium or potassium in respect of food, such as ham, pickle, meat 4. Sorbic acid, including salts thereof	NA	NA	1. Sodium or potassium nitrites 2. Benzoic acid and salts thereof 3. Sulfurous acid and sulfur dioxide	1. Sorbic acid 2. Benzoic acid 3. Sulfur dioxide 4. Biphenyl, diphenyl 5. Orthophenylphenol 6. Nisin 7. Potassium nitrite 8. Sodium nitrite 9. Propionic acid

Source: Food regulations of South Asia Subregional Economic Cooperation countries.

(iii)   **Alignment of national and international standards.** SASEC countries have a long way to go in aligning national standards with global standards. For example, Bangladesh, Bhutan, India, Maldives, Nepal, and Sri Lanka have adopted global best practices such as Hazard Analysis Critical Control Point (HACCP) and Good Hygienic Practices (GHP) as voluntary programs. Yet currently, only large firms adopt these practices. SASEC countries face multidimensional challenges in the implementation of HACCP and GAP, including the absence of state body and industry guidance; unavailability of quality raw materials; lack of officials, guidance, and technical know-how; shortage of trained consultants; and trainee and cost-related implications.

(iv) **Infrastructure gaps.** Another key issue in the SASEC region is the huge SPS and TBT-related infrastructure deficit which, in turn, affects efficiency of export and import operations at ports.

(v) **Information asymmetries.** Significant asymmetries exist in the availability of information on SPS and TBT regulations. Bangladesh, India, Nepal, and Sri Lanka have developed trade portals which become focal points for providing comprehensive information on various SPS and TBT regulations for the trading community; Bhutan and Maldives have yet to establish such trade portals. Information is not always available in English translation.

(vi) **Absence of national single window systems.** SASEC countries are at different levels in establishing and implementing national single window (NSW) systems. Bangladesh, India, and Sri Lanka have established NSW systems, while Bhutan, Nepal, and Maldives are at different stages of developing national systems.

(vii) **Divergent IT application for customs clearance.** Current procedures for electronic clearance of goods through customs vary across India, Nepal, and Bangladesh. For instance, Petrapole (India) and Raxaul (India) use ICEGATE software, whereas their corresponding border points in Benapole (Bangladesh) and Birgunj (Nepal), as well as Male (Maldives) use Automated Systems for Customs Data (ASYCUDA) software, which has significant cost implications.

(viii) **Absence of accreditation bodies.** Among the SASEC countries, Bangladesh, India, and Sri Lanka have accreditation bodies that confirm laboratories' capacity to provide certification for goods, after assessing their technical competence to test, and other related parameters. Other SASEC countries, including Nepal and Bhutan, are at much earlier stages of developing national accreditation bodies. The Nepal Bureau of Standards and Metrology is currently engaged in setting up accreditation bodies under the Nepal Laboratory Accreditation Scheme program. Bhutan has a National Accreditation Focal Point under the South Asian Association for Regional Cooperation-German National Metrology Institute cooperation, and accreditation in Bhutan is mainly done by NABL and the National Accreditation Board for Certification Bodies (NABCB) in India. In February 2018, however, FSSAI issued an order confirming recognition of the National Food testing Laboratory in Thimphu, Bhutan for analysis of samples under Food Safety and Standards Regulations, 2011. This could significantly ease the complexity and time required by Bhutanese traders to test food products for export to India.[25]

[25] Order of the Food Safety and Standards Authority of India. File No. 12012/45/2017-QA.

4.5   India's Evolving Position on Sanitary and Phytosanitary and Technical Barriers to Trade Measures

India's increased integration with the global economy has created a need to overhaul its domestic laws, regulations, and institutions to keep economic and trade interests updated in the ever-changing global economic and political environment. As a result, India has significantly invested in enhancing the capacity of domestic institutions to enable better visibility and influence at both regional and multilateral levels. Substantial progress has been made in reforming the SPS and TBT environments. India's evolving position on SPS and TBT measures is shaped by three major developments: (i) entry into the WTO SPS and TBT agreements; (ii) the rise of regional trade agreements; and (iii) increased integration with the world, coupled with the growing importance of higher standards in the domestic economy.

The WTO agreements on SPS and TBT have facilitated India's trade with the world by improving transparency at the national level, promoting harmonization, and reducing the implementation of SPS and TBT measures that cannot be justified scientifically.[26] India has made considerable efforts to streamline its domestic legislation and align with the global trading system. As a result, India's track record on the international stage is satisfactory with respect to the WTO-led SPS and TBT frameworks: according to the United Nations Conference on Trade and Development (UNCTAD), India has currently developed and enforced 72 measures for SPS and 46 for TBT.[27] And the WTO database shows only three complaints initiated against India through the WTO Dispute Settlement Body involving India's SPS measures, and one involving India's TBT measures. Of these disputes, the Dispute Settlement Body ruled against India in only one case, which India duly complied with.[28] In another dispute, India and the complainant country (European Communities) reached a "mutually agreed solution," indicating India's cooperation in international deal-making.[29]

With respect to bilateral and regional trade agreements, India has emphasized inclusion of MRAs: its free trade agreements with advanced countries contain provisions on MRAs, mostly agreeing to the standards of those countries. For example, the India–Japan Comprehensive Economic Partnership Agreement underpins the importance of promoting greater coherence in standards through "conformity assessment procedures."[30] Similarly, The India–Singapore Comprehensive Economic Partnership contains provisions on mutual

26   S.J. Henson. 2012. *Impact of Sanitary and Phytosanitary Measures on Developing Countries.* Report of Department of Agricultural and Food Economics of University of Reading. http://www.cepaa. esalq.usp.br/pdfs/134.pdf.
27   UNCTAD. http://i-tip.unctad.org/Forms/MemberView.aspx?mode=modify&action=search.
28   India: Measures Concerning the Importation of Certain Agricultural Products. DS 430. The World Trade Organization, https://www.wto.org/english/tratop_e/dispu_e/cases_e/ds430_e.htm
29   India: Quantitative Restrictions on Imports of Agricultural, Textile, and Industrial Products. DS 96. The World Trade Organization, https://www.wto.org/english/tratop_e/dispu_e/cases_e/ds90_e.htm
30   The India–Japan Comprehensive Economic Partnership Agreement: https://www.mofa.go.jp/region/ asia-paci/india/pdfs/joint0612.pdf

recognition of standards and regulations.[31] India's increased interest in including MRAs and agreeing to the standards of other countries in FTAs is influenced by several factors, including the upgrading of national measurement methods, and the scientific advancement of increasingly important standards in value chain-led trade.[32] These provisions are largely in line with what India negotiates at a multilateral level.

Waves of globalization have contributed to deeper integration of markets, increased consumers' income, and spurred higher aspirations and consumer demand. The demand is not merely for a myriad of goods and services to cater to consumer needs, but also for an efficient, safe, and consumer-friendly demand and supply regime to pass the litmus test of consumer "satisfaction." Catering to consumer satisfaction led to the birth of modern international trade governance mechanisms through which consumer welfare is ensured, and the safety and security of plant, animal, and human life is positively maintained. These mechanisms come in the form of standards and regulations.

The world is moving fast toward standardization through various international and regional initiatives. In a highly interconnected world, standards-related policies (i.e., SPS and TBT policies and frameworks) focus on five areas: (i) challenges related to cross-border trade; (ii) ensuring a higher level of transparency, and sharing relevant information with all stakeholders; (iii) the opportunity to provide feedback and comments on standards while they are being formulated; (iv) bringing trade-related concerns to the attention of the implementing party and seeking solutions; and (v) developing domestic capacity in the context of standards.[33]

India has long recognized the growing importance and need for higher standards in global value chains and that participation in modern trade largely hinges on the ability of producers to meet global standards. India further understands clearly that domestic reforms are essential to comply with global standards to create trade opportunities. However, it is also important to recognize that meeting standards for exports in the international market is not a permanent guarantee for effective market access. Accepted conformity assessment procedures are vital to get unhindered market access in other markets and they become the new fulcrum of meeting standards in the global market.

Ultimately, India still has some distance to go in upgrading its domestic standards to meet global standards. It recognizes that standards-related policies should take into account the changed realities of the global trading system, such as aligning policies and capabilities toward international standards; recognizing the importance of private and voluntary standards, and conformity assessment; and improving the capacity of small and medium enterprises through effective training programs. In this overall context, India deepens its roots in a strong capacity-based environment to meet international standards

[31] Center for the Analysis of Regional Integration at Sussex and CUTS International. 2007. A Report on Qualitative Analysis of a Potential Free Trade Agreement between the European Union and India. http://trade.ec.europa.eu/doclib/docs/2007/june/tradoc_135101.pdf.

[32] (Kallummal, 2012), SPS Measures and Possible Market Access Implications for Agricultural Trade in the Doha Round: An analysis of systemic issues, International Development Economic Associates.

[33] H. Singh. 2016. Trade Policy Reforms in India since 1991. Brooking India. Special Import License Regulations. 2013. Extraordinary Gazette, Democratic Socialist Republic of Sri Lanka. 5 June 2013. http://www.imexport.gov.lk/web/images/PDF_upload/Gazettes/english/1813-14_e.pdf.

and to upgrade its own standards at the same time. India unequivocally understands that alignment of domestic standards with international standards is critical to prevent friction when it comes to the application of these standards in the international trade regime.

The Government of India, through its Ministry of Commerce and Industry and various agencies and institutions, has been actively participating in the rule-making process of SPS and TBT standards and regulations, not only at the national level, but also through regional and international platforms. BIS – the pan-Indian standards body – facilitates a quality-based trade regime and has been ceaselessly working toward harmonization of India's standards with the two known international standards bodies:[34] the ISO and the IEC.

BIS has entered into various MOUs and MRAs with other countries' national standards bodies in conformity assessment procedures,[35] as well as mutual recognition of standards.[36] Progress is good: India already harmonized 17% of its domestic standards with international standards. BIS has also framed the draft "conformity assessment regulations" under the BIS Act,[37] which will increase global acceptance of India's standards and enhance potential market access for exporters.

The Quality Council of India (QCI) plays an important role in improving the capacity of domestic manufacturers to adhere to a set of uniform practices that help create a stable and consumer-friendly trade climate in India. One landmark QCI initiative is the zero defect zero effect (ZED) certification scheme, designed especially for micro- small- and medium-sized enterprises (MSMEs) and based on the current "Make in India" agenda, calling for zero defect in manufacturing of products for both domestic and export purposes, along with zero negative impact on consumer welfare. The ZED scheme also incorporates a subsidy plan for MSME capacity building. Another QCI initiative, in association with the Ministry of Ayurveda, Yoga and Naturopathy, Unani, Siddha and Homoeopathy (AYUSH), is the AYUSH Mark Scheme,[38] which incorporates domestic regulation requirements,[39] together with World Health Organization (WHO) guidelines and product requirements.[40]

In another historical move toward uniformity in standards setting, the Ministry of Commerce and Industry, in collaboration with the Confederation of Indian Industry, BIS, NABCB, and other knowledge partners, developed the Indian National Strategy for Standardization.[41]

---

[34]   In fact, certain India standards are already harmonized with these international standards. See Bureau of International Standards. International Co-operation. http://www.bis.org.in/sf/international_ cooperation.asp.

[35]   These countries include Afghanistan, Bangladesh, Bhutan, Egypt, France, Germany, Ghana, Greece, Israel, Iran, Mauritius, Nigeria, Slovenia, United Arab Emirates, US, Ukraine, Uzbekistan, Brazil, and South Africa.

[36]   S. B. S. Reddy. 2006. Policy Brief on SPS and TBT Measures–India's Concerns. Regional Trade Policy Course. Hong Kong, China.

[37]   Raj. 2016. ZED Certification Scheme for MSMEs. Quality India Magazine. August–October 2016.

[38]   Quality Council of India. Voluntary Certification Scheme for AYUSH Products. http://www.qcin. org/ voluntary-certification-scheme-for-ayush-products.php.

[39]   The domestic regulation requirements have to be met for the AYUSH standard mark certification.

[40]   The WHO guidelines have to be met for the AYUSH Premium mark certification.

[41]   Press Information Bureau. 4th National Standards Conclave. Ministry of Commerce, Government. of India. 28 April 2017. http://pib.nic.in/newsite/PrintRelease.aspx?relid=161366.

> ### Box 2: Key Elements of India's National Strategy for Standardization
>
> - Policy formulation through an inclusive participatory mechanism.
>
> - A proper policy framework for selecting goods for which technical regulations are required to be issued in the public interest.
>
> - A proper policy framework for selecting the services for which technical regulations are required to be commonly notified.
>
> - A national common strategy for effective capacity building and capacity utilization of accreditation and conformity assessment models by the various institutions in India.
>
> - Development of a harmonized system of inclusive quality standard setting.
>
> Source: Indian National Strategy for Standardization Evolving a Quality Ecosystem, National Accreditation Board for Certification Bodies.

The Government of India has launched the Indian Standards Portal to build a common information platform on India's standards and regulations, conformity assessment procedures, and others, and to ensure maximum outreach of updates and policies.[42] India is also an active member of Codex Alimentarius: India's FSSAI and EIC are responsible for compliance with Codex Standards. Through these institutions, India further ensures its participation in international decision- and rule-making.

In short, India has fully recognized the need to improve its domestic SPS and TBT institutions and already developed several initiatives to this end, including a comprehensive national standardization strategy; launching of a standards information portal; rolling out of the AYUSH Mark Scheme; and development of the ZED certification scheme. Such initiatives serve as constructive examples of India's evolving stance on SPS and TBT measures in the current global trading environment, where gold standards are of immense importance. India is firmly on the path toward global standards compliance, while simultaneously making its own national frameworks more coherent and uniform across states.

---

[42] Capital Market. Nirmala Sitharaman Launches India Standards Portal. *Business Standard.* 8 May 2017. www.business-standard.com/article/news-cm/nirmala-sitharaman-launches-india-standards-portal-117050800738_1.html.

Chapter 5
Standards, Regulations, and Procedural Obstacles That Impede Trade

This diagnostic study has identified potential export items of India to five SASEC countries and also noted that India exports the same products to non-SASEC countries at lower unit prices. The reason of less exports or no exports to five SASEC countries are many, ranging from India's trade policy restrictiveness, to the importing countries' restrictions on imports. This chapter explores the mid-ground between these two extremes, and explores by country some of the SPS and TBT-related challenges that India's traders face when exporting the potential products to other SASEC countries.

5.1. Impediments Exporting to Bangladesh

India's current major exports to Bangladesh include cotton, milled rice, motor vehicles, wheat, onions, and chemicals, among others (Table A1.1), while potential exports to Bangladesh include 108 products using the HS 6-digit level of product classification (Table A2.1). These products are subject to different kinds of SPS and TBT measures in Bangladesh as per the UNCTAD database, India trade portal. The details of specific NTMs on these products are found in Table A4.1.

Bangladesh applies seven SPS and three TBT measures on India's potential export items (Table 7). UNCTAD broadly defines these SPS measures in Chapter A, and TBT measures in Chapters B.[43] Chapter A classifies SPS measures and includes legitimate restrictions by the importing country to ensure food safety and prevention of diseases. Chapter B classifies technical measures related to labeling and imposition of standards on technical specifications and quality requirements.

A detailed description of these SPS and TBT measures imposed by Bangladesh on India's potential exports is in Table 7. All potential products at HS 6-digit level were aggregated to their corresponding 2-digit HS codes to show the product-wise relevant NTMs imposed by Bangladesh. The measures listed in Table are legitimate and imposed by the importing country to maintain minimum quality and to ensure food safety.

Procedural Obstacles in Obtaining Import License

The BSTI Ordinance 1985 and the BSTI (Amendment) Act, 2003 made it mandatory to have an import license when importing products in the list prepared under the Mandatory Certification Marks Scheme (MCMS). There are 166 products aggregated into food and

---

[43]   UNCTAD. 2015. *International Classification of Non-Tariff Measures.* Geneva.

Table 7: Sanitary and Phytosanitary and Technical Barriers to Trade Measures Applied by Bangladesh on India's Potential Exports

NTM Code	Measure Description by UNCTAD	2-Digit HS Codes
A: Sanitary and Phytosanitary Measures		
A14	Special authorization requirement for SPS reasons: A requirement that importers should receive authorization, permits, or approval from a relevant government agency of the destination country for SPS reasons. To obtain the authorization, importers may need to comply with other related regulations and conformity assessments. Example: An import authorization from the Ministry of Health is required.	13, 30
A15	Registration requirements for importers: The requirement that importers should be registered before they can import certain products: To register, importers may need to comply with certain requirements, provide documentation, and pay registration fees. Example: Importers of a certain food item need to be registered at the Ministry of Health.	30
A21	Tolerance limits for residues of or contamination by certain (nonmicrobiological) substances: A measure that establishes a maximum residue limit (MRL) or tolerance limit of substances such as fertilizers, pesticides, and certain chemicals and metals in food and feed, which are used during their production process, but are not their intended ingredients: It includes a permissible maximum level (ML) for nonmicrobiological contaminants. Measures related to microbiological contaminants are classed under A4 below. Examples: (i) MRL is established for insecticides, pesticides, heavy metals, and veterinary drug residues; (ii) POPs and chemicals generated during processing; and (iii) residues of dithianon in apples and hop.	13, 30
A3	Labeling, marking, and packaging requirements	29, 30
A31	Labeling requirements: Measures defining the information directly related to food safety, which should be provided to the consumer: Labeling is any written, electronic, or graphic communication on the consumer packaging or on a separate but associated label. Examples: (i) Labels that must specify the storage conditions such as "5 degrees C maximum"; and (ii) potentially dangerous ingredients such as allergens, e.g., "contains honey not suitable for children under 1 year of age."	13, 29
A42	Hygienic practices during production: Requirements principally intended to give guidance on the establishment and application of microbiological criteria for food at any point in the food chain from primary production to final consumption: The safety of foods is principally assured by control at the source, product design, and process control, and the application of good hygienic practices during production, processing (including labeling), handling, distribution, storage, sale, preparation, and use. Example: Milking equipment on the farm should be cleaned daily with a specified detergent.	29
A83	Certification requirement: Certification of conformity with a given regulation required by the importing country but may be issued in the exporting or the importing country. Example: Certificate of conformity for materials in contact with food (containers, papers, plastics, and others) is required.	13

continued on next page

Table 7 continued

NTM Code	Measure Description by UNCTAD	2-Digit HS Codes
B: Technical Barriers to Trade (TBT) Measures		
B31	Labeling requirements: Measures regulating the kind, color, and size of printing on packages and labels and defining the information that should be provided to the consumer. Labeling is any written, electronic, or graphic communication on the packaging or on a separate but associated label, or on the product itself. It may include requirements on the official language to be used as well as technical information on the product, such as voltage, components, instruction on use, safety, and security advice. Example: Refrigerators need to carry a label indicating its size, weight, and electricity consumption level.	32, 34, 35, 38, 39, 40, 41, 48, 51, 52, 54, 55, 58, 60, 62, 64, 71, 72, 73, 83, 84, 85, 87, 88, 90, 94
B8	Conformity assessment related to TBT: Requirement for verification that a given TBT requirement has been met: This could be achieved by one or combined forms of inspection and approval procedure, including procedures for sampling, testing and inspection; evaluation, verification and assurance of conformity; accreditation and approval.	25, 27, 28, 29, 32, 34, 35, 38, 39, 40, 41, 48, 51, 52, 54, 55, 58, 60, 62, 64, 71, 72, 73, 83, 84, 85
B82	Testing requirement: A requirement for products to be tested against a given regulation, such as performance level – includes sampling requirement. Example: A testing on a sample of motor vehicle imports is required against the required safety compliance and its equipment.	87, 90

Main Headings of Nontariff Measures:

A1: Prohibitions or restrictions of imports for SPS reasons; A2: Tolerance limits for residues and restricted use of substances; A3: Labeling, marking, and packaging requirements; A4: Hygienic requirements; A8: Conformity assessment related to SPS; B3: Labeling, marking, and packaging requirements; B8: Conformity assessment related to TBT.

HS = Harmonized Commodity Description and Coding System, NTM = nontariff measure, SPS = sanitary and phytosanitary, TBT = technical barriers to trade, UNCTAD = United Nations Conference on Trade and Development.

Sources: Table A4.1; UNCTAD. 2012. *International Classification of Non-Tariff Measures.*

agricultural products (71 items), chemical products (42 items), jute and textile products (11 items), electricals and electronics products (27 items), and engineering products (15 items).[44] For example, the potential products' HS codes (690890 and 690790) are put under the MCMS, which means that the import of these products is subject to the MCMS in Bangladesh (Table A2.1). Furthermore, the majority of these products have significant potential for exports from India.

However, the import of products classified under the MCMS requires a special import license, and the procedure to obtain the license is arcane and cumbersome. Moreover, the license is valid for only 3 years, requiring frequent renewal to maintain its validity. The entire process to obtain the license takes a 19–94 days.[45] Testing samples takes more time than the process to obtain the license (the maximum time for testing is 90 days). One of the key reasons for this delay is the lack of laboratories competent to test the products recognized under the MCMS. Only four laboratories – located in Dhaka, Khulna, Chittagong, and Rajshahi – are able to conduct this testing. The unavailability of laboratories in Bangladesh

---

[44] For the list of 155 products, visit http://bsti.portal.gov.bd/site/page/d2b5d505-31ef-420a-a4bf-b1855fb734de/Product-List-under-Certification-Marks-Scheme.

[45] Procedure for Certification Marks License, Bangladesh Standards Testing Institute: http://bsti.portal.gov.bd/site/page/fb161b66-d269-4173-94ad-4148cc2f5895/Procedure-for-Certification-Marks---License.

thus remains a key challenge which, in turn, causes delays in clearance of cargo at border points.

Challenges Related to Trade Infrastructure

The current state of infrastructure at border points with Bangladesh is very weak. Field surveys conducted for this diagnostic study revealed some of the infrastructure-related challenges, frustrations, and economic disadvantage Indian exporters face, for example, while exporting to Bangladesh via the Petrapole-Benapole border point (Box 3).

Box 3: Infrastructure

A leading tractor manufacturing company, based in Mumbai, trades regularly with Bangladesh through the Benapole land port. It described the difficulties and cost relating to the detention of vehicles.

The per-day detention cost of a trailer is US$ 27 at the India–Bangladesh border. On average, the waiting time of a trailer at the border is 20 days, so the total cost of waiting per trailer is about Rs.40,000. In one month, the company has 30 trailers involved in exports, which makes the total detention cost to the company for 30 trailers about Rs.12,000,000. And the annual cost is huge: Rs14,400,000.

This estimate of detention cost is only for farm vehicles. The company also exports other vehicles which add to its total detention cost: the auto division of the company, for example, sends an additional 400–500 vehicles on a monthly basis.

The cost of vehicles sitting in detention, waiting to cross the border is huge. Only larger companies are able to absorb these costs due to their scale of operations. Effectively, smaller-scale traders cannot bear such costs.

Source: Primary field surveys of Asian Development Bank consultant.

Labeling-Related Obstacles

According to the Food Safety (Labeling) Regulations 2017 of Bangladesh and Product Labelling Policy 2006, imported packaged food products must be in the Bengali language, even if the label of the product is already in English and any foreign language.[46] On the other hand, the Food Safety and Standards (Packaging and Labelling) Regulations, 2011 of India, states that the labeling language should be English or Hindi (Devnagri script).[47] Due to Bangladesh's specific labeling requirement (in Bengali), India's producers have to follow India's labeling regulation for domestic sales and Bangladesh's labeling regulation when exporting to Bangladesh. Moreover, Bangladesh's labeling regulation also makes it mandatory to give the importer's name and address, along with the manufacturer's name

---

[46]   Gadget notification of Food Safety (Labeling) Regulations. 2017.
[47]   Food Safety and Standards (Packaging and Labeling) Regulation, 2011. http://www.fssai. gov.in/dam/jcr:2d48f646-d9f9-4bc1-af03-493f29cc45a9/Packaging_Labelling_Regulations.pdf.

and address, batch number, slot number, date of expiry, and, if applicable, should provide the repackaging, refilling, and distributing agent's name and address.[48] Different labeling standards add to exporters' costs and often affect India's exports of potential products to Bangladesh.

Language-Related Obstacles

Language barriers are of the most common problems faced by India's exporters to Bangladesh. Most of Bangladesh's SPS and TBT regulations are in the Bengali language, causing significant hurdles for exporters from other countries. Recently, Bangladesh released a list of approved export and import goods through land ports in the Bengali language,[49] which was uploaded by the Indian Export Organization (FIEO) to the India Trade Portal without translating it to English. Such practices continue to unnecessarily increase the time and cost of trade for Indian exporters.

Unaligned Food Safety Regulations

Bangladesh Food Safety (Contaminants, Toxins, and Harmful Residues) Regulation, 2017 specifies the maximum permissible limit of contaminants, toxins, and harmful residues of products under HS Chapter 13 (in Table A4.1, the product 130239 is in the list of India's potential export items).[50] However, Indian Food Safety and Standards (Contaminants, Toxins, and Residues) Regulation, 2011 does not specify maximum permissible limits of the same parameters of this product. Different prescribed limits for usage of contaminants, toxins, and harmful residues of products creates market access-related impediments for India's food products.

Divergent Motor Vehicles Standards

Divergent specifications for maximum safe weights of axle and laden weights of vehicles in the Motor Vehicles Ordinance 1983 of Bangladesh and Central Motor Vehicles Rules 1989 of India affect the hassle-free movement of cargo between the two countries. For example, the maximum permissible weight limit for a transport vehicle axle that has two closely spaced axles (center lines of axles not more than 2.5 meters and not less than 1.02 meters apart) with 2 tires each is 6.25 tons;[51] and the permissible maximum laden weight limit is 13 tons.[52] For the same type of vehicle, the maximum weight limit for an axle is 6 tons and permissible laden weight limit is 12 tons.[53] To import vehicles from Bangladesh, the importing vehicles have to comply with the specified axle weight and laden weight of

[48] Product Labeling Policy 2006. http://www.clcbd.org/document/download/782.html.

[49] Bangladesh – List of Approved Export/Import Goods in Bangladesh Land Port. http://files. indiantradeportal.in/
     download.aspx?file=uploads/General%20Documents/Alert/01-02-2018/List_Of_Approved_Export_-_Import_
     Goods_In_Bangladesh_Land_Port.pdf.

[50] Gadget notification of Food Safety (Contaminants, Toxins, and Harmful Residues) Regulations, 2017. http://bfsa.gov.
     bd/images/pdf/tanzid.pdf.

[51] See Notification No. RRD/BRTA/Overload – 38/96 (P-1) – 653, published in Bangladesh Extraordinary Gazette, dated
     5 May 2004,

[52] Bangladesh Government Press, 2004: http://www.rthd.gov.bd/assets/docs/brta/ordinance/ bangladesh_gazette.pdf.

[53] Published in the *Extraordinary Gazette of India*. 18 October 1996. Ministry of Surface Transport, Notification, 1996,
     http://tis.nhai.gov.in/Admin/pdf/2301201732PM04_ 9567.pdf

vehicles in the *Extraordinary Gazette* by the vested power of the government in Chapter VI of The Motor Vehicles Ordinance 1983.[54]

National Drug Policy

The National Drug Policy 1982 and the Drug (Control) Ordinance 1982 had the mandatory requirement of registration of imported drugs. The new National Drug Policy 2005 (import restrictive measures A14, A15, and A21) restricts the import of drugs. The National Drug Policy 2005 of Bangladesh was formulated with the objective to become a drug-exporting country, instead of a drug-importing country. The procedure for exporting pharmaceutical products to Bangladesh is cumbersome. The regulatory authority only considers the application for the registration to import pharmaceutical products into Bangladesh if the drug is registered under the same brand name in at least one of the following developed countries: Australia, France, Germany, Japan, Switzerland, the United Kingdom, and the US.[55]

Letter of Credit-Related Concerns

Indian traders note the challenges that arise when Bangladesh banks are reluctant to open letters of credit in favor of India's exporters until the importer has a contract from international buyers.

5.2. Impediments Exporting to Bhutan

Current major export items of India to Bhutan are mineral oils and fuels, machines and their parts, and motor vehicles, among others (Table A1.2 in Appendix 1). As per the list of India's potential export items to Bhutan, India has export potential in 35 products using the HS 6-digit level of product classification (Table A2.1 in Appendix 2), and this list contains many items subject to SPS and TBT measures. Information on these measures imposed by Bhutan on India's potential export items is found in Table A4.2 in Appendix 4. As per available information, Bhutan mainly applies two SPS and nine TBT measures on 33 potential export items of India to Bhutan (Table 8).[56] All potential products at HS 6-digit level are aggregated to their corresponding 2-digit HS codes to show the product-wise relevant NTMs imposed by Bhutan.

Exports from India to Bhutan do not face any SPS and TBT impediments. India's exporters easily comply with legal and regulatory formalities prescribed by the Bhutan Agriculture and Food Regulatory Authority (BAFRA) and the Bhutan Standards Bureau (BSB) for the import of products. However, India's exporters do encounter challenges of a more generic nature in Bhutan such as human resources constraints and the lack of sufficient qualified skilled professionals, which affects the efficient functioning of laboratories and leads to delays in obtaining clearance for imported goods.

---

[54] The Motor Vehicles Ordinance, 1983 (Ordinance No. LV of 1983). http://www.rthd.gov.bd/ assets/docs/brta/acts/the_motor_vehicles_ordinance_1983_ordinance_no_lv_of_1983.pdf.
[55] National Drug Policy 2005. Ministry of Health and Family Welfare. Government of People's Republic of Bangladesh.
[56] Information is not available on the remaining two potential export products.

Table 8: Sanitary and Phytosanitary and Technical Barriers to Trade Measures Applied by Bhutan on India's Potential Exports

NTM Code	Measure Description by UNCTAD	2-Digit HS Codes
A: Sanitary and Phytosanitary (SPS) Measures		
A3	Labeling, marking, and packaging requirements	22
A83	Certification requirement: Certification of conformity with a given regulation required by the importing country, but may be issued in the exporting or the importing country. Example: Certificate of conformity for materials in contact with food (containers, papers, plastics, and others) is required.	22
B: Technical Barriers to Trade (TBT) Measures		
B14	Authorization requirement for TBT reasons: Requirement that the importer should receive authorization, permits, or approval from a relevant government agency of the destination country, for reasons such as national security, environment protection, and others. Example: Imports must be authorized for drugs, waste and scrap, and firearms.	30
B15	Registration requirement for importers for TBT reasons: Requirement that importers should be registered to import certain products. To register, importers may need to comply with certain requirements, documentation, and registration fees. It also includes the cases when the registration of establishments producing certain products is required. Example: Importers of sensitive products, such as medicines, drugs, explosives, firearms, alcohol, cigarettes, game machines may be required to be registered in the importing country.	30
B31	Labeling requirements: Measures regulating the kind, color, and size of printing on packages and labels and defining the information that should be provided to the consumer. Labeling is any written, electronic, or graphic communication on the packaging or on a separate but associated label, or on the product itself. It may include requirements on the official language to be used as well as technical information on the product, such as voltage, components, instruction on use, safety, and security advice. Example: Refrigerators need to carry a label indicating its size, weight, and electricity consumption level.	73, 84, 85, 94
B41	TBT regulations on production processes: Requirement on production processes not classified under SPS above. It also excludes those specific measures under B2: Tolerance limits for residues and restricted use of substances (or its subcategories). Example: Use of environmentally friendly equipment is mandatory.	38, 39, 40, 49, 61, 62, 63, 65, 69, 73, 84, 85, 90, 94, 95
B7	Product-quality or -performance requirement: Conditions to be satisfied in terms of performance (e.g., durability, hardness) or quality (e.g., content of defined ingredients). Example: Door must resist a certain minimum high temperature.	38, 39, 40, 49, 61, 62, 63, 65, 69, 73, 84, 85, 90, 94, 95
B8	Conformity assessment related to TBT: Requirement for verification that a given TBT requirement has been met: This could be achieved by one or combined forms of inspection and approval procedures, including procedures for sampling, testing and inspection; evaluation, verification and assurance of conformity, accreditation, and approval.	38, 39, 40, 49, 61, 62, 63, 65, 69, 73, 84, 85, 90, 95

continued on next page

Table 8 continued

NTM Code	Measure Description by UNCTAD	2-Digit HS Codes
B82	Testing requirement: A requirement for products to be tested against a given regulation, such as performance level. Includes sampling requirement. Example: Testing on a sample of motor vehicle imports is required against the required safety compliance and its equipment.	38, 39, 40, 49, 61, 62, 63, 65, 69, 73, 84, 85, 90, 95
B83	Certification requirement: Certification of conformity with a given regulation: required by the importing country, but may be issued in the exporting or the importing country. Example: Certificate of conformity for electric products is required.	38, 39, 40, 49, 61, 62, 63, 65, 69, 73, 84, 85, 90, 95
B89	Conformity assessment related to TBT, n.e.s.	38, 39, 40, 49, 61, 62, 63, 65, 69, 73, 84, 85, 90, 95

Main Headings of Nontariff Measures:
A1: Prohibitions or restrictions of imports for SPS reasons; A3: Labeling, marking, and packaging requirements; A4: Hygienic requirements; A8: Conformity assessment related to SPS; B1: Prohibitions or restrictions of imports for objectives set out in the TBT agreement; B3: Labeling, marking, and packaging requirements; B8: Conformity assessment related to TBT.

HS = Harmonized Commodity Description and Coding System, n.e.s. = not elsewhere specified, NTM = nontariff measure, SPS = sanitary and phytosanitary, TBT = technical barriers to trade, UNCTAD = United Nations Conference on Trade and Development.

Sources: Table A4.2 in Appendix 4; UNCTAD. 2012. *International Classification of Non-Tariff Measures.*

5.3. Impediments Exporting to Maldives

Current major export items of India to Maldives include crushed stones for concrete aggregates, milled rice, pharmaceutical products (medicaments), cement, iron and steel rods, meat, onions, printed books, fresh eggs, and areca nuts, among others (Table A1.3 in Appendix 1). According to the list of India's potential export items to Maldives, the highest export potential is in machinery, electrical equipment, furniture items, plastic items, edible fruits and nuts, articles of iron and steel, and beverages, among other potential products (Table A2.2 in Appendix 2)—many of which are subject to SPS and TBT measures.

Most regulatory documents are in the national language Dhivehi which causes difficulty for exporters in obtaining information on precise measures imposed by Maldives on India's potential export items. For this diagnostic study, existing literature is used to understand the impediments faced by India's exporters in the Maldives market. Table 9 presents the laws and regulations related to SPS measures with the names of their implementation agency.

Procedural and Infrastructure-Related Hurdles

India's exporters tend not to experience difficulties while exporting to Maldives, given India's relatively advanced domestic regulatory system. However, some challenges do exist, including (i) a lack of SPS-related and general trade infrastructure, (ii) the use of multiple regulators, (iii) the absence of testing agencies, and others. Maldives has one of the least-developed regulatory frameworks among SASEC countries, which is exacerbated by weak institutional development and inadequate supply of human resources.

Table 9: Sanitary and Phytosanitary Regulations and their Implementing Authorities in Maldives

No.	Laws and Regulations	Implementing Authority
1	Plant Protection Act	Ministry of Fisheries and Agriculture
2	Public Health Act	Health Protection Agency, Ministry of Health
3	Port Health Regulation	Health Protection Agency
4	Animal Health and Production Bill	Ministry of Fisheries and Agriculture
5	Plant Import Regulation (in Attorney General's office for comment)	Ministry of Fisheries and Agriculture
6	Animal Quarantine Regulation	Ministry of Fisheries and Agriculture
7	Food Safety and Quality Bill	Maldives Food and Drug Authority
8	Food Import Regulation (Draft)	Maldives Food and Drug Authority

Source: SASEC. 2013. Brain Storming Meeting on Sanitary and Phytosanitary Priorities and Challenges, SASEC. Bangkok. 24 and 25 November.

Shortages of skilled personnel lead to suboptimal diagnostic capacity and lack of awareness in quarantine procedures. Weak coordination among stakeholders further complicates the import/export environment.

Multiple Regulators

Although Maldives is heavily dependent on imported food products – 95% of food consumed in Maldives is imported – it has neither a comprehensive policy framework for domestic and imported food products, nor specific food safety policies. Available information indicates that the Ministry of Economic Development (MED) is responsible for issuing licenses to trade to importers and exporters and for overall trade facilitation, and it also helps respond to SPS and TBT-related inquiries. The Maldives Health Protection Agency (HPA) under the Ministry of Food regulates food imports and local productions. Currently, different regulators are assigned to different imported food articles, which leads to divergent parameters being used to assess the quality of imported articles. For exporters of food products into Maldives, this practice tends to add multiple layers of process and cause delay. Table 10 lists the food safety implementing authorities in Maldives.

5.4. Impediments Exporting to Nepal

Major export items of India to Nepal include mineral oils and fuels, milled rice, semi-finished products of iron or non-alloy steel, motorcycles, motor vehicles and parts, medicaments, among others (Table A1.4 in Appendix 1). As per the list of India's potential export items to Nepal, India has export potential in 63 products using the HS 6-digit level of product classification (Table A2.4 in Appendix 2), some of which are subject to SPS and TBT measures. The information on these measures is culled from the Market Access Map (MAcMap) database.

Table 10: Food Safety Implementing Authorities in Maldives

No.	Food Control Activities	Implementing Authority
1	Fisheries production	MOFA, MFDA, local councils, HSD
2	Agricultural production and harvest	MOFA, local councils
3	Fresh food	MFDA, HPA, MOFA
4	Food processing and marketing	MFDA, HPA, MED, HSD, EPA
5	Licensing of processing plants	MFDA, EPA
6	Coordination of standard	MFDA, MOFA, MED
7	Premarket food product evaluation	MFDA, EPA
8	Food labeling and advertising control	MFDA, HPA, MED
9	Food safety and quality monitoring	MFDA, HPA, HSD
10	Food production and distribution inspection	MFDA, HPA, HSD
11	Food-borne disease surveillance	HPA, IGMH
12	Risk communication and public awareness	HPA, MFDA
13	Food exports	MFDA, MCS, MED
14	Food imports	HPA, MCS, MED, MPL
15	Food retail and food service	HPA, MFDA, HSD, MED
16	Food complaints	MFDA, HPA
17	Food safety education and training	MOE, MFDA, MNU
18	Food safety research	MNU

EPA = Environment Protection Agency, HPA = Health Protection Agency, HSD = Regional and Atoll Health Services Department, IGMH = Indira Gandhi Memorial Hospital, MCS = Maldives Customs Service, MED = Ministry of Economic Development, MFDA = Maldives Food and Drug Authority, MNU = Maldives National University, MOE = Ministry of Education, MOFA = Ministry of Fisheries and Agriculture, MPL = Maldives Port Limited.

Source: Maldives Food and Drug Authority. 2017. National Food Safety Policy (2017-2026). Appendix 1.

Under NTMs, the MAcMap database indicates that Nepal imposes SPS-related measures on only one product (HS code 293040) and TBT-related measures on 52 products (Table A4.3 in Appendix 4). As per the UNCTAD NTM classification, the common TBT-related measures are: B11, B14, B6, B8, and B83; while SPS-related NTMs are A14, A31, and A64 (Table 11). The potential products at 6-digit level are aggregated to their corresponding 2-digit HS codes to show the product-wise relevant NTMs imposed by Nepal.

India's exports to Nepal generally do not face difficulties meeting SPS and TBT compliance requirements, except in a few cases. However, there are some restrictive impediments which do affect India's exports to Nepal.

Restriction on Import of Portland Pozzolana Cement

Nepal's government has restricted the import of Portland Pozzolana Cement grade cement if it contains fly ash that exceeds the 15%–25% threshold limit prescribed by the National

Table 11: Sanitary and Phytosanitary and Technical Barriers to Trade Measures Applied by Nepal on India's Potential Exports

NTM Code	Measure Description by UNCTAD	2-Digit HS Codes
A: Sanitary and Phytosanitary (SPS) Measures		
A14	Special authorization requirement for SPS reasons: A requirement that importers should receive authorization, permits, or approval from a relevant government agency of the destination country for SPS reasons. To obtain the authorization, importers may need to comply with other related regulations and conformity assessments. Example: An import authorization from the Ministry of Health is required.	29
A31	Labeling requirements: Measures defining the information directly related to food safety, which should be provided to the consumer: Labeling is any written, electronic, or graphic communication on the consumer packaging or on a separate but associated label. Examples: (i) Labels that must specify the storage conditions such as "5°C maximum"; and (ii) potentially dangerous ingredients such as allergens, e.g., "contains honey not suitable for children under 1 year of age."	29
A64	Storage and transport conditions: Requirements on certain conditions under which food and feed, plants, and animals should be stored and/or transported. Example: Certain foodstuffs should be stored in a dry place, or below a certain temperature.	29
B: Technical Barriers to Trade (TBT) Measures		
B11	Prohibition for TBT reasons: Import prohibition for reasons set out in B1. Example: Imports are prohibited for hazardous substances, including explosives, certain toxic substances covered by the Basel Convention such as aerosol sprays containing CFCs, a range of HCFCs and BFCs, halons, methyl chloroform, and carbon tetrachloride.	85, 87
B14	Authorization requirement for TBT reasons: Requirement that the importer should receive authorization, permits, or approval from a relevant government agency of the destination country, for reasons such as national security, environment protection. Example: Imports must be authorized for drugs, waste and scrap, and firearms.	18, 21, 22, 26, 33, 37, 38, 39, 40, 42, 49, 59, 68, 71, 72, 73, 76, 80, 83, 90, 94
B6	Product identity requirement: Conditions to be satisfied to identify a product with a certain denomination (including biological or organic labels). Example: For a product to be identified as "chocolate," it must contain a minimum of 30% cocoa.	04
B8	Conformity assessment related to TBT: Requirement for verification that a given TBT requirement has been met. This could be achieved by one or combined forms of inspection and approval procedure, including procedures for sampling, testing and inspection; evaluation, verification and assurance of conformity; accreditation and approval.	18, 21, 22, 26, 33, 37, 38, 39, 40, 42, 49, 59, 68, 71, 72, 73, 76, 80, 83, 90, 94
B83	Certification requirement: Certification of conformity with a given regulation required by the importing country, but may be issued in the exporting or the importing country. Example: Certificate of conformity for electric products is required.	32, 87

Main Headings of Nontariff Measures:

A1: Prohibitions or restrictions of imports for SPS reasons; A3: Labeling, marking, and packaging requirements; A6: Other requirements on production or post-production processes; B1: Prohibitions or restrictions of imports for objectives set out in the TBT agreement; B6: Product identity requirement; B8: Conformity assessment related to TBT.

BFC = bromofluorocarbon, CFC = chlorofluorocarbon, HCFC = hydrofluorocarbon, HS = Harmonized Commodity Description and Coding System, NTM = nontariff measure, UNCTAD = United Nations Conference on Trade and Development.

Sources: Table A4.3 in Appendix 4; UNCTAD. 2012. *International Classification of Non-Tariff Measures.*

Bureau of Standards (NBSM). Conversely, the content of fly ash is permissible up to 15%–35% per the Bureau of Indian Standards. Divergent permissible limits of fly ash in Portland Pozzolana Cement between India and Nepal adversely affect India's cement exports.

Registration-Related Requirements

During field surveys for this diagnostic study, pharmaceutical exporters in India expressed difficulties faced over Nepal's registration procedures. according to exporters, any firm intending to export to Nepal must be associated with local Nepalese importers who, in turn, apply for registration of pharmaceutical products to be sold and marketed against the name of the local importer. For imported pharmaceutical products to be sold through the second importer, the exporter should obtain a No Objection Certificate (NOC) through the existing importer—a cumbersome and time-consuming procedure. In addition, the Government of Nepal has mandated that all pharmaceutical imports from India must have a Certificate of Good Manufacturing Practices and a Certificate of Pharmaceutical Product, although this rule is not applicable to domestic drug manufacturers. Such issues hamper India's export of pharmaceutical products to Nepal's market.

Restrictions on Product Registration

Nepal has very strict guidelines for product registration for common drugs. The registration of each product has many steps, requires excessive paperwork, and routine follow-up with drug regulators. This detailed and exhaustive process often proves problematic for Indian pharmaceutical exporting firms.

Other Obstacles

(i)   An agriculture reform fee of 5% is applied by Nepal on imported primary articles from India which, in turn, affects India's exports. Moreover, the fee is neither compatible with the existing trade treaty between India and Nepal, nor with the WTO-led multilateral trading system.

(ii)   India exports key value-added products to Nepal, such as nonalcoholic beverages (30%), pineapple juice (30%), and tomato juice (30%). High import duties affect the export of these value-added products to Nepal's market. In addition, Nepal has placed Chapter 42 (leather) and Chapter 64 (footwear) in its entirety on the sensitive list, which adversely affects India's exports of leather products to Nepal's market.

(iii)   Exporters in India have concerns over the calculation of duty of imported paper into Nepal. Nepal's customs officials do not assess the value of imported paper on the basis of the export invoice, but rather make the assessment on a flat value $0.50 (₹43) per kilogram, irrespective of the quality of the paper imported. If the value of duty calculated at this rate is higher than the value quoted in the export invoice, it is accepted. Otherwise, duty is calculated based on ₹43 per kilogram.

(iv)   The export of agricultural products from India to Nepal is affected by suboptimal infrastructure facilities at border points, which is particularly important for perishable products. Lack of cold storage and warehousing are major issues in particular at the Raxual–Birganj border-crossing point, which accounts for more than 70% of trade between the two countries.

(v)   Nepal has very limited quality food-testing laboratories and quarantine laboratories: only four food testing laboratories exist at customs border-crossing points—Kakarbhitta, Birgunj, Mahendranagar, and Tatopani/Kodari. These central laboratories are accredited by NABL to conduct 27 test parameters for chemical testing of food, agricultural products, and water,[57] although inadequate infrastructure facilities result in only a limited number of laboratory tests being carried out.

5.5   Impediments Exporting to Sri Lanka

Current major export items of India to Sri Lanka include aircraft, mineral oils and preparations, motor cars and motorcycles, medicaments, among others (Table A1.5 in Appendix 1). As per the list of India's potential export items to Sri Lanka, India has export potential in 66 products using the HS 6-digit level of product classification. The MAcMap database contains information on NTMs for only 34 potential products and has no information for the remaining 32 products. According to available information, Sri Lanka mainly applies nine SPS measures and eight TBT measures (Table 12). Detailed information on these measures is in Table A4.4 in Appendix 4. The potential products at 6-digit level are aggregated to their corresponding 2-digit HS codes to show the product-wise relevant NTMs imposed by Sri Lanka.

India's exports to Sri Lanka are growing at a consistent pace and face few specific SPS and TBT-related challenges for two reasons. First, India and Sri Lanka have a free trade agreement that is instrumental in facilitating bilateral trade flows;[58] and secondly, India has an Agreement for Recognition of Export Inspection and Certification System of Export Inspection Council, while the Sri Lanka Standards Institution operates an Import Inspection Scheme.[59] However, these agreements and frameworks do not prevent all standards and regulation-related impediments from affecting India's potential exports to Sri Lanka.

Registration Requirement for the Import of Cosmetic Products

Sri Lanka's Cosmetic Device and Drug Act 1980 and its subsequent amendments require the registration of imported cosmetics, meaning that exporters of cosmetics to Sri Lanka should be registered with the State Pharmaceutical Corporation under Sri Lanka's Ministry of Health. With no registration, the exporter is obliged to submit to the Sri Lankan importer a detailed report of all tests conducted in India, with samples. These samples are further tested in Sri Lanka before the registration certificate is awarded based on the sample report.

---

[57]   *Managing Quality in Nepal: A Directory of Services for SMEs.* http://www.intracen. org/publication/Managing-Quality-in-Nepal-A-directory-of-services-for-SMEs1/.

[58]   The Free Trade Agreement Between the Democratic Socialist Republic of Sri Lanka and the Republic of India is available at http://www.doc.gov.lk/index.php?option=com_content&view= article& id=44&Itemid=169&lang=en.

[59]   Agreement for Recognition of Export Inspection & Certification System of Export Inspection Council of India and Import Inspection Scheme of Sri Lanka Standards Institutions. https://eicindia.gov.in/int_recognition/05_SLSI Srilanka.pdf.

Table 12: Sanitary and Phytosanitary and Technical Barriers to Trade Measures Applied by Sri Lanka on India's Potential Exports

NTM Code	Measure Description by UNCTAD	2-Digit HS Codes
A: Sanitary and Phytosanitary (SPS) Measures		
A14	Special authorization requirement for SPS reasons: A requirement that importers should receive authorization, permits, or approval from a relevant government agency of the destination country for SPS reasons. To obtain the authorization, importers may need to comply with other related regulations and conformity assessments. Example: An import authorization from the Ministry of Health is required.	04, 18, 19, 21, 22, 38, 39, 84, 85, 87
A15	Registration requirements for importers: The requirement that importers should be registered before they can import certain products: To register, importers may need to comply with certain requirements, provide documentation, and pay registration fees. Example: Importers of a certain food item need to be registered at the Ministry of Health.	04, 18, 19, 21, 22
A21	Tolerance limits for residues of or contamination by certain (nonmicrobiological) substances: A measure that establishes a maximum residue limit (MRL) or tolerance limit of substances such as fertilizers, pesticides, and certain chemicals and metals in food and feed, used during their production process, but are not their intended ingredients: It includes a permissible maximum level for nonmicrobiological contaminants. Measures related to microbiological contaminants are classified under A4 below. Examples: (i) MRL is established for insecticides, pesticides, heavy metals, and veterinary drug residues; (ii) POPs and chemicals generated during processing; and (iii) residues of dithianon in apples and hop.	04
A22	Restricted use of certain substances in food and feed and their contact materials: Restriction or prohibition on the use of certain substances contained in food and feed. It includes the restrictions on substances contained in the food containers that might migrate to food. Examples: (i) Certain restrictions exist for food and feed additives used for coloring, preservation, or sweeteners; and (ii) For food containers made of polyvinyl chloride plastic, vinyl chloride monomer must not exceed 1 microgram per kilogram.	04, 18, 19, 21, 22
A31	Labeling requirements: Measures defining the information directly related to food safety, which should be provided to the consumer: Labeling is any written, electronic, or graphic communication on the consumer packaging or on a separate but associated label. Examples: (i) Labels that must specify the storage conditions such as "5°C maximum"; and (ii) potentially dangerous ingredients such as allergens, e.g., "contains honey not suitable for children under 1 year of age."	04, 18, 19, 21, 22
A4	Hygienic requirements: Requirements related to food quality, composition, and safety, usually based on hygienic and good manufacturing practices, recognized methods of analysis and sampling. The requirements may be applied on the final product (A41) or on the production processes (A42).	04, 18, 19, 21, 22
A49	Hygienic requirements, n.e.s.	04, 18, 19, 21, 22
A83	Certification requirement: Certification of conformity with a given regulation required by the importing country, but may be issued in the exporting or the importing country. Example: Certificate of conformity for materials in contact with food (containers, papers, plastics, and others) is required.	04, 18, 19, 21, 22

continued on next page

Table 12 continued

NTM Code	Measure Description by UNCTAD	2-Digit HS Codes
A84	Inspection requirement: Requirement for product inspection in the importing country. It may be performed by public or private entities. It is similar to testing, but it does not include laboratory testing. Example: Animal or plant parts must be inspected before entry is allowed.	04, 18, 19, 21, 22
B: Technical Barriers to Trade (TBT) Measures		
B11	Prohibition for TBT reasons: Import prohibition for reasons set out in B1. Example: Imports are prohibited for hazardous substances, including explosives, certain toxic substances covered by the Basel Convention such as aerosol sprays containing CFCs, a range of HCFCs and BFCs, halons, methyl chloroform, and carbon tetrachloride.	38
B14	Authorization requirement for TBT reasons: Requirement that the importer should receive authorization, permits, or approval from a relevant government agency of the destination country, for reasons such as national security, environment protection, and others. Example: Imports must be authorized for drugs, waste and scrap, and firearms.	04, 18, 19, 21, 22, 38, 39, 84, 85, 87, 90
B15	Registration requirement for importers for TBT reasons: Requirement that importers should be registered to import certain products. To register, importers may need to comply with certain requirements, documentation, and registration fees. It also includes the cases when the registration of establishments producing certain products is required. Example: Importers of sensitive products such as medicines, drugs, explosives, firearms, alcohol, cigarettes, game machines, and others may be required to be registered in the importing country.	04, 18, 19, 21, 22, 38, 39, 71, 84, 85, 87, 90
B3	Labeling, marking, and packaging requirements	04, 18, 19, 21, 22
B31	Labeling requirements: Measures regulating the kind, color, and size of printing on packages and labels and defining the information that should be provided to the consumer. Labeling is any written, electronic, or graphic communication on the packaging or on a separate but associated label, or on the product itself. It may include requirements on the official language to be used as well as technical information on the product, such as voltage, components, instruction on use, safety and security advice. Example: Refrigerators need to carry a label indicating its size, weight, and electricity consumption level.	04, 18, 19, 21, 22
B4	Production or post-production requirements	22
B7	Product-quality or -performance requirement: Conditions to be satisfied in terms of performance (e.g., durability, hardness) or quality (e.g., content of defined ingredients). Example: Door must resist a certain minimum high temperature.	04, 19, 87
B83	Certification requirement: Certification of conformity with a given regulation required by the importing country, but may be issued in the exporting or the importing country. Example: Certificate of conformity for electric products is required.	04, 18, 19, 21, 22, 87
B84	Inspection requirement: Requirement for product inspection in the importing country may be performed by public or private entities. It is similar to testing, but does not include laboratory testing. Example: Textile and clothing imports must be inspected for size and materials used before entry is allowed.	04, 18, 19, 21, 22

Main Headings of Nontariff Measures:

A1: Prohibitions or restrictions of imports for SPS reasons; A2: Tolerance limits for residues and restricted use of substances; A3: Labeling, marking, and packaging requirements; A4: Hygienic requirements; A8: Conformity assessment related to SPS; B1: Prohibitions or restrictions of imports for objectives set out in the TBT agreement; B3: Labeling, marking, and packaging requirements; B7: Product-quality or -performance requirement; B8: Conformity assessment related to TBT.

BFC = bromofluorocarbon, CFC = chlorofluorocarbon, HCFC = hydrofluorocarbon, HS = Harmonized Commodity Description and Coding System, n.e.s. = not elsewhere specified, NTM = nontariff measure, POP = persistent organic pollutant, UNCTAD = United Nations Conference on Trade and Development.

Sources: Table A4.4 in Appendix 4; UNCTAD. 2012. *International Classification of Non-Tariff Measures.*

Mandatory Standards

Sri Lanka has mandatory standards for a range of product categories, including food products, electric products, cement and cement products, steel products, polyvinyl chloride products, and others. Any imported products must contain the SLS Mark Scheme and conform to Sri Lanka's specifications and standards.[60] The annual fee for the SLS Mark Scheme for overseas suppliers depends on total sales.

Milk Products

Milk is one the identified potential items of export from India to Sri Lanka. However, the permissible limit of milk fat and the minimum percentage of milk solids (not fat) is different in India and Sri Lanka. The buffalo milk fat limit varies between 5%–6% in India (figures vary across states), and 7% in Sri Lanka. For skimmed milk, the fat content should be more than 0.5% in India, and 0% in Sri Lanka.

Labeling-Related Issues with Milk Products

The labeling requirement for milk products is almost the same in both countries, but does have slight differences. For example, the caps of milk bottles, pouches, and tetra-packs of standardized milk in India should be labeled with "S," while in Sri Lanka, the label for standardized milk of sterilized designation is "SS" and for pasteurized designation is "SP." These divergent labels become punitive measures and restrict exports.

Divergent Labeling Requirement of Packaging Food Products

The labeling requirements on packages and containers of flavor-added food products are not harmonized. In India, the Food Safety and Standards (Packaging and Labeling) Regulation, 2011 states that if extraneous flavoring agent is added to any article of food, the statement "contains added flavor" should be written beneath the list of ingredients on the label. The Regulation also specifies that where artificial flavoring substances are added to the food, the label of that food product should print the common name of the added flavor; and in natural flavoring and nature-identical flavoring added food, the class name of the flavors should be printed on the label.[61]

On the other hand, the Food (Labeling and Advertising) Regulations, 2005 of Sri Lanka includes a provision stating that if any article of food has added natural flavoring substances, the label printed on or attached to the package containing food should have the words "natural (insert description of flavor) flavoring." For added nature-identical flavoring, the printed words should be "nature-identical (insert description of flavor) flavoring"; and for artificial flavoring articles of food, the words to add are "artificial (insert description of flavor) flavoring." Other items to be printed on the label are the common

---

[60] Sri Lanka Standards Institutions, Procedure for Granting SLS Mark for Products Manufactured Overseas: http://www.slsi.lk/index.php?option=com_content&view=article&id=65&Itemid=274&lang=en and http://www.gic.gov.lk/gic/pdf/sls-mandatory.pdf.

[61] Food Safety and Standards (Packaging and Labeling) Regulation, 2011. http://www.fssai.gov.in/dam/jcr:2d48f646-d9f9-4bc1-af03-493f29cc45a9/Packaging_Labelling_Regulations.pdf.

name; the INS number, if any, of other substances added; and a statement on any restrictions that the food may have to those with health issues or a specific reference to the food's intended use.[62]

Special Import License

Sri Lanka has imposed a special import license requirement for a number of products and many of the identified potential exports items from India to Sri Lanka are included under special import license categories. The key product codes are HS codes: 220710, 382490, 392690, 847130, 847150, 851712, 853620, 853931, 870323, 870332, 870333, 870870 (for descriptions of these products, see Table A4.4 in Appendix 4). Special import regulations fall under UNCTAD's A14 for SPS measures and B14 for TBT measures.[63]

High Import Duties on Automobile Products

Sri Lanka imposes very high import duty of 150% on automobile products, which increases to 175% for cars: this clearly adversely affects India's automobile exports to Sri Lanka's market.

Overall, some SPS and TBT-related measures and impediments for Indian exporters are common among several of the SASEC countries. For example, a lack of harmonized compliance procedures due to the typically large number of bodies involved in setting standards at a national level disadvantages many exporters. While large exporters with the necessary resources (agents and connections) are more easily able to meet the importing country's required standards and thus gain competitive advantage over smaller exporters, for which the costs involved in meeting the same standards are relatively more demanding. An international body should be established to harmonize standards across countries to eliminate ambiguity in meeting these required standards.

All standards should be transparent and acceptable to all member countries: this will indirectly reduce the time to trade, and the associated benefits will go directly to consumers. Transparent and acceptable standards would lead to greater market access, less distortions, and enhanced regional trade. Such an international body should ensure the technical capacity of the member countries and provide necessary recommendations.

Another critical common factor is the lack of adequate quality infrastructure among SASEC countries, including testing laboratories, inspection agencies, and adequately trained staff.

Aside from SPS and TBT measures, there are other instances in which the imposition of legitimate measures can become a barrier to smooth and transparent international transactions: for example, inspection and payments, and the physical inspection of goods which adds time to clearing goods at a border. In such cases, all exporters—large and small—face the same barriers, which negatively affect trade between the partner

---

[62]   Food (Labeling and Advertising) Regulations – 2005. *Gazette of the Democratic Socialist Republic of Sri Lanka (Extraordinary)*. 1456/22.

[63]   Special Import License Regulations, 2013, *Gazette of the Democratic Socialist Republic of Sri Lanka (Extraordinary)*. 1813/14.

countries, and can lead to full trade diversion. Inevitably, small exporters find it more challenging to hurdle such barriers and end up with market loss. In the field survey of exporters undertaken for this diagnostic study, one case of policy barriers led to very significant barriers and an Indian exporter lost the Afghanistan market.

Chapter 6
Prioritized Recommendations for Action

This diagnostic study attempts to identify and understand existing laws, policies, and regulations related to SPS and TBT measures of SASEC countries that hinder India's potential exports. Based on these identified impediments, the recommendations proposed in this chapter map three critical areas of possible reform at national (India) and regional (SASEC) levels: (i) the legislative and regulatory environment, (ii) institutional structures, and (iii) SPS and TBT-related infrastructure. The common inextricable areas of reform are noted where India and other SASEC countries should make concerted efforts to address SPS and TBT impediments to cross-border trade in identified potential export items.

6.1 Recommendations for National Action: India

6.1.1 Legislative and Regulatory Environment

(i) **Review and Consolidate Outdated Legislation.** India has made serious efforts to overhaul its domestic laws, rules, and regulations related to SPS and TBT regulations, yet several outdated laws remain. For example, the Agricultural Produce (Grading and Marking) Act 1937 is a pre-independence Act and deals with grading and marking of agricultural and other produce. The Act should be overhauled as it does not capture the realities of contemporary trade where standards related to grading and marking have significantly improved. Likewise, the Essential Commodities Act 1954 is outdated. A comprehensive review of existing older acts should be carried out and efforts made to consolidate or render inactive, as appropriate, all legislative and regulatory documentation.

(ii) **Develop Additional Necessary Regulations.** India has a huge deficit of technical regulations and there is growing need for new technical regulations in sectors such as chemicals, toys, telecom, agriculture products, and plastics. While some of these sectors are currently being brought under technical regulations, the process is far from complete and should be expedited to protect the health and safety of consumers and to regulate the imports of spurious products. A task force should be established with the mandate to better understand the current deficit of technical regulations in various sectors and develop a comprehensive plan for the development and implementation of technical regulations.

(iii) **Increase Supporting Infrastructure for Standards Development.** There is considerable focus in India on developing horizontal regulations in the food sector relating to residue limits for pesticide, veterinary drugs, contaminants, and other chemicals. However, there is scant progress in developing a scientific basis for some standards: this is particularly evident in new areas where standards have yet to be developed as notification of such standards should be made to the WTO before domestic notifications are made. Failure to do so may lead to overseas markets challenging India to provide a reasonable scientific basis for the standards. Currently, FSSAI lacks adequate infrastructure and facilities to conduct comprehensive scientific risk assessments, and develop data on maximum residue levels and acceptable daily intakes, and others. The development of such infrastructure is vital to avoid potential issues and FSSAI should consider leveraging the work carried out by the Food and Agriculture Organization of the United Nations (FAO) and the World Health Organization (WHO) in this area.

6.1.2   Institutional Structures

(i)   **Consolidate Regulations under One Single Act.** The current regulatory environment is convoluted with a large number of regulators active in the export of food products, which poses major challenges for India's exporters. The Export Inspection Council (EIC) is an apex body which regulates export of food products, but other bodies have also entered the regulatory landscape and set standards for exported products: for example, the APEDA; AGMARK; MPEDA; Chemical and Allied Export Promotion Council of India; and Chemicals, Cosmetics, and Dyes Export Promotion Council. A plethora of regulators not only adds costs, but also compounds procedural and process-related complications. The relevant agency of the Government of India should consolidate regulations under one single act, with a task force constituted to review overlapping regulations to bring them under a single act. Such a task force should seek the expertise of the Bureau of Indian Standards (BIS), FSSAI, and other relevant agencies.

(ii)   **Improve Access to Information on SPS and TBT Measures of Trading Partners and Other Countries.** India's SPS and TBT institutions continue to operate without sufficient and easily accessible information food regulations of more developed countries and their agreements, quarantine procedures, hazardous procedures, performance requirements, and other related procedures. Free and open access to such information is critical not only for exports, but also for imports in the world of value chain-led trade. India should recognize the importance of information in protecting its interest in international markets and consider positioning technical officers in strategic locations such as Brussels; Geneva; and Washington, DC. A deeper understanding of more advanced countries' SPS and TBT regulations would help India avert challenges emanating from the ever-changing global economic and regulatory environment. In addition, this type of technical presence would help India in negotiating bilateral, regional, and multilateral agreements.

(iii)   **Create Synergy between Standard-Setting Bodies, Domestic Regulators, and Industry.** The BIS is an apex standard-setting body and actively participates in the SARSO work program committee on the harmonization of standards. However, to date, the BIS does not have a mandate to regulate standards, which is problematic when it must negotiate standards at regional or bilateral levels without consulting domestic regulators in respective sectors. Commitments the BIS makes in SARSO, without adequate consultation with domestic regulators, can become a source of conflict which, in turn, can affect negotiations at the regional level. Dynamic synergies should be created between standard-setting bodies and domestic regulators and industries. A national coordinating agency could be established under the Department of Commerce to supervise the ecosystem of standards, and to promote coordination and coherence.

(iv)   **Bolster Coordination between State and Central Government Institutions.** In India, agriculture is governed and managed at a state level while central government of India governs the overall policy regime dealing with production, marketing, and imports of agriculture products. This requires the primary agriculture production of India's states to be coherent with national standards and inspection procedures. Efficient exchange of information between central and state governments is essential—particularly related to the banning of pesticides or chemicals in other countries—to effectively promote agricultural exports. The Ministry of Agriculture and Farmers Welfare should consider requesting state governments to develop agriculture business offices within their agriculture departments, which would work closely with key departments of the central government on critical areas of policy coordination.

(v)   **Correct Structures for Industry Demonstration of Regulatory Compliance.** A major area of concern are the current structures in place to enforce regulations in India. Currently, SPS and TBT regulators rely on their own inspection machinery and facilities (government laboratories and other agencies) to verify compliance. However, the onus of compliance with regulations rests on industry, and full regulatory compliance should be fulfilled before any inspection takes place. Therefore, a system should be developed in which industry demonstrates compliance with regulations, and the role of regulators should be confined to verification of compliance.

(vi)   **Complete Recruitment Processes at FSSAI to Ensure Adequate Technical Expertise.** India faces a very significant shortage of competent technicians at food laboratories. A recent report of the Comptroller and Auditor General (CAG) of India raised serious concerns about technical competencies of laboratory technicians, citing a shortage of qualified manpower and functional food testing equipment in state food laboratories and referral laboratories, resulting in deficient testing of food samples. The CAG noted that the Ministry of Health and Family Welfare requisitioned 356 positions for FSSAI at different levels, yet most of these were not yet filled by permanent employees. Further, many employees are appointed on a contractual basis. The FSSAI should develop a comprehensive plan and processes to complete recruitment of qualified professionals to fill the current gap. The FSSAI should also consider collaborating with universities and other tertiary level education institutions to train young students in this area.

6.1.3   Sanitary and Phytosanitary and Technical Barriers to Trade-Related Infrastructure

(i)   **Address the Imbalance of Laboratory Infrastructure.** The current domestic laboratory testing infrastructure is highly skewed across India. In Eastern

India, there are no NABL-accredited laboratories in Assam, Bihar, Jharkhand, Manipur, Meghalaya, Mizoram, Nagaland, Sikkim, and Tripura even if these states are good producers of organic products, spices, floriculture, horticulture, and ginger and have tremendous potential for the development of exports. The NABL, FSSAI, and EIC should collaborate to identify potential locations for new NABL-accredited laboratories in these states. With a justified case of possible commercial feasibility for increased export production, Assistance could be sought from the Department of Commerce through its Viability Gap Funding Program since these states have products that are ripe for increased commercial export production. The private sector could also be offered incentives to invest in the development of testing laboratories and other facilities in these states. Discussions should be tabled through relevant public–private platforms.

(ii) **Address the Imbalance of Plant Quarantine Stations.** The current infrastructure of plant quarantine stations is also uneven in the country. The northern, western, and southern regions have more plant quarantine stations than the eastern side of the country. Of 52 plant quarantine stations, nearly 79% are located in the northern, western, and southern regions; and the remaining 21% are located in the eastern region. States such as Sikkim, Mizoram, and Meghalaya do not have plant quarantine stations. This reflects the existing lab and testing infrastructure deficit across states and creates massive challenges for local producers, exporters, and importers. The Directorate of Plant Protection, Quarantine, and Storage should make the effort to identify specific locations for development of plant quarantine and testing laboratories at Agartala, Meghalaya, Manipur, and Mizoram.

6.2 Recommendations for Regional Action: SASEC Countries

6.2.1 Legislative and Regulatory Environment

(i) **Align National Standards with Global Standards.** There are significant gaps in the development of SPS and TBT standards across SASEC countries. Food safety regulations of each country, for example, demonstrate the range of development and enforcement. India continuously upgrades its food regulations (original regulations in 2006, with amendments in 2011, 2017, and 2018) and its food laws are relatively advanced and comprehensive, providing detailed information on the usage of various types of contaminants, preservatives, toxins, residues, sampling analysis, and packaging labeling; and these are also consistent with international standards such as CODEX. However, other SASEC countries lag behind in upgrading food regulations in a comprehensive manner. In addition, food-related legislation is sometimes available only in the national language, which is a barrier for foreign traders. All SASEC countries should try to align their national standards with CODEX and the World Organisation for Animal Health.

(ii)   **Review of Food Regulations as First Step Toward Mutual Recognition Agreements.** India's existing technical regulations pertaining to labeling requirements and product standards, specifications, weights, and measurements is relatively advanced compared with other SASEC countries. While Sri Lanka has well developed technical regulations, regulations in Bangladesh and Maldives in the local language, and Nepal and Bhutan have yet to develop technical regulations in many sectors. This reflects asymmetries in the regulatory and institutional frameworks of SASEC countries. To help increase intraregional trade within SASEC countries, a comprehensive review of existing food regulations could be the first step in exploring a possible road map for mutual recognition arrangements in this area.

6.2.2   Institutional Structures

(i)   **Consolidate Multiple Regulators.** SASEC countries tend to have many regulators that deal with single products, which is challenging for compliance. Multiple regulators not only increase compliance costs, but also add complexity to the process. This is most apparent in Bangladesh, Maldives, and Nepal, where multiple regulators regulate the import of food products. For example, the BSTI regulates the import of food products in Bangladesh; at the same time, the Bangladesh Food Safety Authority under the Bangladesh Food Safety Act, 2013 is also mandated to regulate food products. A similar situation exists in other SASEC countries. SASEC countries may consider consolidating their existing regulations under a single regulation or act to resolve this problem.

(ii)   **Provide SPS and TBT Information on Trade Portals.** Bangladesh, India, Nepal, and Sri Lanka have well established trade portals, while Bhutan and Maldives do not have comprehensive trade portals. It is important for all SASEC countries to upgrade or establish their existing trade portals with comprehensive product-wise information on SPS and TBT-related regulations. Moreover, SASEC countries could also explore possible opportunities for creating a common integrated SPS and TBT portal for SASEC countries along the lines of the Association of Southeast Asian Nations (ASEAN) Trade Repository.

(iii)   **Strengthen National Accreditation Bodies.** Among the SASEC countries, Bangladesh, India, and Sri Lanka have accreditation bodies that provide accreditation to laboratories after assessing their technical competence for testing and other related parameters. Bhutan and Nepal do not have accreditation bodies yet. The Nepal Bureau of Standards and Metrology is currently engaged in setting up accreditation bodies under the Nepal Laboratory Accreditation Scheme program. Bhutan has the National Accreditation Focal Point (NAFP) under the SAARC-PTB cooperation, although the actual accreditation in Bhutan is mainly done by National Accreditation Board for Testing and Calibration Labs (NABL) and NABCBs in India. Bhutan, Maldives, and Nepal could explore seeking assistance from the Government of India to develop national accreditation bodies. India could provide technical and capacity building assistance.

(iv) **Collaborate to Better Align National Standards with Global Standards.** SASEC countries continue to work toward alignment of national standards with global standards. Bangladesh, Bhutan, India, Maldives, Nepal, and Sri Lanka have adopted global best practices, such as Hazard Analysis Critical Control Point (HACCP), and GAP as voluntary programs, but only in few sectors. Currently, large-scale firms adopt these best practices, but HACCP, GHP, and GAP have yet to be applied in many sectors (including food, fish, and meat). Some of the challenges are a lack of state body and industry guidance, unavailability of quality raw materials, lack of officials, lack of guidance and technical know-how, a shortage of trained consultants, and trainee and cost-related implications. To address these challenges, the SASEC countries should consider a regionwide collaboration to map sectors and subsectors where such practices should be introduced on a priority basis, and explore possible support from international bodies, such as FAO and WHO.

(v) **Establish a Joint Task Force to Address Procedural and Registration-Related Hurdles.** Procedural and product registration measures of some SASEC countries directly impact India's exports. Bangladesh has a mandatory certificate marks scheme (MCMS) categorizing 155 products including most of India's potential export items. Under the MCMS, an importer should obtain a special license for the import of products—yet the procedure to obtain a license is complex and takes a minimum of 19 days and a maximum of 94 days. Likewise, Nepal and Sri Lanka have registration-related requirements for exporters for pharmaceuticals and cosmetic products. These create challenges for exporters in India and other countries, and discourage trade. SASEC countries should consider establishing a joint task force to gather as much as information on such procedural and registration-related hurdles, and developing a concrete action plan to address them either through bilateral or regional mechanisms.

6.2.3 Sanitary and Phytosanitary and Technical Barriers to Trade-Related Infrastructure

(i) **Upgrade Testing and Laboratory Infrastructure.** Insufficient access to necessary testing and laboratory infrastructure, and the significant time and costs involved, are recognized as major challenges for exporters within South Asia. Existing testing laboratories in Bangladesh, Bhutan, and Nepal, for example, are not equipped to conduct all kinds of laboratory tests. As a result, delays are incurred in the clearance of goods at land ports which increase the cost of doing trade. Existing testing and laboratory infrastructure should be upgraded by exploring possible opportunities through public–private partnership initiatives.

(ii) **Development of Technical Laboratory Expertise.** The quality of human resources remains a key concern in all SASEC countries where qualified human resources (especially laboratory technicians and microbiologists) are in short supply and adversely affects the efficient functioning of laboratories. SASEC countries should undertake an in-depth review of existing gaps in human resource skills and develop time-bound programs, also seeking support from FAO and WHO in this area.

(iii)   **Conduct Laboratory Facilities Assessment.** SASEC countries often have limited information about their existing laboratory facilities and standard operating procedures (SOPs). An in-depth assessment of laboratory facilities, including SOPs, would help government agencies better understand critical areas with gaps in soft and hard infrastructure, and develop industry guidelines and uniform SOPs across laboratories.

Chapter 7
Conclusion

In the SASEC region, India is the center of gravity and has a strong impact on the economic and trade relations of all member countries. Its significance comes from its land connectivity to most of the South Asian countries that helped India expand its trade ties with the other SASEC countries. In general, the SASEC countries' many bilateral and regional trading arrangements with each other help lower the region's high tariff walls. Yet on the other hand, this region has many nontariff barriers imposed by the importing country behind the legitimate nontariff measures. Two such nontariff barriers are SPS and TBT requirements, which are often used as NTMs to limit imports coming from other countries.

This diagnostic study has attempted to identify only those barriers to trade associated with legitimate SPS and TBT measures imposed on India's exports by the relevant importing SASEC country. The study also provides a country-wise list of potential items for export from India to five SASEC countries and finds that India has export potential mainly in machinery and electrical products in the markets of all the other SASEC countries. For these products, India's share in total imports of SASEC countries currently remains modest, which gives room for further improvement.

The study highlights several policy-level barriers that could be the reasons for India's low export share of these potential products in the other SASEC markets. Such policy-level barriers include, among others, lack of harmonized standards, lack of quality infrastructure availability, lack of updated regulations on standards, and the presence of multiple regulatory agencies. On the basis of its primary survey, the study also observes that impediments have a greater negative effect on small exporters than large exporters: while the latter can easily fulfil the importing country's requirements with the help of their resources, contacts, and network within the importing country, small exporters most often do not have that advantage. The identified challenges should be addressed to further facilitate trade among the SASEC countries.

Overall, this diagnostic study finds tremendous potential to increase trade between India and SASEC countries if impediments related to NTBs are removed and provides prioritized recommendations to help achieve this target.

Appendix 1
Top 10 Export Products from India to Other SASEC Countries in 2015 at the 6-Digit HS Code Level

Table A1.1: Top 10 Exports to Bangladesh in 2015

S.N.	HS Code (6-digit)	Description	Export Value ($ million)
1	520100	Cotton, not carded or combed	677.65
2	520524	Single cotton yarn, of combed fibers, containing >= 85% cotton by weight and with a linear density of 125 decitex to < 192,31 decitex "> MN 52 to MN 80" (excluding sewing thread and yarn put up for retail sale)	188.12
3	100630	Semi-milled or wholly milled rice, whether or not polished or glazed	168.47
4	520523	Single cotton yarn, of combed fibers, containing >= 85% cotton by weight and with a linear density of 192,31 decitex to < 232,56 decitex "> MN 43 to MN 52" (excluding sewing thread and yarn put up for retail sale)	151.48
5	520942	Denim, containing >= 85% cotton by weight and weighing > 200 g/m^2, made of yarn of different colors	130.19
6	871120	Motorcycles, including mopeds, with reciprocating internal combustion piston engine of a cylinder capacity > 50 cm^3 but <= 250 cm^3	129.13
7	100199	Wheat and meslin (excluding seed for sowing, and durum wheat)	88.08
8	070310	Fresh or chilled onions and shallots	80.73
9	320416	Synthetic organic reactive dyes; preparations based on synthetic organic reactive dyes of a kind used to dye fabrics or produce colorant preparations (excluding preparations of heading 3207, 3208, 3209, 3210, 3213, and 3215)	77.42
10	720711	Semi-finished products of iron or non-alloy steel containing, by weight, < 0,25% of carbon, of square or rectangular cross-section, the width measuring < twice the thickness	74.41
Total of Top 10 Products			**1,765.68**
Share of Value of Top 10 Exports in Total Export to Bangladesh (in %)			**32.05**

HS = Harmonized Commodity Description and Coding System, S.N. = serial number.

Source: UN Comtrade under World Integrated Trade Solution.

Table A1.2: Top 10 Exports to Bhutan in 2015

S.N.	HS Code (6-digit)	Description	Export Value ($ million)
1	271019	Medium oils and preparations, of petroleum or bituminous minerals, not containing biodiesel, n.e.s.	56.70
2	846249	Punching or notching machines, including presses, and combined punching and shearing machines, not numerically controlled, for working metal	21.97
3	870321	Motor cars and other motor vehicles principally designed for the transport of persons, including station wagons and racing cars, with spark-ignition internal combustion reciprocating piston engine of a cylinder capacity <= 1.000 cm³ (excluding vehicles for the transport of persons on snow and other specially designed vehicles of subheading 8703.10)	16.23
4	271012	Light oils and preparations, of petroleum or bituminous minerals which >= 90% by volume "including losses" distil at 210°C "ASTM D 86 method" (excluding containing biodiesel)	14.28
5	852910	Aerials and aerial reflectors of all kinds; parts suitable for use therewith, n.e.s.	10.19
6	270119	Coal, whether or not pulverized, non-agglomerated (excluding anthracite and bituminous coal)	8.22
7	847990	Parts of machines and mechanical appliances, n.e.s.	6.54
8	190590	Bread, pastry, cakes, biscuits and other bakers' wares, whether or not containing cocoa; communion wafers, empty cachets of a kind suitable for pharmaceutical use, sealing wafers, rice paper and similar products (excluding crisp bread, gingerbread, and the like, sweet biscuits, waffles, wafers not mentioned, rusks, toasted bread, and similar toasted products)	6.50
9	730890	Structures and parts of structures, of iron or steel, n.e.s. (excluding bridges and bridge-sections, towers and lattice masts, doors and windows and their frames, thresholds for doors, props, and similar equipment for scaffolding, shuttering, propping, or pit-propping)	6.37
10	730820	Towers and lattice masts, of iron or steel	6.26
Total of Top 10 Products			**153.27**
Share of Value of Top 10 Exports in Total Export to Bhutan (in %)			**45.98**

HS = Harmonized Commodity Description and Coding System, n.e.s. = not elsewhere specified, S.N. = serial number.

Source: UN Comtrade under World Integrated Trade Solution.

Table A1.3: Top 10 Exports to Maldives in 2015

S.N.	HS Code (6-digit)	Description	Export Value ($ million)
1	251710	Pebbles, gravel, broken or crushed stone, for concrete aggregates, for road metaling or for railway or other ballast, shingle and flint, whether or not heat-treated	20.41
2	100630	Semi-milled or wholly milled rice, whether or not polished or glazed	12.09
3	300490	Medicaments consisting of mixed or unmixed products for therapeutic or prophylactic purposes, put up in measured doses, including those in the form of transdermal administration or in forms or packings for retail sale (excluding medicaments containing antibiotics, medicaments containing hormones or steroids used as hormones, but not containing antibiotics, medicaments containing alkaloids or derivatives thereof, but not containing hormones or antibiotics and medicaments containing provitamins, vitamins, or derivatives thereof used as vitamins)	8.38
4	252329	Portland cement (excluding white, whether or not artificially colored)	5.92
5	721410	Bars and rods, of iron or non-alloy steel, not further worked than forged (excluding in irregularly wound coils)	4.81
6	020230	Frozen, boneless meat of bovine animals	4.33
7	070310	Fresh or chilled onions and shallots	3.90
8	490110	Printed books, brochures, and similar printed matter, in single sheets, whether or not folded (excluding periodicals and publications which are essentially devoted to advertising)	3.36
9	040721	Fresh eggs of domestic fowls, in shell (excluding fertilized for incubation)	2.81
10	080280	Fresh or dried areca nuts, whether or not shelled or peeled	2.60
Total of Top 10 Products			68.61
Share of Value of Top 10 Exports in Total Export to Maldives (in %)			41.13

HS = Harmonized Commodity Description and Coding System, S.N. = serial number.
Source: UN Comtrade under World Integrated Trade Solution.

Table A1.4: Top 10 Exports to Nepal in 2015

S.N.	HS Code (6-digit)	Description	Export Value ($ million)
1	271019	Medium oils and preparations, of petroleum or bituminous minerals, not containing biodiesel, n.e.s.	434.37
2	271119	Gaseous hydrocarbons, liquefied, n.e.s. (excluding natural gas, propane, butane, ethylene, propylene, butylene, and butadiene)	133.03
3	100630	Semi-milled or wholly milled rice, whether or not polished or glazed	129.30
4	271012	Light oils and preparations, of petroleum or bituminous minerals which >= 90% by volume "including losses" distil at 210°C "ASTM D 86 method" (excluding containing biodiesel)	104.53
5	720719	Semi-finished products of iron or non-alloy steel containing, by weight, < 0,25% of carbon, of circular cross-section, or of a cross-section other than square or rectangular	103.26
6	871120	Motorcycles, including mopeds, with reciprocating internal combustion piston engine of a cylinder capacity > 50 cm³ but <= 250 cm³	82.96
7	720918	Flat-rolled products of iron or non-alloy steel, of a width of >= 600 mm, in coils, simply cold-rolled "cold-reduced", not clad, plated or coated, of a thickness of < 0.5 mm	70.65
8	870600	Chassis fitted with engines for tractors, motor vehicles for the transport of ten or more persons, motor cars and other motor vehicles principally designed for the transport of persons, motor vehicles for the transport of goods and special purpose motor vehicles of heading 8701 to 8705 (excluding those with engines and cabs)	65.90
9	300339	Medicaments containing hormones or steroids used as hormones, not containing antibiotics, not in measured doses or put up for retail sale (excluding those containing insulin)	51.54
10	100590	Maize (excluding seed for sowing)	46.32
Total of Top 10 Products			**1,221.86**
Share of Value of Top 10 Exports in Total Export to Nepal (in %)			**38.26**

HS = Harmonized Commodity Description and Coding System, n.e.s. = not elsewhere specified, S.N. = serial number.

Source: UN Comtrade under World Integrated Trade Solution.

Table A1.5: Top 10 Exports to Sri Lanka in 2015

S.N.	HS Code (6-digit)	Description	Export Value ($ million)
1	880240	Airplanes and other powered aircraft of an of an unladen weight > 15000 kg (excluding helicopters and dirigibles)	777.25
2	271019	Medium oils and preparations, of petroleum or bituminous minerals, not containing biodiesel, n.e.s.	629.55
3	870321	Motor cars and other motor vehicles principally designed for the transport of persons, including station wagons and racing cars, with spark-ignition internal combustion reciprocating piston engine of a cylinder capacity <= 1.000 cm³ (excluding vehicles for the transport of persons on snow and other specially designed vehicles of subheading 8703.10)	319.05
4	880220	Airplanes and other powered aircraft of an unladen weight <= 2000 kg (excluding helicopters and dirigibles)	275.85
5	871120	Motorcycles, including mopeds, with reciprocating internal combustion piston engine of a cylinder capacity > 50 cm³ but <= 250 cm³	218.64
6	890690	Vessels, including lifeboats (excluding warships, rowing boats, and other vessels of heading 8901 to 8905 and vessels for breaking up)	179.55
7	271012	Light oils and preparations, of petroleum or bituminous minerals which >= 90% by volume "including losses" distil at 210°C "ASTM D 86 method" (excluding containing biodiesel)	158.46
8	870421	Motor vehicles for the transport of goods, with compression-ignition internal combustion piston engine "diesel or semi-diesel engine" of a gross vehicle weight <= 5 t (excluding dumpers for off-highway use of subheading 8704.10 and special purpose motor vehicles of heading 8705)	123.25
9	300490	Medicaments consisting of mixed or unmixed products for therapeutic or prophylactic purposes, put up in measured doses including those in the form of transdermal administration or in forms or packings for retail sale (excluding medicaments containing antibiotics, medicaments containing hormones or steroids used as hormones, but not containing antibiotics, medicaments containing alkaloids or derivatives thereof but not containing hormones or antibiotics and medicaments containing provitamins, vitamins or derivatives thereof used as vitamins)	121.90
10	252329	Portland cement (excluding white, whether or not artificially colored)	80.89
Total of Top 10 Products			**2,884.39**
Share of Value of Top 10 Exports in Total Export to Sri Lanka (in %)			**52.45**

HS = Harmonized Commodity Description and Coding System, n.e.s. = not elsewhere specified, S.N. = serial number.

Source: UN Comtrade under World Integrated Trade Solution.

Appendix 2
Identification of Potential Export Items

Table A2.1: Potential Export Products of India in Bangladesh Market at Harmonized System 6-Digit Level of Product Classification
($10 million filter)

S.N.	HS Code 6-Digit (2007)	Short Description	Export Value (India to Bangladesh) ($)	Global Export Value of India ($)	Unit Value of Exports of India	Global Import Value of Bangladesh ($)	Unit Value of Imports of Bangladesh	India's Share of Exports in Bangladesh Imports (%)
1	130239	Mucilages and thickeners	190,848	11,096,224	2.33	14,550,323	3.55	1.31
2	252310	Cement clinkers	7,835,355	90,912,104	0.04	399,258,816	0.05	1.96
3	271011	Light petroleum oils and preparations	445,757	18,901,563,392	0.88	98,613,944	1.03	0.45
4	271019	Petroleum oils and oils	66,396,016	33,841,328,128	0.79	1,932,698,112	0.79	3.44
5	280920	Phosphoric and polyphosphoric acids	839,762	13,918,603	0.41	11,177,631	0.65	7.51
6	293040	Methionine	19,962	11,959,766	4.01	11,870,374	4.52	0.17
7	300210	Antisera and other blood fractions	305,899	43,399,924	94.12	19,405,954	186.94	1.58
8	300490	Medicaments	7,188,731	7,581,884,416	28.54	41,834,172	43.55	17.18
9	320411	Disperse dyes and preparations	1,788,522	56,259,692	6.05	28,575,294	6.84	6.26
10	320611	Pigments and preparations	1,197,797	25,247,110	1.96	19,423,888	2.63	6.17
11	320710	Prepared pigments, prepared opacifiers	495,903	17,966,148	2.43	10,592,147	4.85	4.68
12	320890	Paints and varnishes (including enamels and distempers	1,548,641	17,949,770	3.46	10,123,647	3.90	15.30
13	340213	Non-ionic surface-active agents	1,939,224	98,747,872	2.06	11,783,318	2.27	16.46
14	350691	Adhesives based on polymers of 39.0	2,099,574	41,066,644	1.97	21,241,668	2.92	9.88
15	382200	Diagnostic/laboratory reagents on a backing prepared diagnostic	1,276,895	35,966,912	23.05	14,023,226	24.32	9.11
16	382311	Stearic acid	66,018	35,340,592	0.86	13,283,842	0.97	0.50

continued on next page

Table A2.1 continued

S.N.	HS Code 6-Digit (2007)	Short Description	Export Value (India to Bangladesh) ($)	Global Export Value of India ($)	Unit Value of Exports of India	Global Import Value of Bangladesh ($)	Unit Value of Imports of Bangladesh	India's Share of Exports in Bangladesh Imports (%)
17	390390	Polymers of styrene, in primary forms	1,560,509	22,520,956	1.42	16,003,907	1.71	9.75
18	390690	Acrylic polymers other than polymers	5,078,535	59,598,152	1.50	40,573,640	1.67	12.52
19	391910	Self-adhesive plates, sheets, film	446,598	22,577,618	3.13	11,520,098	6.46	3.88
20	392321	Sacks and bags (including cones), of poly propylene	104,889	109,520,160	2.34	12,968,620	6.69	0.81
21	392329	Sacks and bags (including cones), of plastics	872,112	197,250,448	1.69	10,349,668	5.64	8.43
22	392690	Articles of plastics and articles of other materials	1,981,553	457,590,752	2.28	70,876,840	6.35	2.80
23	400219	Styrene-butadiene rubber (SBR), other materials	1,559,276	12,355,130	2.35	10,363,448	2.40	15.05
24	401699	Articles of vulcanized rubber other hard rubber	1,700,477	190,370,976	5.16	10,223,807	6.36	16.63
25	410799	Leather further prepared after tanning	2,300,754	258,967,728	12.92	18,241,234	17.93	12.61
26	480256	Paper and paperboard	165,373	45,312,068	0.85	10,307,444	0.96	1.60
27	480257	Paper and paperboard	64,499	79,765,664	0.84	17,321,628	2.45	0.37
28	481019	Paper and paperboard of a kind used	258,383	40,810,488	0.65	41,050,496	0.71	0.63
29	481159	Paper and paperboard coated or impregnated	957,283	57,742,440	2.08	17,162,784	4.24	5.58
30	482390	Paper, paperboard, cellulose wadding	1,755,878	207,590,416	2.24	12,348,675	2.37	14.22
31	510710	Yarn of combed wool, not put up for retail sale	543,647	61,982,524	15.23	11,738,216	19.53	4.63
32	520532	Cotton yarn, multiple (folded) or cable	1,605,041	56,979,144	3.31	46,179,244	3.94	3.48
33	520911	Woven fabrics of cotton	566,927	42,075,992	7.61	10,624,275	27.77	5.34
34	540110	Sewing thread of manmade filaments	1,096,190	11,148,101	6.66	13,582,640	7.03	8.07
35	540247	Yarn other than high tenacity or texture	265,561	35,297,696	1.87	26,056,972	2.11	1.02
36	550130	Synthetic filament towel, acrylic or modacrylic	1,265,635	15,635,872	2.49	27,095,680	2.83	4.67
37	550921	Yarn other than sewing thread,	726,696	44,852,504	2.62	15,527,261	3.76	4.68

continued on next page

Table A2.1 *continued*

S.N.	HS Code 6-Digit (2007)	Short Description	Export Value (India to Bangladesh) ($)	Global Export Value of India ($)	Unit Value of Exports of India	Global Import Value of Bangladesh ($)	Unit Value of Imports of Bangladesh	India's Share of Exports in Bangladesh Imports (%)
38	550922	Yarn other than sewing thread,	1,349,412	50,801,072	2.85	55,795,740	2.91	2.42
39	550969	Yarn other than sewing thread,	224,714	13,630,380	1.42	25,659,590	6.69	0.88
40	551012	Yarn other than sewing thread,	1,405,615	44,270,160	3.58	35,535,976	4.22	3.96
41	580620	Narrow woven fabrics (excluding of 5806)	1,338,675	20,269,482	6.93	49,661,872	12.03	2.70
42	580632	Narrow woven fibers, Nesoi, of manmade fibers (excluding of 5806)	50,717	10,028,036	3.57	26,124,042	8.91	0.19
43	600624	Knitted/crocheted fabrics, n.e.s.	1,053,499	12,423,871	3.32	11,054,478	7.39	9.53
44	600690	Knitted/crocheted fabrics, n.e.s.	1,845,624	31,879,240	4.07	14,806,564	8.16	12.46
45	621710	Made up clothing accessories	1,097,755	34,160,312	7.24	26,077,956	12.16	4.21
46	640299	Other footwear with outer soles	94,342	73,018,016	3.94	26,837,212	4.20	0.35
47	640699	Removable insoles, heel cushions	555,790	13,557,773	8.21	24,863,290	8.73	2.24
48	690790	Unglazed ceramic flags and paving	58,649	20,659,064	5.98	27,953,950	6.59	0.21
49	690890	Glazed ceramic flags and paving	453,470	208,177,696	3.35	31,015,308	7.50	1.46
50	711319	Articles of jewelry and parts thereof	1,182,937	11,825,043,456	39,084.77	187,136,032	6,047,937.00	0.63
51	720839	Flat-rolled products of iron or non-aluminum	9,583,050	228,085,280	0.57	329,354,560	0.58	2.91
52	730300	Tubes, pipes and hollow profiles	542,367	171,545,456	0.77	17,678,850	1.29	3.07
53	730890	Structures (excluding prefabricated	3,566,738	376,832,064	1.77	65,712,256	2.23	5.43
54	830210	Hinges of base metal	430,195	54,384,860	2.30	10,674,508	3.08	4.03
55	830242	Mountings, fittings and similar articles	159,011	39,398,792	3.03	15,533,088	6.48	1.02
56	840690	Parts of the steam turbines	840,100	44,541,128	21.46	20,447,134	42.89	4.11
57	840890	Internal combustion piston engines	195,692	313,166,848	1,144.99	102,003,176	158,901.83	0.19
58	840991	Parts suitable for use	1,984,963	244,003,840	8.45	24,447,312	13.89	8.12

continued on next page

Table A2.1 continued

S.N.	HS Code 6-Digit (2007)	Short Description	Export Value (India to Bangladesh) ($)	Global Export Value of India ($)	Unit Value of Exports of India	Global Import Value of Bangladesh ($)	Unit Value of Imports of Bangladesh	India's Share of Exports in Bangladesh Imports (%)
59	841480	Air pumps, air or other gas compressor	2,120,748	356,367,968	145.49	51,155,684	726.23	4.15
60	841590	Parts of the air conditioning machines	689,115	62,476,280	7.30	20,257,910	10.02	3.40
61	841869	Refrigerating/freezing equipment, n.e.s	3,652,452	32,952,800	8.61	23,742,930	10.01	15.38
62	841950	Heat exchange units	1,230,089	125,707,904	690.06	22,498,898	34,043.02	5.47
63	842139	Filtering or purifying machinery and appliances	1,941,111	83,358,440	26.10	14,799,088	293.77	13.12
64	842290	Parts of the machinery of 8422.11-8	1,371,369	33,909,700	16.58	11,139,386	74.62	12.31
65	842619	Overhead traveling cranes	1,316,221	35,506,260	21,824.01	10,506,748	120,180.01	12.53
66	843149	Parts suitable for use solely	822,388	273,704,384	4.57	24,343,142	14.44	3.38
67	843710	Machines for cleaning, sorting	2,673,752	15,318,067	704.25	16,201,720	6,636.29	16.50
68	843880	Machinery n.e.s. in Chapter 84	2,136,751	25,521,894	1,655.31	12,931,973	5,436.46	16.52
69	844839	Parts and accessories of the machines	2,153,894	17,989,476	14.25	23,338,522	17.15	9.23
70	844849	Other parts and accessories of weaving	573,555	15,421,935	8.31	27,858,558	8.97	2.06
71	845140	Washing, bleaching, dyeing machines	1,959,157	17,222,002	18,279.22	60,528,776	61,145.09	3.24
72	847130	Portable automatic data	90,459	43,145,560	363.58	97,427,336	385.64	0.09
73	847150	Processing units	91,638	76,407,896	546.76	21,829,752	1,384.44	0.42
74	847170	Storage units	108,510	62,931,436	50.53	26,913,672	105.85	0.40
75	847290	Other office machines	656,649	56,011,224	2.88	10,392,932	3.57	6.32
76	847480	Machinery for agglomerating or shaping	1,287,212	17,524,962	3,029.36	16,693,562	20,181.48	7.71
77	847710	Injection-molding machines	236,901	44,092,164	27,877.85	24,127,100	35,648.45	0.98
78	847780	Machinery for working rubber or plastic	779,060	34,247,812	6,453.56	22,105,080	14,637.35	3.52
79	847982	Mixing, kneading, crushing, grinding machines	2,647,588	24,153,358	988.84	13,310,570	9,456.76	19.89
80	847989	Other machines and mechanical appliances	10,658,642	253,923,808	2,124.14	65,063,924	3,467.76	16.38
81	847990	Parts of machines and mechanical appliances	3,548,938	164,488,320	9.49	21,040,664	14.95	16.87
82	850164	AC generators (alternators)	155,146	47,647,520	64,264.29	22,114,018	362,974.88	0.70

continued on next page

Table A2.1 continued

S.N.	HS Code 6-Digit (2007)	Short Description	Export Value (India to Bangladesh) ($)	Global Export Value of India ($)	Unit Value of Exports of India	Global Import Value of Bangladesh ($)	Unit Value of Imports of Bangladesh	India's Share of Exports in Bangladesh Imports (%)
83	850211	Electric generating sets	1,458,103	52,196,940	4,153.62	18,377,218	5,897.91	7.93
84	850213	Electric generating sets	1,179,968	48,119,768	27,316.27	133,191,624	59,180.89	0.89
85	850220	Electric generating sets	905,188	31,369,762	629.77	93,791,776	13,950.23	0.97
86	850239	Electric generating sets	435,684	15,849,924	9,257.14	27,277,476	269,970.53	1.60
87	850300	Parts suitable for use	4,062,859	291,101,248	6.98	57,594,288	19.20	7.05
88	850490	Parts of the machines of 85.04	2,444,296	173,042,128	4.43	16,512,222	9.53	14.80
89	852340	Optical media for the recording	323,078	147,849,728	0.22	73,459,592	3.25	0.44
90	853190	Parts of the apparatus of 85.31	133,608	21,061,334	27.74	24,826,180	35.08	0.54
91	853590	Electrical apparatus for switching	1,911,710	48,750,904	10.61	12,923,378	24.78	14.79
92	853620	Automatic circuit breakers	673,173	85,156,336	11.34	14,625,495	17.22	4.60
93	853650	Switches other than isolating switches	1,266,574	97,804,256	14.84	12,259,678	16.43	10.33
94	853710	Boards, panels, consoles, desks	7,411,651	240,336,928	19.32	48,549,404	29.79	15.27
95	853931	Electric discharge lamps	1,001,510	19,863,334	0.77	19,861,986	0.81	5.04
96	854460	Electric conductors (excluding 8544)	3,693,452	225,960,016	5.38	21,438,306	7.54	17.23
97	870210	Motor vehicles for transport	1,937,701	227,730,208	27,605.72	15,021,860	47,030.70	12.90
98	870322	Vehicles (excluding of 87.02 and 8703.10)	1,003,894	2,901,425,408	6,375.43	127,081,952	10,538.56	0.79
99	870323	Vehicles (excluding of 87.02 and 8703.10)	176,077	555,554,752	10,134.74	61,188,016	17,440.69	0.29
100	870333	Vehicles principally designed	2,027,931	12,166,162	7,806.30	10,723,456	26,081.99	18.91
101	880330	Parts of airplanes, helicopters	261,065	1,312,559,744	562.72	17,241,716	567.81	1.51
102	901839	Catheters, cannulae, and the like	2,511,693	178,340,656	0.17	12,463,246	0.21	20.15
103	901890	Instruments and appliances used	3,117,753	177,094,400	0.86	31,572,122	1.78	9.88
104	902214	Apparatus based on the use of X-ray	1,124,977	83,440,264	1,380.17	10,203,330	17,343.57	11.03
105	902780	Instruments and apparatus	1,112,652	21,018,526	85.19	14,559,227	312.01	7.64
106	903289	Automatic regulating or controlling	1,103,699	115,576,296	62.88	14,087,084	134.72	7.83

continued on next page

Table A2.1 continued

S.N.	HS Code 6-Digit (2007)	Short Description	Export Value (India to Bangladesh) ($)	Global Export Value of India ($)	Unit Value of Exports of India	Global Import Value of Bangladesh ($)	Unit Value of Imports of Bangladesh	India's Share of Exports in Bangladesh Imports (%)
107	940320	Metal furniture (excluding 94.01)	421,975	53,438,436	2.69	16,257,759	4.48	2.60
108	940389	Furniture of other materials	721	12,026,776	7.85	52,472,680	9.73	0.00

HS = Harmonized Commodity Description and Coding System, n.e.s. = not elsewhere specified, S.N. = serial number.

Source: Asian Development Bank data analysis using trade data from World Integrated Trade Solution.

Table A2.2: Potential Export Products of India in Bhutan Market at Harmonized System 6-Digit Level of Product Classification
(no filter)

S.N.	HS Code 6-Digit (2007)	Short Description	Export Value (India to Bhutan) ($)	Global Export Value of India ($)	Unit Value of Exports of India	Global Import Value of Bhutan ($)	Unit Value of Imports of Bhutan	India's Share of Exports in Bhutan Imports (%)
1	10511	Live fowls of species Gallus	10,362.00	330,735.75	2.01	65,791.00	5.14	15.75
2	220830	Whiskies	32,008.00	107,400,264	3.56	1,552,890.00	14.40	2.06
3	251512	Marble and travertine, cut	35,042.25	34,155,516	0.18	517,410.75	0.21	6.77
4	300220	Vaccines for human medicine	40,980.00	487,710,880	157.72	521,241.81	351.60	7.86
5	382200	Diagnostic or laboratory reagents on	7,243.80	35,966,912	23.05	120,542.20	117.19	6.01
6	392410	Tableware and kitchenware, of plastic	18,821.00	141,296,400	3.11	207,229.67	3.55	9.08
7	392640	Statuettes and other ornamental articles	10,348.50	15,795,247	6.01	207,348.50	10.28	4.99
8	401693	Gaskets, washers, and other seals of	22,980.00	65,912,132	7.50	121,645.34	21.97	18.89
9	491110	Trade advertising material,	879.75	15,902,464	4.60	18,201.00	33.28	4.83
10	610910	T-shirts, singlets, and other vests	413.67	1,735,263,104	3.11	22,449.00	4.82	1.84
11	621490	Shawls, scarves, mufflers, mantilla	88.50	456,096,704	3.10	13,487.50	7.61	0.66
12	630720	Life-jackets and life-belts	363.50	11,424,459	7.05	4,284.50	36.49	8.48
13	650610	Safety headgear, whether or not lined	2,093.50	13,055,173	5.55	22,767.25	59.49	9.20
14	691110	Tableware and kitchenware, of porcelain	9,868.25	12,999,715	2.55	75,669.75	14.17	13.04
15	731822	Washers (excluding of 7318.21) of iron	19.00	38,001,440	2.42	15,736.50	15.21	0.12
16	732620	Articles of iron or steel wire	46,317.00	50,533,392	2.94	294,517.50	3.23	15.73
17	841319	Pumps for liquids, fitted or designed	1,436.50	14,220,382	51.03	22,470.00	4,172.19	6.39
18	841850	Refrigerating or freezing chests, cabinets	2,618.50	23,185,774	359.34	23,971.50	918.89	10.92
19	844332	Other printers, copying machines,	7,610.67	5,538,467.50	448.52	61,958.00	605.53	12.28
20	847130	Portable automatic data	66,446.00	46,189,520	331.98	649,808.25	607.11	10.23
21	847170	Storage units	17,347.50	42,431,320	78.35	267,042.50	2,025.54	6.50
22	847330	Parts and accessories of the machines	127,072.40	132,644,784	74.74	1,023,855.81	106.04	12.41

continued on next page

Table A2.2 continued

S.N.	HS Code 6-Digit (2007)	Short Description	Export Value (India to Bhutan) ($)	Global Export Value of India ($)	Unit Value of Exports of India	Global Import Value of Bhutan ($)	Unit Value of Imports of Bhutan	India's Share of Exports in Bhutan Imports (%)
23	848180	Taps, cocks, valves, and similar appliances	5,916.40	674,439,680	12.85	151,005.80	60.15	3.92
24	850300	Parts suitable for use solely or /	235,796.75	294,134,336	7.20	671,666.00	42.88	35.11
25	851770	Parts of telephone sets, including	48,831.40	615,033,728	53.19	1,539,489.00	140.54	3.17
26	852580	Television cameras, digital cameras	19,278.00	22,393,540	239.10	176,295.50	450.66	10.94
27	853650	Switches other than isolating switches	54,959.50	93,654,368	14.76	254,383.50	23.69	21.60
28	901831	Syringes, with or without needles	169.00	32,407,684	0.04	12,938.33	172.00	1.31
29	901849	Instruments and appliances used in	931.00	6,388,771	3.28	45,285.00	2,447.88	2.06
30	902300	Instruments, apparatus, and models	10,224.00	35,528,156	86.61	59,413.67	97.30	17.21
31	902680	Instruments and apparatus for measuring	1,187.00	21,984,690	10.61	14,777.50	124.62	8.03
32	902690	Parts and accessories of the instruments	274.00	30,065,100	20.69	4,582.00	176.95	5.98
33	902790	Microtomes; parts and accessories	1,136.00	18,224,658	70.06	25,405.00	304.66	4.47
34	940540	Electric lamps and lighting fittings	1,464.00	15,555,260	29.89	256,138.50	37.09	0.57
35	950699	Articles and equipment for sports, n.e.s	2,111.00	75,686,760	4.25	929,069.50	12,378.45	0.23

HS = Harmonized Commodity Description and Coding System, n.e.s. = not elsewhere specified, S.N. = serial number.

Source: Asian Development Bank data analysis using trade data from World Integrated Trade Solution.

Table A2.3: Potential Export Products of India in Maldives Market at Harmonized System 6-Digit Level of Product Classification
($1 million filter)

S.N.	HS Code 6-Digit (2007)	Short Description	Export Value (India to Maldives) ($)	Global Export Value of India ($)	Unit Value of Exports of India	Global Import Value of Maldives ($)	Unit Value of Imports of Maldives	India's Share of Exports in Maldives Imports (%)
1	20712	Meat of fowls of species Gallus	701,697.19	7,893,420	1.75	10,548,908.00	1.89	6.65
2	20714	Cuts and edible offal of species	116,991.75	1,222,655.50	0.88	7,409,262.50	2.24	1.58
3	30612	Lobsters (*Homarus* spp.)	391,792.41	28,241,366	13.03	2,660,678.00	17.55	14.73
4	40120	Milk and cream, not concentrated	9,249.00	5,341,516	0.66	2,245,042.75	2.12	0.41
5	40210	Milk in powder/granules or other	483.67	122,230,776	3.12	3,129,348.75	5.15	0.02
6	40229	Milk in powder/granules or other	4,404.20	7,625,320.50	3.75	12,042,417.00	6.09	0.04
7	70200	Tomatoes, fresh or chilled	438,225.00	73,913,408	0.33	3,886,654.00	2.06	11.28
8	70960	Fruits of the genera capsicum	53,016.00	25,174,258	0.59	2,949,309.75	3.86	1.80
9	71390	Dried leguminous vegetables, n.e.s.	1,909.33	7,186,328	1.07	1,173,625.63	1.14	0.16
10	80430	Pineapples, fresh or dried	261,911.60	2,015,382.63	0.66	3,399,471.75	1.32	7.70
11	80450	Guavas, mangoes and mangosteens, fresh or dried	268,982.40	190,197,312	0.88	3,988,390.00	4.51	6.74
12	80510	Oranges, fresh or dried	1,222.25	8,412,042	0.36	2,469,425.25	0.89	0.05
13	80550	Lemons (Citrus limon or limonum)	287,412.19	9,194,247	0.44	2,976,836.50	2.22	9.65
14	80610	Grapes, fresh	45,029.20	149,884,272	1.35	1,321,688.25	5.33	3.41
15	80719	Melons (excluding watermelons), fresh	5,308.00	1,196,557	0.54	2,839,861.75	3.95	0.19
16	80810	Apples, fresh	267.50	11,395,748	0.46	3,017,952.75	1.38	0.01
17	81090	Fresh fruit, n.e.s.	254,164.41	63,367,408	1.12	3,512,555.00	4.87	7.24
18	90230	Tea, black (fermented) and partly fermented	49,088.40	71,945,336	4.09	1,228,330.75	6.73	4.00
19	170490	Sugar confectionery other than chewing products	126,501.00	66,515,932	1.30	1,695,660.00	2.31	7.46
20	190219	Uncooked pasta, not stuffed	825.75	7,956,517	1.73	4,814,021.50	1.87	0.02
21	190531	Sweet biscuits	209,232.60	154,066,064	1.16	6,486,686.50	1.97	3.23
22	190532	Waffles and wafers	21,542.20	8,395,390	1.86	1,015,428.63	2.48	2.12

continued on next page

Table A2.3 continued

S.N.	HS Code 6-Digit (2007)	Short Description	Export Value (India to Maldives) ($)	Global Export Value of India ($)	Unit Value of Exports of India	Global Import Value of Maldives ($)	Unit Value of Imports of Maldives	India's Share of Exports in Maldives Imports (%)
23	190590	Bread, pastry, cakes, biscuits	584,434.37	105,447,376	1.69	3,672,237.25	3.22	15.91
24	200799	Preparations of fruit (excluding citrus)	13,548.60	103,189,360	1.12	1,243,219.25	2.90	1.09
25	200819	Nuts (excluding ground-nuts), including mixed nuts	102,783.60	34,991,116	2.62	2,433,333.50	2.88	4.22
26	210390	Sauces and preparations therefor n.e.s.	14,152.60	27,528,826	2.17	3,093,190.50	2.37	0.46
27	220210	Waters, including mineral waters	76,489.20	2,134,282.25	0.64	10,063,107.00	1.66	0.76
28	220290	Non-alcoholic beverages	128,374.80	8,431,592	1.04	7,874,759	1.37	1.63
29	220300	Beer made from malt	9,485.50	31,572,964	0.86	2,038,249.25	0.89	0.47
30	220410	Sparkling wine of fresh grapes	117,417.50	1,308,844.75	6.01	2,882,869.25	9.28	4.07
31	220421	Wine other than sparkling wine	69,282.50	1,124,430.75	3.78	4,285,507.00	5.43	1.62
32	240220	Cigarettes containing tobacco	9,380,866.81	99,800,992	14.44	13,581,218.00	30.24	6.91
33	252329	Portland cement (excluding white cement)	3,261,480.75	132,797,248	0.06	1,6460,237.00	0.10	19.81
34	271019	Petroleum oils and oils obtained	3,763,269.50	33,841,328,128	0.79	393,046,464.00	0.87	0.96
35	320890	Paints and varnishes (including enamels	44,256.00	17,949,770	3.46	6,505,477.00	5.06	0.68
36	320990	Paints and varnishes (including enamels	31,933.60	4,178,773.50	2.38	1,197,106.00	4.48	2.67
37	330129	Essential oils	33,850.00	60,399,844	48.19	1,003,558.81	54.60	3.37
38	330300	Perfumes and toilet waters	141,629.60	129,798,192	7.09	7,612,478.50	35.58	1.86
	330499	Beauty or make-up preparations and preparations	872,516.18	132,579,656	3.86	6,787,370.00	16.54	12.85
40	330510	Shampoos	227,073.20	22,476,172	2.56	1,801,140.62	4.30	12.61
41	330590	Preparations for use on the hair	213,091.41	90,987,696	3.27	2,197,885.50	6.29	9.70
42	330720	Personal deodorants and antiperspirants	12,857.40	10,138,594	5.20	1,533,598.25	6.92	0.84
43	340111	Soap and organic surface-active products	31,218.00	60,152,536	2.42	1,141,407.63	2.43	2.74
44	340130	Organic surface-active products	144,217.79	8,713,560	2.62	2,653,105.50	4.01	5.44

continued on next page

Table A2.3 continued

S.N.	HS Code 6-Digit (2007)	Short Description	Export Value (India to Maldives) ($)	Global Export Value of India ($)	Unit Value of Exports of India	Global Import Value of Maldives ($)	Unit Value of Imports of Maldives	India's Share of Exports in Maldives Imports (%)
45	382200	Diagnostic or laboratory reagents	323,066.60	35,966,912	23.05	2,930,910.50	123.26	11.02
46	382490	Chemical products and preparations	24,016.40	170,987,808	0.83	2,074,974.25	3.25	1.16
47	390791	Polyesters (excluding of 3907.10-3907.6)	502,832.66	24,451,568	2.10	2,466,009.75	2.27	20.39
48	391721	Tubes, pipes and hoses, rigid	8,7421.40	36,650,656	2.57	1,001,208.81	3.75	8.73
49	391740	Fittings (e.g., joints, elbows,	109,785.00	18,880,534	3.50	3,591,986.50	9.64	3.06
50	392310	Boxes, cases, crates, and similar articles	127,770.00	39,632,764	2.97	2,163,111.50	4.37	5.91
51	392330	Carboys, bottles, flasks, and similar articles	17,866.60	20,374,688	2.92	3,004,820.00	5.21	0.59
52	392410	Tableware and kitchenware, of plastic	35,929.20	130,356,936	3.08	1,528,431.75	5.53	2.35
53	392490	Household articles and toilet articles	158,683.40	36,730,200	2.39	1,583,708.25	5.42	10.02
54	392690	Articles of plastics and articles	463,555.19	457,590,752	2.28	5,468,806.50	10.37	8.48
55	401693	Gaskets, washers, and other seals	3,798.50	65,493,140	8.19	1,862,203.50	26.91	0.20
56	480256	Paper and paperboard	63,797.80	45,312,068	0.85	1,725,220.25	1.23	3.70
57	481730	Boxes, pouches, wallets	7,562.20	2,153,035	3.42	1,030,620.00	5.76	0.73
58	481840	Sanitary towels and tampons, napkins	232,076.20	10,238,807	3.44	4,795,077.50	4.56	4.84
59	481910	Cartons, boxes and cases	35,364.60	33,164,910	1.46	1,115,349.63	2.07	3.17
60	490199	Printed books, brochures, leaflets	90,258.60	40,349,264	3.37	3,986,404.75	10.09	2.26
61	610342	Men's or boys' trousers, bib	6,278.60	90,533,480	3.45	1,545,728.62	3.95	0.41
62	630291	Toilet linen and kitchen linen	6,932.00	46,446,148	4.75	1,884,247.38	8.62	0.37
63	630533	Sacks and bags, of a kind used	51,854.50	15,234,084	2.46	1,132,082.75	2.89	4.58
64	681099	Articles of cement, concrete	25,303.00	16,920,320	1.24	1,380,467.00	1.28	1.83
65	690710	Unglazed ceramic tiles, cubes	12,421.75	44,536,160	5.87	2,032,178.75	8.97	0.61
66	690810	Glazed ceramic tiles, cubes	29,522.80	16,046,964	3.46	2,151,363.25	4.49	1.37
67	690890	Glazed ceramic flags and paving	386,421.00	208,177,696	3.35	6,895,202.00	4.65	5.60

continued on next page

Table A2.3 continued

S.N.	HS Code 6-Digit (2007)	Short Description	Export Value (India to Maldives) ($)	Global Export Value of India ($)	Unit Value of Exports of India	Global Import Value of Maldives ($)	Unit Value of Imports of Maldives	India's Share of Exports in Maldives Imports (%)
68	691090	Ceramic sinks, wash basins	47,035.75	53,653,932	25.62	2,576,863.00	54.75	1.83
69	691200	Ceramic tableware, kitchenware,	30,766.60	5,752,985.5	1.84	1,800,739.25	3.02	1.71
70	721041	Flat-rolled products of iron	174,584.80	315,956,960	0.92	1,609,547.25	1.09	10.85
71	721049	Flat-rolled products of iron	110,064.60	848,482,944	0.82	5,324,567.00	1.42	2.07
72	721669	Angles, shapes, and sections of iron	111,438.40	1,060,597	1.10	1,760,547.75	1.26	6.33
73	730690	Tubes, pipes, and hollow profiles	143,358.67	111,472,248	0.97	1,690,186.00	2.88	8.48
74	730890	Structures (excluding prefabricated	341,594.00	376,832,064	1.77	3,996,646.00	2.78	8.55
75	731815	Screws and bolts (excluding 7318.11-73)	52,515.60	278,744,256	1.85	2,411,317.50	4.96	2.18
76	732393	Table, kitchen, or other household articles	98,513.20	284,887,776	3.89	1,148,643.38	9.05	8.58
77	732394	Table, kitchen, or other household articles	7,171.80	184,045,104	3.80	1,378,050.00	5.20	0.52
78	732490	Sanitary ware and parts thereof	15,456.40	6,035,606	3.39	1,566,564.38	11.34	0.99
79	732690	Articles of iron or steel, n.e.s.	83,080.00	464,460,032	3.14	5,262,095.00	7.03	1.58
80	761010	Doors, windows, and their frames	7,666.00	1,541,457.5	6.05	2,782,250.00	9.66	0.28
81	761090	Aluminum structures (excluding prefabricated	132,403.60	27,731,448	4.83	2,057,403.38	7.69	6.44
82	830140	Locks, key, combination	21,164.60	21,266,436	5.83	1,187,985.63	17.50	1.78
83	840999	Parts suitable for use solely	318,113.81	571,931,264	8.53	7,433,707.00	29.69	4.28
84	841391	Parts of the pumps of 8413.11	235,837.41	240,727,184	8.75	1,753,450.63	34.14	13.45
85	841480	Air pumps, air or other gas compressor	32,935.40	356,367,968	145.49	2,475,334.50	265.29	1.33
86	841510	Window or wall type air conditioning machines	51,471.80	20,803,408	332.67	7,948,722.00	395.66	0.65
87	841590	Parts of the air conditioning machines	44,816.75	65,418,836	7.30	2,845,846.00	17.44	1.57
88	841829	Refrigerators, household type	539.00	12,949,004	151.00	2,243,724.00	231.87	0.02
89	841850	Refrigerating or freezing chests, cabinets	59,938.00	22,849,120	460.10	2,978,610.50	1,095.14	2.01

continued on next page

Table A2.3 continued

S.N.	HS Code 6-Digit (2007)	Short Description	Export Value (India to Maldives) ($)	Global Export Value of India ($)	Unit Value of Exports of India	Global Import Value of Maldives ($)	Unit Value of Imports of Maldives	India's Share of Exports in Maldives Imports (%)
90	841869	Refrigerating or freezing equip. n.e.s.	34,387.60	32,952,800	8.61	2,661,251.50	17.46	1.29
91	841899	Parts of the refrigerating	49,815.00	30,977,398	6.72	1,030,574.81	13.92	4.83
92	842121	Filtering or purifying machinery and appliances	227,068.00	84,932,840	65.92	4,075,628.50	642.90	5.57
93	842123	Oil or petrol-filters for internal	1,517.20	31,581,084	2.51	1,472,013.25	10.96	0.10
94	842199	Parts of the filtering or purifying machines	99,792.80	107,798,464	8.65	3,701,980.00	26.26	2.70
95	842810	Lifts (i.e., passenger elevators)	47,391.75	7,561,066.50	3,920.56	1,239,144.25	20,799.12	3.82
96	842959	Self-propelled mechanical shovels	251,232.00	104,632,640	25,464.15	3,725,211.25	63,251.16	6.74
97	843149	Parts suitable for use solely	16,457.80	273,704,384	4.57	1,446,702.00	11.24	1.14
98	846729	Tools for working in the hand	16,587.25	3,251,241.50	42.37	1,294,463.75	55.47	1.28
99	847130	Portable automatic data	37,065.40	43,145,560	363.58	7,553,450.50	415.74	0.49
100	847170	Storage units	4,863.80	62,931,436	50.53	4,547,179.50	67.57	0.11
101	848180	Taps, cocks, valves, and similar appliances	69,230.80	674,439,680	12.85	5,932,512.50	26.15	1.17
102	850134	DC motors (excluding universal AC or DC motors)	2,676.50	16,618,051	7,830.65	1,077,168.50	34,884.39	0.25
103	850213	Electric generating sets	345,032.00	47,388,020	34,092.68	2,984,897.00	65,547.84	11.56
104	851610	Electric instantaneous or storage	4,325.50	13,102,490	61.38	1,272,609.75	87.90	0.34
105	851679	Electro-thermic appliances n.e.s.	35,437.20	5,873,409	1.83	1,115,547.38	12.82	3.18
106	851712	Telephones for cellular networks	15,361.25	1,465,620,992	40.25	15,610,959.00	86.71	0.10
107	852340	Optical media for recording	22,205.40	147,849,728	0.22	2,670,795.00	9.68	0.83
108	852872	Other color reception apparatus	149,073.00	35,071,288	134.03	6,819,049.00	361.44	2.19
109	853650	Switches other than isolating switches	73,245.50	105,979,728	15.36	2,481,749.75	60.91	2.95
110	853690	Electrical apparatus for switching	43,883.60	200,086,080	16.07	1,880,164.38	39.13	2.33
111	853710	Boards, panels, consoles, desks	84,656.25	270,379,648	20.09	2,037,925.75	99.72	4.15

continued on next page

Table A2.3 continued

S.N.	HS Code 6-Digit (2007)	Short Description	Export Value (India to Maldives) ($)	Global Export Value of India ($)	Unit Value of Exports of India	Global Import Value of Maldives ($)	Unit Value of Imports of Maldives	India's Share of Exports in Maldives Imports (%)
112	853929	Electric filament lamps (excluding	5,572.80	23,021,592	0.13	1,067,488.63	1.15	0.52
113	854140	Photosensitive semiconductor devices	12,345.00	192,239,328	12.60	2,729,935.50	23.04	0.45
114	854370	Other machines and apparatus	20,446.60	33,519,314	10.68	1,478,048.38	101.78	1.38
115	854442	Other electric conductors	14,554.50	38,379,624	13.22	2,084,657.25	29.01	0.70
116	854449	Other electric conductors	79,248.60	47,433,472	8.54	5,917,735.50	9.18	1.34
117	854460	Electric conductors	88,783.80	225,960,016	5.38	3,301,285.00	9.11	2.69
118	870323	Vehicles (excluding of 87.02 and 8703.10)	67,756.00	501,942,528	10,617.02	1,037,469.50	13,774.30	6.53
119	870421	Motor vehicles for the transport	44,775.33	298,334,528	6085.02	1,305,784.00	10,532.83	3.43
120	870899	Other parts and accessories	136,593.20	2,422,961,408	4.64	1,957,610.25	12.53	6.98
121	871120	Motorcycles (including mopeds) and cycles	34,064.20	1,507,454,208	690.74	5,327,206.00	950.22	0.64
122	880310	Propellers and rotors and parts thereof	12,608.67	9,067,729	281.85	1,187,557.00	460.06	1.06
123	901890	Instruments and appliances	608,045.81	177,094,400	0.86	3,763,878.50	7.02	16.15
124	940169	Seats (excluding of 9401.10-9401.50)	3,439.00	40,166,144	14.99	1,495,151.50	117.81	0.23
125	940320	Metal furniture (excluding of 94.01	35,316.60	53,438,436	2.69	2,882,147.50	5.04	1.23
126	940340	Wooden furniture	446.67	1,317,730.63	30.16	1,015,312.69	85.85	0.04
127	940350	Wooden furniture of a kind used	33,234.00	4,183,111.5	47.78	5,205,461.00	122.46	0.64
128	940360	Wooden furniture (excluding of 94.01)	49,362.60	387,466,688	25.34	8,235,468.50	122.25	0.60
129	940390	Parts of the furniture	31,849.25	10,140,963	3.77	1,623,931.00	4.17	1.96
130	940490	Other articles of bedding	202,044.80	244,179,952	5.67	2,550,218.50	9.28	7.92
131	940600	Prefabricated buildings	107,032.33	42,788,228	3.43	4,338,958.00	3.46	2.47
132	950691	Articles and equip. for general	14,042.00	9,944,919	4.58	1,519,062.63	7.44	0.92

HS = Harmonized Commodity Description and Coding System, n.e.s. = not elsewhere specified, S.N. = serial number.

Source: Asian Development Bank data analysis using trade data from World Integrated Trade Solution.

Table A2.4: Potential Export Products of India in Nepal Market at Harmonized System 6-Digit Level of Product Classification
($1 Million Filter)

S.N.	HS Code 6-Digit (2007)	Short Description	Export Value (India to Nepal) ($)	Global Export Value of India ($)	Unit Value of Exports of India	Global Import Value of Nepal ($)	Unit Value of Imports of Nepal	India's Share of Exports in Nepal Imports (%)
1	40229	Milk in powder/granules or other solids	671,961.00	7,625,320.50	3.75	5,382,547.50	4.89	12.48
2	80131	Cashew nuts, in shell	147,989.20	8,521,558	1.36	1,220,543.37	4.09	12.12
3	120991	Vegetable seeds, of a kind used	468,903.81	38,151,864	7.32	2,668,794.50	12.58	17.57
4	180610	Cocoa powder, containing added sugar	43,247.40	1,017,253.38	4.84	2,060,764.00	5.20	2.10
5	210390	Sauces and preparations therefor, n.e.s.	595,051.81	27,528,826	2.17	3,217,034.00	2.55	18.50
6	220830	Whiskies	170,419.75	106,762,024	3.71	6,007,280	11.70	2.84
7	261800	Granulated slag (slag sand)	1,911,033.63	10,800,434	0.02	11,242,229.00	0.03	17.00
8	262190	Slag and ash, including seaweed ash	972,702.83	22,323,460	0.03	13,519,191.00	0.03	7.19
9	293040	Methionine	28,291.00	5,625,586.50	3.26	4,006,948.00	3.47	0.71
10	320611	Pigments and preparations	839,413.19	25,247,110	1.96	4,172,097.50	3.07	20.12
11	330510	Shampoos	1,341,545.00	22,476,172	2.56	8,238,637.00	4.35	16.28
12	370790	Chemical preparations for photographs	106,470.40	8,579,340	4.02	2,488,099.50	7.59	4.28
13	380894	Disinfectants, put up in forms	156,389.41	12,244,885	1.60	1,203,647.38	3.07	12.99
14	381900	Hydraulic brake fluids and other	187,795.80	6,930,358.50	1.66	1,025,048.37	2.21	18.32
15	390120	Polyethylene having a specific grade of 0.9	8,263,483.50	176,413,200	1.40	37,975,564.00	1.42	21.76
16	390230	Propylene copolymers, in primary	29,986.67	6,115,673.5	1.25	2,481,689.75	1.47	1.21
17	390421	Poly(vinyl chloride), non-plasticized	164,958.80	4,752,596	1.91	1,318,224.00	2.25	12.51
18	390422	Poly(vinyl chloride), plasticized	734,890.63	14,387,404	1.46	7,897,172.50	1.53	9.31
19	390720	Polyethers other than polyacetals	389,641.81	29,191,670	2.27	1,944,694.38	2.30	20.04
20	392410	Tableware and kitchenware, of plastic	287,398.81	130,356,936	3.08	1,556,111.38	5.46	18.47
21	392590	Builders' ware of plastics, n.e.s.	81,844.80	14,093,826	2.81	1,213,181.75	5.00	6.75

continued on next page

Table A2.4 continued

S.N.	HS Code 6-Digit (2007)	Short Description	Export Value (India to Nepal) ($)	Global Export Value of India ($)	Unit Value of Exports of India	Global Import Value of Nepal ($)	Unit Value of Imports of Nepal	India's Share of Exports in Nepal Imports (%)
22	401290	Solid or cushion tires, tire treads	708,168.19	34,428,604	3.31	5,965,800.50	4.06	11.87
23	420222	Handbags	60,093.40	181,071,264	1.38	1,494,989.38	1.79	4.02
24	420330	Belts and bandoliers, of leather	36,140.40	80,779,864	11.57	1,045,411.63	61.89	3.46
25	490199	Printed books, brochures, leaflets	209,481.80	40,349,264	3.37	5,257,155.50	10.09	3.98
26	590699	Rubberized textile fabrics	59,761.00	8,614,496	5.26	5,389,420.50	6.19	1.11
27	681381	Friction material and articles thereof	184,601.00	41,274,836	1.83	1,133,661.00	2.45	16.28
28	710692	Silver (including silver plated with gold)	2,537.50	4,856,660	188.47	100,895,400.00	538.79	0.00
29	720827	Flat-rolled products of iron	37,893.25	52,981,732	0.62	9,491,441.00	0.62	0.40
30	720838	Flat-rolled products of iron	3,846,877.50	85,151,136	0.55	18,699,824	0.56	20.57
31	720839	Flat-rolled products of iron	14,212,406.00	228,085,280	0.57	78,599,640	0.61	18.08
32	720916	Flat-rolled products of iron	750,096.19	46,849,696	0.62	5,238.71	0.69	14.32
33	730690	Tubes, pipes and hollow profiles	517,511.19	119,228,248	1.03	6,047,865	1.06	8.56
34	730810	Bridges and bridge-sections of iron	299,277.59	5,132,518	2.18	3,083,506.75	2.70	9.71
35	761410	Stranded wire, cables, plaited band	712,348.75	111,214,256	2.61	5,909,611	2.62	12.05
36	800110	Tin, not alloyed, unwrought	122,202.80	31,236,894	17.80	1,234,307.75	21.44	9.90
37	830110	Padlocks, of base metal	46,244.00	1,680,196.25	2.86	1,079,344.75	10.76	4.28
38	842123	Oil or petrol-filters for internal	131,776,60	31,581,084	2.51	2,669,281.25	4.25	4.94
39	843610	Machinery for preparing animal feed	284,833.81	2,780,058.75	273.17	2,905,682.25	3,933.21	9.80
40	844316	Flexographic printing machinery	100,272.25	4,848,475	8,265.78	1,171,842.25	17,355.57	8.56
41	844540	Textile winding (including weft-winding)	23,797.20	6,060,221.5	6021.03	1,035,442.37	11,278.79	2.30
42	847149	Other automatic data processing machines	66,701.00	3,672,532	705.21	3,864,617.75	1,387.69	1.73
43	847160	Input or output units	38,604.25	20,599,132	43.70	6,566,282.50	87.03	0.59
44	848071	Molds for rubber or plastics	409,156.75	45,628,984	24.98	2,144,744.75	40.31	19.08
45	848390	Toothed wheels, chain sprockets	395,220.41	109,027,648	7.14	2,981,170.50	20.99	13.26

continued on next page

Table A2.4 continued

S.N.	HS Code 6-Digit (2007)	Short Description	Export Value (India to Nepal) ($)	Global Export Value of India ($)	Unit Value of Exports of India	Global Import Value of Nepal ($)	Unit Value of Imports of Nepal	India's Share of Exports in Nepal Imports (%)
46	851660	Electric ovens other than microwave	157,905.20	5,504,510	27.35	3,318,078.50	36.68	4.76
47	851679	Electro-thermic appliances n.e.s.	82,537.75	6,080,380.5	1.78	1,346,082.00	3.02	6.13
48	851712	Telephones for cellular networks	412,349.00	1,826,057,472	37.48	94,310,864.00	53.75	0.44
49	852351	Semi-conductor media, solid-state	1,566.50	38,309,884	4.58	3,747,988.00	5.37	0.04
50	852851	Other monitors	25,907.00	5,199,950.50	94.15	3,403,520.50	122.20	0.76
51	852872	Other color reception apparatus	1,342,235.63	35,071,288	134.03	9,777,011.00	141.15	13.73
52	853529	Automatic circuit breakers	103,686.00	29,811,662	8.87	1,081,124.63	23.25	9.59
53	853630	Apparatus for protecting electrical	131,660.60	7,030,249	18.81	1,065,244.63	60.57	12.36
54	853929	Electric filament lamps	310,746.25	24,072,882	0.12	1,864,713.75	0.21	16.66
55	854011	Cathode-ray television picture tube	366,903.81	2,752,232	17.54	4,277,492.50	34.92	8.58
56	870323	Vehicles (excluding of 87.02 and 8703.10)	2,394,882.50	534,109,856	10,327.66	15,610,401.00	11,353.75	15.34
57	901812	Ultrasonic scanning apparatus	165,774.00	50,539,172	121.13	1,996,224.00	2,674.01	8.30
58	902190	Appliances which are worn or carried	141,436.50	15,599,102	63.57	2,088,083.00	980.63	6.77
59	902212	Computed tomography apparatus	6,493.67	1,049,760.38	9,161.88	3,703,930.75	22,386.65	0.18
60	902730	Spectrometers, spectrophotometers	55,242.50	7,847,975	628.48	1,037,561.50	757.62	5.32
61	940310	Metal furniture of a kind used	245,079.00	15,233,491	3.14	2,020,033.00	5.28	12.13
62	940320	Metal furniture	320,092.19	53,438,436	2.69	3,427,884.00	4.97	9.60
63	940360	Wooden furniture	187,893.20	387,466,688	25.34	2,567,677.50	39.98	7.32

HS = Harmonized Commodity Description and Coding System, n.e.s. = not elsewhere specified, S.N. = serial number.

Source: Asian Development Bank data analysis using trade data from World Integrated Trade Solution.

Table A2.5: Potential Export Products of India in Sri Lanka Market at Harmonized System 6-Digit Level of Product Classification
($10 Million Filter)

S.N.	HS Code 6-Digit (2007)	Short Description	Export Value (India to Sri Lanka) ($)	Global Export Value of India ($)	Unit Value of Exports of India	Global Import Value of Sri Lanka ($)	Unit Value of Imports of Sri Lanka	India's Share of Exports in Sri Lanka Imports (%)
1	40210	Milk in powder/granules or other solids	786,684.00	236,246,720	3.31	30,491,676	3.78	2.58
2	80290	Nuts, n.e.s. in 08.01 and 08.02	235,171.20	13,369,242	2.00	11,049,388	4.82	2.13
3	100190	Wheat other than durum wheat;	7,944,574.00	586,091,456	0.28	360,491,808	0.32	2.20
4	180690	Chocolate and other food preparations	1,780,260.00	61,164,120	4.97	13,427,231	8.33	13.26
5	190110	Preparations for infant use	1,454,860.38	31,313,318	3.99	10,222,166	6.77	14.23
6	210690	Food preparations, n.e.s.	3,961,757.50	147,435,424	3.04	34,048,596	7.67	11.64
7	220710	Undenatured ethyl alcohol	2,550,816.50	126,937,488	0.80	16,183,016	0.86	15.76
8	220830	Whiskies	536,779.00	107,400,264	3.56	21,853,474	12.44	2.46
9	240110	Tobacco, not stemmed or stripped	17,320.00	69,161,320	2.72	61,513,580	21.77	0.03
10	320611	Pigments and preparations	342,850.19	25,247,110	1.96	15,813,039	3.19	2.17
11	320649	Coloring matter and other preparations	1,179,359.62	32,232,676	1.50	11,109,880	2.91	10.62
12	321519	Printing ink (excluding black)	2,891,618.50	88,450,208	3.33	18,240,284	9.35	15.85
13	380991	Finishing agents, dye carriers	1,520,950.25	33,507,190	1.44	19,893,466	2.91	7.65
14	382200	Diagnostic or laboratory reagents	795,763.38	35,966,912	23.05	15,416,867	44.74	5.16
15	382490	Chemical products and preparations	2,556,456.25	170,987,808	0.83	23,479,854	1.71	10.89
16	390120	Polyethylene having a specific grade of 0.9	108,845.60	176,413,200	1.40	48,821,740	1.45	0.22
17	390210	Polypropylene, in primary forms	9,250,994.00	1,105,546,368	1.38	61,107,196	1.48	15.14
18	390319	Polystyrene other than	1,840,332.63	100,420,320	1.67	11,796,150	1.68	15.60
19	390720	Polyethers other than polyacetals	1,380,424.25	29,191,670	2.27	18,488,514	2.33	7.47
20	392020	Plates, sheets, film, foil and strip	2,391,576.25	240,714,064	2.40	23,696,594	3.27	10.09

continued on next page

Table A2.5 continued

S.N.	HS Code 6-Digit (2007)	Short Description	Export Value (India to Sri Lanka) ($)	Global Export Value of India ($)	Unit Value of Exports of India	Global Import Value of Sri Lanka ($)	Unit Value of Imports of Sri Lanka	India's Share of Exports in Sri Lanka Imports (%)
21	392690	Articles of plastics and articles	6,092,082.5	457,590,752	2.28	31,584,378	6.35	19.29
22	400110	Natural rubber latex	1,816,097.50	21,584,678	2.37	10,658,252	2.48	17.04
23	400219	Styrene-butadiene rubber (SBR)	1,249,895.63	12,355,130	2.35	39,140,276	2.53	3.19
24	481092	Paper and paperboard(excluding of 4810.13)	1,437,731.75	15,271,637	0.60	46,023,616	0.76	3.12
25	481190	Paper, paperboard, cellulose wadding	1,383,182.38	22,101,028	1.89	11,915,304	2.63	11.61
26	482110	Paper or paperboard labels of all kind	1,419,684.75	17,865,468	5.36	15,609,097	17.70	9.10
27	490199	Printed books, brochures, leaflets	331,301.81	40,349,264	3.37	10,970,551	7.18	3.02
28	490700	Unused postage, revenue	23,250.00	30,592,360	57.26	13,100,423	1,506.95	0.18
29	520511	Cotton yarn, single, excluding sewing	2,122,170.25	180,011,184	3.05	11,397,216	5.30	18.62
30	520521	Cotton yarn, single, excluding sewing threads	1,541,629.00	111,500,904	3.58	44,349,240	4.83	3.48
31	550410	Artificial staple fibers	2,964,159.00	203,049,792	2.13	23,613,754	2.61	12.55
32	550922	Yarn other than sewing thread,	458,977.59	50,801,072	2.85	17,426,604	4.27	2.63
33	580620	Narrow woven fabrics (excluding of 5806)	3,570,613.00	20,269,482	6.93	52,421,480	20.02	6.81
34	710239	Diamonds, non-industrial	2,263,084.00	25,962,780,672	542.98	90,710,824	1,058.04	2.49
35	710391	Rubies, sapphires, and emeralds	2,278.00	121,542,152	8.31	10,839,781	49.04	0.02
36	721061	Flat-rolled products of iron	3,327,346.50	131,862,656	0.89	24,507,416	1.01	13.58
37	730890	Structures (excluding prefabricated)	3,848,685.75	376,832,064	1.77	38,867,352	2.23	9.90
38	731029	Tanks, casks, drums, cans	147,967.20	27,965,660	3.13	19,257,976	3.85	0.77
39	731815	Screws and bolts (excluding of 7318.11-73	1,144,081.75	278,744,256	1.85	12,933,601	2.69	8.85
40	732690	Articles of iron or steel, n.e.s.	2,730,415.00	497,500,800	3.27	24,224,352	3.27	11.27

continued on next page

Table A2.5 continued

S.N.	HS Code 6-Digit (2007)	Short Description	Export Value (India to Sri Lanka) ($)	Global Export Value of India ($)	Unit Value of Exports of India	Global Import Value of Sri Lanka ($)	Unit Value of Imports of Sri Lanka	India's Share of Exports in Sri Lanka Imports (%)
41	760110	Aluminum, not alloyed, unwrought	17,334.00	1,068,341,376	2.09	14,452,804	2.30	0.12
42	760120	Aluminum alloys, unwrought	204,748.80	162,151,328	2.37	15,572,223	2.42	1.31
43	780110	Unwrought lead, refined	1,679,602.75	111,693,984	2.24	12,873,589	2.26	13.05
44	840490	Parts of the auxiliary plant of 840	35,022.00	29,629,452	6.43	10,665,260	11.21	0.33
45	840690	Parts of the steam turbines and others	687,801.50	44,925,924	20.19	13,915,332	167.96	4.94
46	840999	Parts suitable for use	1,532,112.75	571,931,264	8.53	20,496,992	21.22	7.47
47	842199	Parts of the filtering or purifying	1,567,869.63	107,798,464	8.65	12,313,978	12.99	12.73
48	842619	Overhead traveling cranes	124,863.50	30,794,434	21,288.66	14,708,868	49,653.19	0.85
49	843149	Parts suitable for use	979,375.19	273,704,384	4.57	14,843,540	5.16	6.60
50	843880	Machinery n.e.s. in Chapter 84, for the	1,814,709.75	24,799,240	1,336.78	14,833,395	2,069.06	12.23
51	847130	Portable automatic data	125,601.80	43,145,560	363.58	56,818,220	366.01	0.22
52	847150	Processing units	63,399.50	76,407,896	546.76	16,263,126	823.72	0.39
53	847432	Machines for mixing mineral	267,567.00	11,859,130	30,450.81	10,918,986	36,054.37	2.45
54	848180	Taps, cocks, valves, and similar	1,727,877.63	674,439,680	12.85	33,376,034	13.50	5.18
55	850213	Electric generating sets with C-I	499,616.19	48,119,768	27,316.27	14,024,467	39,435.20	3.56
56	851712	Telephones for cellular networks	2,226,188.75	1,826,057,472	37.48	128,778,240	57.48	1.73
57	852340	Optical media for recording	481,693.50	160,758,064	0.23	14,719,224	0.27	3.27
58	853400	Printed circuits	25,599.25	138,529,952	55.79	14,708,125	70.78	0.17
59	853620	Automatic circuit breakers	1,243,565.63	85,156,336	11.34	10,039,103	18.70	12.39
60	853931	Electric discharge lamps	569,685.81	19,863,334	0.77	20,135,782	1.15	2.83
61	870322	Vehicles (excluding of 87.02 and 8703.10)	5,124,166.50	2,901,425,408	6,375.43	279,818,144	14,548.32	1.83
62	870323	Vehicles (excluding of 87.02 and 8703.10)	1,657,771.38	534,109,856	10,327.66	135,566,752	22,966.13	1.22
63	870332	Vehicles principally designed	745,039.81	57,283,672	12,714.54	62,225,052	24,453.23	1.20
64	870333	Vehicles principally designed	219,946.00	14,577,695	7,289.56	42,823,624	35,843.33	0.51

continued on next page

Table A2.5 continued

S.N.	HS Code 6-Digit (2007)	Short Description	Export Value (India to Sri Lanka) ($)	Global Export Value of India ($)	Unit Value of Exports of India	Global Import Value of Sri Lanka ($)	Unit Value of Imports of Sri Lanka	India's Share of Exports in Sri Lanka Imports (%)
65	870870	Road wheels and parts and accessories	272,487.41	89,974,632	2.80	12,797,231	3.08	2.13
66	901890	Instruments and appliances	2,524,302.25	175,495,184	0.85	39,316,824	1.39	6.42

HS = Harmonized Commodity Description and Coding System, n.e.s. = not elsewhere specified, S.N. = serial number.

Source: Asian Development Bank data analysis using trade data from World Integrated Trade Solution.

Appendix 3
Availability of Food Labs and Physical Accessibility in India, 2015–2016

States and Union Territory	No. of Labs	Food Labs '000 Square Kilometers (Area)	Food Labs '000 metric tons (Production)
Andaman and Nicobar Islands	0	0.000	0.0000
Andhra Pradesh	1	0.000	0.0001
Assam	0	0.000	0.0000
Bihar	0	0.000	0.0000
Chhattisgarh	0	0.000	0.0000
Dadra and Nagar Haveli	0	0.000	0.0000
Daman and Diu	1	0.901	0.0090
Delhi	15	1.011	0.1301
Goa	1	0.027	0.0002
Gujarat	7	0.004	0.0004
Haryana	11	0.025	0.0007
Himachal Pradesh	1	0.002	0.0006
Jharkhand	0	0.000	0.0000
Karnataka	11	0.006	0.0009
Kerala	7	0.018	0.0126
Madhya Pradesh	4	0.001	0.0001
Maharashtra	20	0.006	0.0023
Manipur	0	0.000	0.0000
Meghalaya	0	0.000	0.0000
Mizoram	0	0.000	0.0000
Nagaland	0	0.000	0.0000
Odisha	1	0.001	0.0002
Puducherry	0	0.000	0.0000
Punjab	3	0.006	0.0001
Rajasthan	5	0.001	0.0003
Sikkim	0	0.000	0.0000
Tamil Nadu	14	0.011	0.0012
Tripura	0	0.000	0.0000
Uttar Pradesh	7	0.003	0.0002
Uttarakhand	1	0.002	0.0006
West Bengal	5	0.006	0.0003
Telangana	6	0.005	0.0012
All India	121	0.004	0.0005

Sources: India State and Food Safety and Standards Authority of India.

Appendix 4
Existing Sanitary and Phytosanitary and Technical Barriers to Trade Measures by Other SASEC Countries on Identified India Potential Exports

Table A4.1: Sanitary and Phytosanitary and Technical Barriers to Trade Measures by Bangladesh on India's Potential Products

S.N.	HS Code 6-Digit (2007)	Description	Legislation or Regulation	Details of Regulatory Agency of Bangladesh	Description of NTM of Bangladesh
1	130239	Mucilages and thickeners n.e.s., modified or not, derived from vegetable products	Plant Quarantine Act 2011 (A83, A14)	National Plant Quarantine Authority	The import or export of any plants or plant products which have the potential threat to introduce any pest into plants and plant products may be prohibited, restricted. Plants or plant products, beneficial organisms or packing materials shall not be imported into Bangladesh without an import permit and certificate issued by the Authority. Any plant or plant product, beneficial organism or packing material shall be imported into Bangladesh only through a designated point of entry, and upon notification for importation, the import permit issued against the consignment and the phytosanitary certificate issued by the National Plant Protection Authority of the exporting country shall have to be submitted to the concerned plant quarantine officer for examination. The person who transports or stores any plant or plant product, beneficial organism, or packing material or is in charge of the conveyance or the store shall be bound to make the conveyance or store and its contents available for inspection and treatment, if required, in accordance with the order of a plant quarantine officer.

continued on next page

Table A4.1 continued

S.N.	HS Code 6-Digit (2007)	Description	Legislation or Regulation	Details of Regulatory Agency of Bangladesh	Description of NTM of Bangladesh
			Food Safety (Contaminants, Toxins and Harmful Residues) Regulations, 2017 (A21)	Bangladesh Food Safety Authority (BFSA)	Maximum limit of nitrates is 200 milligrams per kilogram. Maximum limit of agaric acid, hydrocyanic acid, hyperici, syafrol, acrylonitrile, and vinyl chloride monomer is 100, 5, 1, 10, 0.02, and 0.01 ppm, respectively.
			Food Safety (Labeling) Regulations, 2017 (A31)	BFSA	Label of the imported products' container would be written in Bengali. Presence of nutrition substances written on label per 100 grams or 100 milligrams of product. For imported products, irrespective of the name and address of manufacturer and importer, name and address of repackaged packaging unit, transporter is written on the label. There is no word or expression that demonstrates the better quality of imported goods.
2	252310	Cement clinkers	Ordinance 1985 (Mandatory Standard Certificate) (B8)	Bangladesh Standards and Testing Institution (BSTI)	Manufacturers or importers are licensed to use the standard mark on goods produced or imported by them in conformity to the relevant Bangladesh Standard (BDS) (BDS EN 197-1:2003 standards in this product).
3	271019	Medium oils and preparations, of petroleum or bituminous minerals, n.e.s.			
4	280920	Phosphoric acid; polyphosphoric acids, whether or not chemically defined			
5	293040	Methionine	Food Safety (Labeling) Regulations, 2017 (A31, A3, A42)	BFSA	Label of the imported products' container would be written in Bengali. Presence of nutrition substances written on label per 100 grams or 100 milligrams of product. For imported products, irrespective of the name and address of manufacturer and importer, name and address of repackaged packaging unit, transporter is written on the label. There is no word or expression that demonstrates the better quality of imported goods.

continued on next page

Table A4.1 continued

S.N.	HS Code 6-Digit (2007)	Description	Legislation or Regulation	Details of Regulatory Agency of Bangladesh	Description of NTM of Bangladesh
			Ordinance 1985 (Mandatory Standard Certificate) (B8)	Bangladesh Standards and Testing Institution (BSTI)	Manufacturers or importers are licensed to use the standard mark on goods produced / imported by them in conformity to the relevant Bangladesh Standard
6	300490	Medicaments n.e.s., in dosage	National Drug Policy, 2005 (A14, A15, A21)	Director General of Drug Administration (DGDA)	All the medicines cannot be permitted to import unless registered with the license authority. As a general principle, registration for manufacture, import, and sale of combination drugs other than those of Unani, Ayurvedic, and other herbal preparations, vitamins and nutritional preparations should not be allowed in the country. However, combinations like vitamins, nutritional preparations, and other drugs which are therapeutically useful and are registered in the developed countries could be considered for registration. Bioavailability and bioequivalence data will be considered as important criteria for the registration of any imported medicine. Liquid dosage forms of Unani, Ayurvedic, and other herbal drugs, that contain up to 50% (v/v) of 96% ethanol may be allowed to be registered, if use of such high proportion of ethanol is absolutely needed for their better efficacy and keeping quality. However, in exceptional cases, use of ethanol up to a maximum volume of 10% (v/v) may be allowed, if recommended by the DCC.
			Labeling and Packaging of Pharmaceutical (A3)		Applicants should include the proposed or approved texts of the package insert (PI), and the patient information leaflet (PIL). Package Insert requirements: 1. Product name, 2. Name and strength of active ingredient(s), 3. Product description, 4. Pharmacokinetics

continued on next page

Table A4.1 continued

S.N.	HS Code 6-Digit (2007)	Description	Legislation or Regulation	Details of Regulatory Agency of Bangladesh	Description of NTM of Bangladesh
					or pharmacodynamics, 5. Indication(s), 6. Recommended dose, 7. Mode of administration, 8. Contraindication(s), 9. Warnings and precautions, 10. Interactions with other medications, 11. Pregnancy and lactation, 12. Undesirable effects, 13. Overdose and treatment, 14. Storage conditions, 15. Dosage forms and packaging available, 16. Name and address of manufacturer/ marketing authorization holder, 17. Date of revision of PI. Patient information leaflet requirements: 1. Name of product, 2. Description of product, 3. What is the medicine?, 4. Strength of the medicine, 5. What is the medicine used for?, 6. How much and how often should you use this medicine?, 7. When should you not take this medicine?, 8. Undesirable effects?, 9. What other medicine(s) or food(s) should be avoided when taking this. medicine?
7	320411	Disperse dyes and preparations based thereon	Ordinance 1985 (Mandatory Standard Certificate) (B8)	Bangladesh Standards and Testing Institution (BSTI)	Manufacturers or importers are licensed to use the standard mark on goods produced or imported by them in conformity to the relevant Bangladesh Standard (BDS ISO 105-E 11:2004 for this product).
8	320611	C.I. Pigment yellow 157, containing 80% or more by weight of titanium	Product Labeling Policy – 2006 (B31)	Bangladesh Standards and Testing Institution (BSTI)	Manufacturer's name, full address, and country of origin have been incorporated in the product labeling for all products. In addition, ingredients, composition, batch no., code no., expiry date/ or use best before on, and other information which are necessary have been incorporated in chemical, agriculture, and food products. The weights and measures will be expressed in System International Units.

continued on next page

Table A4.1 continued

S.N.	HS Code 6-Digit (2007)	Description	Legislation or Regulation	Details of Regulatory Agency of Bangladesh	Description of NTM of Bangladesh
9	320710	Prepared pigments, prepared opacifiers, prepared colors, and similar preparations			
10	320890	Paints and varnishes based, including enamels and lacquers, on synthetic polymers or chemically modified natural polymers, dispersed or dissolved in a non-aqueous medium, and solutions of products of subheadings 3901 to 3913 in volatile organic solvents, containing > 50% solvent by weight (excluding those based on polyesters and acrylic or vinyl polymers and solutions of collodion)			
11	340213	Organic surface-active agents, whether or not put up for retail sale: non-ionic			
12	350691	Adhesives based on polymers of headings 3901 to 3913 or on rubber			
13	3822000	Diagnostic or laboratory reagents on a backing, prepared diagnostic or laboratory reagents whether or not on a backing, other than those of heading 3002 or 3006; certified reference materials			
14	382311	Stearic acid, industrial			
15	390390	Polymers of styrene, n.e.s., in primary forms			
16	390690	Acrylic polymers, in primary forms (excluding polymethyl methacrylate)			
17	391910	Acetate tapes, self-adhesive, In rolls of a width not exceeding 20 centimeters			
18	392321	Sacks and bags (including cones): Of polymers of ethylene			
19	392329	Sacks and bags (including cones): Of poly (vinyl chloride) and other			
20	392690	Articles of plastics or of other materials of Nos. 39.01 To 39.14, n.e.s.			

continued on next page

Table A4.1 continued

S.N.	HS Code 6-Digit (2007)	Description	Legislation or Regulation	Details of Regulatory Agency of Bangladesh	Description of NTM of Bangladesh
21	400219	Acrylonitrile butadiene rubber			
22	401699	Articles of vulcanized rubber, n.e.s., other than hard rubber			
23	410799	Leather further prepared after tanning or crusting, including parchment-dressed leather, of bovine (including buffalo) or equine animals, without hair on, whether or not split, other than leather of heading 41.14: Other, including sides			
24	480256	Uncoated paper and paperboard, of a kind used for writing, printing or other graphic purposes, and nonperforated punch cards and punch-tape paper, in square or rectangular sheets with one side <= 435 millimeters and the other side <= 297 millimeters in the unfolded state, not containing fibers obtained by a mechanical or chemi-mechanical process or of which <= 10% by weight of the total fiber content consists of such fibers, and weighing 40 grams to 150 grams per meter, n.e.s.			
25	480257	Uncoated paper and paperboard, of a kind used for writing, printing or other graphic purposes, and nonperforated punch cards and punch-tape paper, in rolls or rectangular (including square) sheets, of any size, other than paper of heading 48.01 or 48.03; hand-made paper and paperboard: Other paper and paperboard, not containing fibers obtained by a mechanical or chemi-mechanical process or of which not more than 10 % by weight of the total fiber content consists of such fibers: Other, weighing 40 g/m² or more but not more than 150 g/m² drawing paper			

continued on next page

Table A4.1 continued

S.N.	HS Code 6-Digit (2007)	Description	Legislation or Regulation	Details of Regulatory Agency of Bangladesh	Description of NTM of Bangladesh
27	481159	Paper, paperboard, cellulose wadding and webs of cellulose fibers, coated, impregnated, covered, surface-colored, surface-decorated or printed, in rolls or rectangular (including square) sheets, of any size, other than goods of the kind described in heading 48.03, 48.09, or 48.10: paper and paperboard coated, impregnated or covered with plastics (excluding adhesives): Others			
28	482390	Braille paper, cellulose in sole board or sheet; packing and wrapping paper; paper for cigarette, filter tips; paper cone for loud speaker; patterns made of papers for leather footwear, leather garments and goods; patterns made of paper for articles of apparel and clothing accessories, products consisting of sheets of paper or paperboard, impregnated, coated or covered with plastics (including thermoset resins or mixtures thereof or chemical formulations, containing melamine phenol, or urea formaldehyde with or without curing agents or catalysts), compressed together in one or more operations; decorative laminates			
29	510710	Yarn of combed wool, not put up for retail sale: containing 85% or more by weight of wool: worsted knitted yarn			
30	520532	Cotton yarn (other than sewing thread), containing 85% or more by weight of cotton, not put up for retail sale: multiple (folded) or cabled yarn, of uncombed fibers: measuring per single yarn less than 714.29 decitex but not less than 232.56 decitex (exceeding 14 metric number but not exceeding 43 metric number per single yarn): bleached			

continued on next page

Table A4.1 continued

S.N.	HS Code 6-Digit (2007)	Description	Legislation or Regulation	Details of Regulatory Agency of Bangladesh	Description of NTM of Bangladesh
31	520911	Woven fabrics of cotton, containing 85% or more by weight of cotton, weighing more than 200 g/m2: unbleached: plain weave: handloom: saree			
32	540110	Sewing thread of manmade filaments, whether or not put up for retail sale: of synthetic filaments			
33	540247	Synthetic filament yarn (other than sewing thread), not put up for retail sale, including synthetic monofilament of less than 67 decitex: other yarn, single, untwisted or with a twist not exceeding 50 turns per meter: other, of polyesters			
34	550130	Synthetic filament tow: acrylic or modacrylic			
35	550921	Yarn (other than sewing thread) of synthetic staple fibers, not put up for retail sale: containing 85% or more by weight of polyester staple fiber: single yarn			
36	550922	Yarn (other than sewing thread) of synthetic staple fibers, not put up for retail sale: containing 85% or more by weight of polyester staple fiber: multiple (folded) or cabled yarn			
37	550969	Yarn (other than sewing thread) of synthetic staple fibers, not put up for retail sale: other yarn, of acrylic or modacrylic staple fibers: other			
38	551012	Yarn (other than sewing thread) of artificial staple fibers, not put up for retail sale: containing 85% or more by weight of artificial staple fibers: multiple (folded) or cabled yarn: acetate rayon spun yarn			
39	580620	Narrow woven fabrics, other than goods of heading 58.07; narrow fabrics consisting of warp without weft assembled by means of an adhesive (bolducs):			

continued on next page

Table A4.1 continued

S.N.	HS Code 6-Digit (2007)	Description	Legislation or Regulation	Details of Regulatory Agency of Bangladesh	Description of NTM of Bangladesh
		other woven fabrics, containing by weight 5% or more of elastomeric yarn or rubber thread			
40	580632	Narrow woven fabrics, other than goods of heading 58.07; narrow fabrics consisting of warp without weft assembled by means of an adhesive (bolducs): other woven fabrics: of manmade fibers			
41	600624	Other knitted or crocheted fabrics: of cotton: printed			
42	600690	Other knitted or crocheted fabrics: other			
43	621710	Other made up clothing accessories; parts of garments or of clothing accessories, other than those of heading 62.12: accessories: or articles of apparel of synthetic fibers, for articles of apparel of cotton, for articles of apparel of wool, for articles of apparel of silk, or articles of apparel of regenerated fiber, for articles of apparel of other fibers, stockings, socks, sockettes, and the like of cotton, and other			
44	640299	Other footwear with outer soles and uppers of rubber or plastics: other footwear: other			
45	711319	Articles of jewelry and parts thereof, of precious metal or of metal clad with precious metal: of precious metal whether or not plated or clad with precious metal: of other precious metal, whether or not plated or clad with precious metal: of gold, set with pearls			
46	720839	Flat-rolled products of iron or non-alloy steel, of a width of 600 millimeters or more, hot-rolled, not clad, plated or coated: other, in coils, not further worked than hot-rolled: of a thickness of less than 3 millimeters: Universal plates			
47	730300	Tubes, pipes and hollow profiles, of cast iron: soil pipe			

continued on next page

Table A4.1 continued

S.N.	HS Code 6-Digit (2007)	Description	Legislation or Regulation	Details of Regulatory Agency of Bangladesh	Description of NTM of Bangladesh
48	730890	structures (excluding prefabricated buildings of heading 94.06) and parts of structures (for example, bridges, and bridge-sections, lock-gates, towers, lattice masts, roofs, roofing frameworks, doors, and windows and their frames and thresholds for doors, shutters, balustrades, pillars, and columns), of iron or steel; plates, rods, angles, shapes, sections, tubes, and the like, prepared for use in structures, of iron or steel: other: drop rods			
49	830210	Hinges of base metal			
50	830242	Base metal mountings, fittings and similar articles suitable for furniture, doors, staircases, windows, blinds, coachwork, saddlery, trunks, chests, caskets, or the like; base metal hat racks, hat pegs, brackets, and similar fixtures; castors with mountings of base metal; automatic door closers of base metal: other mountings, fittings, and similar articles: other, suitable for furniture			
51	840690	Parts of steam and vapor turbines			
52	840890	Engines, diesel, n.e.s.			
53	840991	Parts suitable for use solely or principally with spark-ignition internal combustion piston engines, n.e.s.			
54	841480	Air or gas compressors, hoods			
55	841590	Airconditioning machines, comprising a motor-driven fan and elements for changing the temperature and humidity, including those machines in which the humidity cannot be separately regulated: parts			
56	841869	Refrigerators, freezers, and other refrigerating or freezing equipment, electric or other; heat pumps other than airconditioning			

continued on next page

Table A4.1 continued

S.N.	HS Code 6-Digit (2007)	Description	Legislation or Regulation	Details of Regulatory Agency of Bangladesh	Description of NTM of Bangladesh
		machines of heading 84.15: other refrigerating or freezing equipment; heat pumps: other: water cooler			
57	841950	Heat exchanger unit of aluminum			
58	842139	Centrifuges, including centrifugal dryers; filtering or purifying machinery and apparatus, for liquids or gases: filtering or purifying machinery and apparatus for gases: other: air purifiers or cleaners			
59	842290	Dish washing machines; machinery for cleaning or drying bottles or other containers; machinery for filling, closing, sealing, or labeling bottles, cans, boxes, bags, or other containers; machinery for capsuling bottles, jars, tubes, and similar containers; other packing or wrapping machinery (including heat-shrink wrapping machinery); machinery for aerating beverages: parts: of dish washing machines of household type			
60	842619	Overhead traveling cranes, other than those on fixed support			
61	843149	Parts suitable for use solely or principally with the machinery of headings 84.25 to 84.30: of machinery of heading 84.26, 84.29, or 84.30: other: of ships derricks and cranes			
62	843710	Machine for cleaning, sorting, or grading of seeds and grains and others			
63	843880	Machinery, not specified or included elsewhere in this Chapter, for the industrial preparation or manufacture of food or drink, other than machinery for the extraction or preparation of animal or fixed vegetable fats or oils: other: machinery: auxiliary equipment for extrusion cooking			

continued on next page

Table A4.1 continued

S.N.	HS Code 6-Digit (2007)	Description	Legislation or Regulation	Details of Regulatory Agency of Bangladesh	Description of NTM of Bangladesh
		u 12.5% plant, for production of soya milk or other soya products (other than soya oil), diffusing machines (diffusers), tea leaf rolling or cutting machine, and others			
64	844839	Auxiliary machinery for machines of heading 8444, 8445, 8446, or 8447: combs for cotton textile machinery, gills for gill boxes, others			
65	844849	Auxiliary machinery for use with machines of headings 84.44, 84.45, 84.46, or 84.47 (for example, dobbies, jacquards, automatic stop motions, shuttle changing mechanisms); parts and accessories suitable for use solely or principally with the machines of this heading or of headings 84.44, 84.45, 84.46, or 84.47 (for example, spindles and spindle flyers, card clothing, combs, extruding nipples, shuttles, healds and heald-frames, hosiery needles): parts and accessories of weaving machines (looms) or of their auxiliary machinery: other: parts of cotton weaving machinery, jute weaving machinery, silk and manmade fibers weaving machinery, wool weaving machinery, other textile weaving machinery, others			
66	845140	Washing, bleaching, or dyeing machines			
67	847130	Portable digital automatic data processing machines,			
68	847150	Processing units other than those of under 12.5% subheadings 8471 41 or 8471 49, whether or not containing in the same housing one or two of the following types of unit: storage units, input units, output units			
69	847170	Storage units			

continued on next page

Table A4.1 continued

S.N.	HS Code 6-Digit (2007)	Description	Legislation or Regulation	Details of Regulatory Agency of Bangladesh	Description of NTM of Bangladesh
70	847480	Other machinery: category: machinery for sorting, screening, separating, washing, crushing, grinding, mixing or kneading earth, stone, ores or other mineral substances, in solid (including powder or paste) form; machinery for agglomerating, shaping, or mother machinery: category: machinery for sorting, screening, separating, washing, crushing, grinding, mixing or kneading earth, stone, ores or other mineral substances, in solid (including powder or paste) form; machinery for agglomerating, shaping			
71	847710	Injection-molding machines			
72	847780	Machinery for working rubber or plastics or for the manufacture of products from these materials, n.e.s.			
73	847982	Mixing, kneading, crushing, grinding, screening, sifting, homogenizing, emulsifying, or stirring machines			
74	847989	Soap cutting or molding machinery, air humidifiers, or dehumidifiers (other than those falling under heading 8415 or 8424), mechanical sifting machines, ultrasonic transducers, car washing machines, and related appliances, coke oven plants, machinery for the manufacture of chemical and pharmaceuticals goods			
75	847990	Parts: of machines for public works, building or the like, of machines for the extraction of animal or fruit and vegetable fats or oil, of machines and mechanical appliances for treating wood, of machinery used for manufacture of chemicals and pharmaceuticals, other			

continued on next page

Table A4.1 continued

S.N.	HS Code 6-Digit (2007)	Description	Legislation or Regulation	Details of Regulatory Agency of Bangladesh	Description of NTM of Bangladesh
76	850164	Electric motors and generators (excluding generating sets): AC generators (alternators): of an output exceeding 750 kVA: of an output exceeding 2,000 kVA but not exceeding 5,000 kVA, of an output exceeding 5,000 kVA, but not exceeding 15,000 kVA, of an output exceeding 15,000 kVA, but not exceeding 37,500 kVA, of an output exceeding 37,500 kVA, but not exceeding 75,000 kVA, of an output exceeding 75,000 kVA, but not u 12.5% exceeding 1,37,500 kVA, of an output exceeding 1,37,500 kVA, but not u 12.5% exceeding 3,12,500 kVA, of an output exceeding 3,12,500 kVA			
77	850211	Generating sets with compression-ignition internal combustion piston engines (diesel or semi-diesel engines): of an output not exceeding 75 kVA			
78	850213	Generating sets with compression-ignition internal combustion piston engines (diesel or semidiesel engines): of an output exceeding 375 kVA			
79	850220	Generating sets with spark-ignition internal combustion piston engines: electric portable generators of an output u 12.5% not exceeding 3.5 kVA, other			
80	850239	Other generating sets: powered by steam engine, powered by water turbine, other			
81	850300	Parts suitable for use solely or principally with the machines of headings 8501 or 8502			
82	850490	Electrical transformers, static converters (for example, rectifiers) and inductors: parts: other			

continued on next page

Table A4.1 continued

S.N.	HS Code 6-Digit (2007)	Description	Legislation or Regulation	Details of Regulatory Agency of Bangladesh	Description of NTM of Bangladesh
83	853190	Electric sound or visual signaling apparatus (for example, bells, sirens, indicator panels, burglar or fire alarms), other than those of headings 85.12 or 85.30: parts			
84	853590	Electrical apparatus for switching or protecting electrical circuits, or for making connections to or in electrical circuits (for example, switches, fuses, lightning arresters, voltage limiters, surge suppressors, plugs, and other connectors, junction boxes), for a voltage exceeding 1,000 volts: other: control gear and starters for DC motors, other control and switchgears, junction boxes, motor starters for AC motors, control gear and starters for DC motors, and other			
85	853620	Automatic circuit breakers: air circuit breakers, molded case circuit breakers, miniature circuit breakers, earth leak circuit breakers, and other			
86	853650	Electrical apparatus for switching or protecting electrical circuits, or for making connections to or in electrical circuits (for example, switches, relays, fuses, surge suppressors, plugs, sockets, lamp-holders, and other connectors, junction boxes), for a voltage not exceeding 1,000 volts; connectors for optical fibers, optical fiber bundles, or cables: other switches: other switches of plastic, control and switch gears, and other			
87	853710	Boards, panels, consoles, desks, cabinets, and other bases, equipped with two or more apparatus of headings 85.35 or 85.36, for electric control or the distribution of electricity, including those incorporating instruments or apparatus of Chapter 90, and numerical			

continued on next page

Table A4.1 continued

S.N.	HS Code 6-Digit (2007)	Description	Legislation or Regulation	Details of Regulatory Agency of Bangladesh	Description of NTM of Bangladesh
		control apparatus, other than switching apparatus of heading 85.17: for a voltage not exceeding 1,000 volts			
88	853931	Discharge lamps, other than ultraviolet lamps: fluorescent, hot cathode: compact fluorescent lamps and other			
89	854460	Insulated (including enameled or anodized) wire, cable (including coaxial cable), and other insulated electric conductors, whether or not fitted with connectors; optical fiber cables, made up of individually sheathed fibers, whether or not assembled with electric conductors or fitted with connectors: other electric conductors, for a voltage exceeding 1,000 volts			
90	870210	Motor vehicles for the transport of 10 or more persons, including the driver: with only compression-ignition internal combustion piston engine (diesel or semidiesel): vehicles for transport of not more than 13 persons, including the driver	The Motor Vehicles Ordinance 1983 (B82)	Bangladesh Road Transport Authority (BRTA)	Every imported motor vehicle should have to comply with the requirements of Chapter VI (this chapter has given the specification of construction, equipment, and maintenance requirements that should maintain and also has the area to make rule) and the further regulations made thereunder.
91	870322	Motor cars and other motor vehicles principally designed for the transport of persons (other than those of heading 87.02), including station wagons and racing cars: Other vehicles, with only spark-ignition internal combustion reciprocating piston engine: of a cylinder capacity exceeding 1,000 cc but not exceeding 1,500 cc	Product Labeling Policy – 2006 (B31)	Bangladesh Standards and Testing Institution (BSTI)	Manufacturer's name, full address, and country of origin has been incorporated in the product labeling for all products. In addition, ingredients, composition, batch no., code no., expiry date or use best before on and other information which are necessary has been incorporated in chemical, agriculture, and food products. The weights and measures will be expressed in System International Units.
92	870323	Motor cars and other motor vehicles principally designed for the transport of persons (other than those of heading 87.02), including station wagons and racing cars: other vehicles, with only spark-ignition internal combustion reciprocating piston engine: of a cylinder capacity			

continued on next page

Table A4.1 continued

S.N.	HS Code 6-Digit (2007)	Description	Legislation or Regulation	Details of Regulatory Agency of Bangladesh	Description of NTM of Bangladesh
		exceeding 1,500 cc, but not exceeding 3,000 cc			
93	870333	Motor cars and other motor vehicles principally designed for the transport of persons (other than those of heading 87.02), including station wagons and racing cars: other vehicles, with only spark-ignition internal combustion reciprocating piston engine: wagons and racing cars: Other vehicles, with only spark-ignition internal combustion reciprocating piston engine: of a cylinder capacity exceeding 2,500 cc			
94	880330	Parts of goods of headings 88.01 or 88.02: other parts of airplanes or helicopters	Product Labeling Policy – 2006 (B31)	Bangladesh Standards and Testing Institution (BSTI)	Manufacturer's name, full address and country of origin has been incorporated in the product labeling for all products. In addition, ingredients, composition, batch no., code no., expiry date or use best before on and other information which are necessary has been incorporated in chemical, agriculture, and food products. The weights and measures will be expressed in System International Units.
95	940320	Other furniture and parts thereof: other metal furniture: other			
96	940389	Other furniture and parts thereof: furniture of other materials, including cane, osier, bamboo, or similar materials: other			
97	901839	Catheters (for urine, stool), cardiac catheters, cannulae, and other	(B82)	Bangladesh Standards and Testing Institution (BSTI)	ISO/TC 84 standard used to standardization of the performance
98	901890	Instruments and appliances used in medical, surgical, dental, or veterinary sciences, including scintigraphic apparatus, other electromedical apparatus, and sight-testing instruments: other instruments and appliances: diagnostic instruments and apparatus	Product Labeling Policy – 2006 (B31)		Manufacturer's name, full address, and country of origin has been incorporated in the product labeling for all products. In addition, Ingredients, composition, batch no., code no., expiry date or use best before on and other information which are necessary has been incorporated in chemical, agriculture, and food products. The weights and measures will be expressed in System International Units.

continued on next page

Table A4.1 continued

S.N.	HS Code 6-Digit (2007)	Description	Legislation or Regulation	Details of Regulatory Agency of Bangladesh	Description of NTM of Bangladesh
99	902214	Apparatus based on the use of x-rays, whether or not for medical, surgical, dental, or veterinary uses, including radiography or radiotherapy apparatus: other, for medical, surgical, or veterinary uses: X-ray generators and apparatus (non-portable), portable x-ray machine, and other			
100	902780	Instruments and apparatus for physical or chemical analysis (for example, polarimeters, refractometers, spectrometers, gas, or smoke analysis apparatus); instruments and apparatus for measuring or checking viscosity, porosity, expansion, surface tension, or the like; instruments and apparatus for measuring or checking quantities of heat, sound, or light (including exposure meters); microtomes: other instruments and apparatus: calorimeters, viscometers, Instruments, and apparatus for measuring the under 12.5% surface or interfacial tension of liquids, nuclear magnetic resonance instruments, and other			
101	903289	Automatic regulating controlling instruments and apparatus: electronic automatic regulators, and others			

HS = Harmonized Commodity Description and Coding System, n.e.s. = not elsewhere specified, NTM = nontariff measure, S.N. = serial number.

Sources: Asian Development Bank, compiled from information available on Indian Trade Portal at www.indiantradeportal.in/.

Table A4.2: Sanitary and Phytosanitary and Technical Barriers to Trade Measures by Bhutan on India's Potential Products

S.N.	HS Code 6-Digit (2007)	Description	Legislation or Regulation	Details of Regulatory Agency of Bhutan	Description of NTM of Bhutan
1	220830	Whiskies	The Food Act of Bhutan, 2005 (A3, A83)	Royal Government of Bhutan Ministry of Agriculture	All food imported into Bhutan must be certified by the recognized authority in the exporting country, and must meet the applicable standards for that particular food established in Bhutan. The containers, packaging material, labeling and ingredients of food imported into Bhutan are subject to inspection by a food inspector, and fees for such inspection may be levied as established by the Minister after consultation with the Commission. Food may only be imported into Bhutan at an officially designated border point.
2	300220	Vaccines for human medicine	Bhutan Medicines Rules And Regulation 2012 (B14, B15)	Drug Regulatory Authority	The Import Authorization shall be granted only for registered medicines and medicinal products and on products which are exempted from registration (only in certain cases given in Section 34 of this regulation). The Import Authorization shall be granted to the market authorization holder, local pharmacy licensee, government procurement agencies, and international organization or the individual authorized by the Authority. For the purpose of sale and distribution, the importer shall be a market authorization holder or local pharmacy licensee and/or government procurement agencies. The Importer under section 54 and 55 of this Regulation shall have a licensed premise where the imported drugs are stored prior to distribution. All the medicinal raw materials which are required for manufacture of the medicinal

continued on next page

Table A4.2 continued

S.N.	HS Code 6-Digit (2007)	Description	Legislation or Regulation	Details of Regulatory Agency of Bhutan	Description of NTM of Bhutan
3	382200	Diagnostic or laboratory reagents on a backing, prepared diagnostic or laboratory reagents, whether or not on a backing, and certified reference materials (excluding compound diagnostic reagents designed to be administered to the patient, blood-grouping reagents, animal blood prepared for therapeutic, prophylactic or diagnostic uses, and vaccines, toxins, cultures of microorganisms, and similar products)			products by the pharmaceutical manufacturers shall require the Import Authorization from the Authority. Import authorization for vaccines and biologicals shall be issued only if the conditions prescribed under schedule F of this Regulation are complied with.
4	392410	Tableware and kitchenware, of plastic	BTS ISO 9000: 2005, BTS ISO 9001: 2008 (B7)	Bhutan Standards Bureau (BSB)	Quality Management System
5	392640	Statuettes and other ornamental articles, of plastic			
6	401693	Gaskets, washers and other seals, of vulcanized rubber, other than hard rubber (excluding those of cellular rubber)	BTS ISO14001:2004 (B41)	Bhutan Standards Bureau (BSB)	Environmental Management System (Requirements with guidance for use)
7	491110	Trade advertising material, commercial catalogues, and the like	BTS ISO/IEC 17021:2006 (B83)		Conformity assessment (Requirements for bodies providing audit and certification of management systems)
8	610910	T-shirts, singlets, and other vests, of cotton, knitted	BTS ISO/IEC 17025:2005 (B82)		General requirements for the competence of testing and calibration laboratories
9	621490	Shawls, scarves, veils, and the like, of other textile materials, not knitted			
10	630720	Life jackets and life belts, of all types of textile materials	BTS ISO 26000:2010 (B89)		Guidance on social responsibility
11	650610	Safety headgear, whether or not lined or trimmed	BTS ISO/IEC 17011:2013 (B8)		Conformity Assessment (General requirements for accreditation bodies accrediting conformity assessment bodies)
12	691110	Tableware and kitchenware, of porcelain or china (excluding ornamental articles, pots, jars, carboys, and similar receptacles for the conveyance or packing of goods, and coffee grinders and spice mills with receptacles made of ceramics and working parts of metal)			

continued on next page

Table A4.2 continued

S.N.	HS Code 6-Digit (2007)	Description	Legislation or Regulation	Details of Regulatory Agency of Bhutan	Description of NTM of Bhutan
13	841850	Refrigerators, freezers, and other refrigerating or freezing equipment, electric or other; heat pumps other than airconditioning machines of heading 84.15: other furniture (chests, cabinets, display counters, showcases and the like) for storage and display, incorporating refrigerating or freezing equipment			
14	844332	Machines which only perform one of the functions of printing, copying, or facsimile transmission, capable of connecting to an automatic data processing machine or to a network			
15	847130	Data processing machines, automatic, portable, weighing <= 10 kilograms, consisting of at least a central processing unit, a keyboard and a display (excluding peripheral units)			
16	847170	Storage units for digital automatic data processing machines			
17	847330	Parts and accessories of automatic data processing machines and units thereof			
18	848180	Taps, cocks, valves, and similar appliances, n.e.s.			
19	850300	Parts suitable for use solely or principally with electric motors and generators, electric generating sets and rotary converters, n.e.s.			
20	851770	Parts of telephone sets, telephones for cellular networks or for other wireless networks and of other apparatus for the transmission or reception of voice, images or other data, n.e.s.			
21	852580	Television cameras, digital cameras, and video camera recorders			

continued on next page

Table A4.2 continued

S.N.	HS Code 6-Digit (2007)	Description	Legislation or Regulation	Details of Regulatory Agency of Bhutan	Description of NTM of Bhutan
22	853650	Switches for a voltage <= 1.000 volts (excluding relays and automatic circuit breakers)	Product Brand Approval Scheme 2010 (B7, B31, B41)	Bhutan Standards Bureau (BSB)	Construction-related products (imported) having health, safety, environment, and reliability concerns are screened for minimum quality specifications, and approved or rejected accordingly
23	901831	Syringes, with or without needles, used in medical, surgical, dental, or veterinary sciences	All above measures (B7, B41, B8, B82, B83, B89)		
24	901849	Instruments and appliances, used in dental sciences, n.e.s.			
25	902300	Instruments, apparatus, and models designed for demonstrational purposes			
26	902680	Instruments and apparatus for measuring or check variables of liquids or gases, n.e.s.			
27	902690	Parts of instruments and apparatus for measuring or checking variables of liquid or gases, n.e.s.			
28	902790	Microtomes; parts and access of instruments and apparatus for physical or chemical analysis, n.e.s.			
29	940540	Electric lamps and lighting fittings, n.e.s.	Product Brand Approval Scheme 2010 (B7, B31, B41)	Bhutan Standards Bureau (BSB)	Construction-related products (imported) having health, safety, environment, and reliability concerns are screened for minimum quality specifications, and approved or rejected accordingly.
30	950699	Articles and equipment for sports and outdoor games, n.e.s., and swimming and paddling pools	All above measures (B7, B41, B8, B82, B83, B89)		
31	731822	Washers, iron, or steel, n.e.s.	All above measures (A83, B7, B41, B8, B82, B83, B89) Product Brand Approval Scheme 2010 (B7, B31, B41)	Bhutan Standards Bureau (BSB)	Construction-related products (imported) having health, safety, environment, and reliability concerns are screened for minimum quality specifications, and approved or rejected accordingly.
32	732620	Articles of wire, iron, or steel, n.e.s.			
33	841319	Pumps for liquids, fitted or designed to be fitted with a measuring device (excluding pumps for dispensing fuel or lubricants, of the type used in filling stations or in garages)			

HS = Harmonized Commodity Description and Coding System, n.e.s. = not elsewhere specified, NTM = nontariff measure, S.N. = serial number.

Sources: Asian Development Bank, compiled from information available on Indian Trade Portal at www.indiantradeportal.in/, and other websites of India and Bhutan.

Table A4.3: Sanitary and Phytosanitary and Technical Barriers to Trade Measures by Nepal on India's Potential Products

S.N.	HS Code 6-Digit (2007)	Description	Legislation or Regulation	Details of Regulatory Agency of Nepal	Description of NTM of Nepal
1	293040	Methionine	Animal Quarantine Directives 2064 (A14, A31, A64)	Central Animal Quarantine Office Nepal	A14: A requirement that importer should receive authorization, permit, or approval from a relevant government agency of the destination country for SPS reasons: to obtain the authorization, importers may need to comply with other related regulations and conformity assessments. Example: An import authorization from the Ministry of Health is required.

A31: Measures defining the information directly related to food safety, which should be provided to the consumer: labeling is any written, electronic, or graphic communication on the consumer packaging or on a separate but associated label. Example: i) labels that must specify the storage conditions such as "5 degrees C maximum"; ii) potentially dangerous ingredients such as allergens, e.g., "contains honey not suitable for children under 1 year of age."

A64: Requirements on certain conditions under which food and feed, plants and animal should be stored and/or transported: Example: Certain foodstuffs should be stored in a dry place, or below certain temperature. |
| 2 | 040299 | Milk and cream, concentrated and sweetened (excluding in solid forms) | Minimum Quality Standard Determined for Food and Feed (B6) | Department of Food Technology and Quality Control | Conditions to be satisfied to identify a product with a certain denomination (including biological or organic labels): Example: For a product to be identified as "chocolate," it must contain a minimum of 30% cocoa. |

continued on next page

Table A4.3 continued

S.N.	HS Code 6-Digit (2007)	Description	Legislation or Regulation	Details of Regulatory Agency of Nepal	Description of NTM of Nepal
3	180610	Cocoa powder, sweetened	Collection of Environmental Standard and Related Information (B14)	Ministry of Environment, Government of Nepal	Requirement that the importer should receive authorization, permit, or approval from a relevant government agency of the destination country, for reasons such as national security reasons, environment protection and others. Example: Imports must be authorized for drugs, waste, and scrap, firearms, and others.
4	210390	Sauces and preparations, n.e.s., and mixed condiments and mixed seasonings			
5	220830	Whiskies			
6	261800	Granulated slag (slag sand) from the manufacture of iron or steel			
7	262190	Slag and ash, including seaweed ash kelp" (excluding slag, including granulated, from the manufacture of iron or steel, ashes, and residues containing arsenic, metals, or metal compounds and those from the incineration of municipal waste)"	Foreign Exchange Regulation Circular, E. Pra. Circular no. 569 (B8)	Nepal Rastra Bank	Requirement for verification that a given TBT requirement has been met: it could be achieved by one or combined forms of inspection and approval procedure, including procedures for sampling, testing and inspection, evaluation, verification, and assurance of conformity, accreditation, and approval, and others
8	330510	Shampoos			
9	370790	Preparation of chemicals for photographic uses, including unmixed products put up in measured portions or put up for retail sale in a form ready for use (excluding varnishes, glues, adhesives, and similar preparations, sensitizing emulsions and salts and compounds of precious metals, and others of headings 2843 to 2846)			
10	380894	Disinfectants			
11	381900	Hydraulic brake and transmission fluids not counting or counting <70% of petroleum oils			
12	390120	Hydraulic brake and transmission fluids not counting or counting <70% of petroleum oils			
13	390230	Propylene copolymers, in primary forms			
14	390421	Polyvinyl chloride, n.e.s., not plasticized			
15	390422	Polyvinyl chloride, n.e.s., plasticized			
16	390720	Polyethers, in primary forms (excluding polyacetals)			

continued on next page

Table A4.3 continued

S.N.	HS Code 6-Digit (2007)	Description	Legislation or Regulation	Details of Regulatory Agency of Nepal	Description of NTM of Nepal
17	392410	Tableware and kitchenware, of plastics			
18	392590	Building elements for the manufacture of floors, walls, partition walls, ceilings, roofs, and others, of plastics; gutters and accessories of plastics; railings, fences, and similar barriers, of plastics; large shelves, for assembly and permanent installation in shops, workshops, and others, of plastics; architectural ornaments, e.g., friezes, of plastics; fittings and similar products for permanent mounting on buildings, of plastics			
19	401290	Solid or cushion tires, interchangeable tire treads and tire flaps, of rubber			
20	420222	Handbags, whether or not with shoulder straps, including those without handles, with outer surface of plastic sheeting or textile materials			
21	420330	Belts and bandoliers, of leather or composition leather			
22	490199	Printed books, brochures, and similar printed matter (excluding those in single sheets; dictionaries, encyclopaedias, periodicals, and publications which are essentially devoted to advertising)			
23	590699	Rubberized textile fabrics (excluding knitted or crocheted textile fabrics, adhesive tape of a width of <= 20 centimeters, and tire cord fabric of high tenacity yarn of nylon or other polyamides, polyesters, or viscose rayon)			

continued on next page

Table A4.3 continued

S.N.	HS Code 6-Digit (2007)	Description	Legislation or Regulation	Details of Regulatory Agency of Nepal	Description of NTM of Nepal
24	681381	Brake linings and pads with a basis of asbestos, of other mineral substances or of cellulose, whether or not combined with textile or other materials, not containing asbestos			
25	710692	Silver, including silver plated with gold or platinum, semi-manufactured			
26	720827	Flat-rolled products of iron or non-alloy steel, of a width of >= 600 millimeters, in coils, simply hot-rolled, not clad, plated, or coated, of a thickness of < 3 millimeters, pickled, without patterns in relief			
27	720838	Flat-rolled products of iron or non-alloy steel, of a width of >= 600 millimeters, in coils, simply hot-rolled, not clad, plated, or coated, of a thickness of >= 3 millimeters but < 4,75 millimeters, not pickled, without patterns in relief			
28	720839	Flat-rolled products of iron or non-alloy steel, of a width of >= 600 millimeters, in coils, simply hot-rolled, not clad, plated, or coated, of a thickness of < 3 millimeters, not pickled, without patterns in relief			
29	720916	Flat-rolled products of iron or non-alloy steel, of a width of >= 600 millimeters, in coils, simply cold-rolled cold-reduced, not clad, plated, or coated, of a thickness of > 1 millimeters but < 3 millimeters"			
30	730690	Tubes, pipe and hollow profiles, iron, or steel, welded, n.e.s.			
31	730810	Bridges and bridge-sections, of iron or steel			
32	761410	Stranded wire, cables, plaited bands, and others, aluminum, steel core, not electric insulated			

continued on next page

Table A4.3 continued

S.N.	HS Code 6-Digit (2007)	Description	Legislation or Regulation	Details of Regulatory Agency of Nepal	Description of NTM of Nepal
33	800110	Unwrought tin, not alloyed			
34	830110	Padlocks of base metal			
35	901812	Ultrasonic scanning apparatus			
36	902190	Orthopaedic and other appliances, worn, carried or implanted in the body, n.e.s.			
37	902212	Computer tomography apparatus			
38	902730	Spectrometers, spectrophotometers, and spectrographs using optical radiations			
39	940310	Office furniture, metal, n.e.s.			
40	940320	Metal furniture (excluding for offices, seats, and medical, surgical, dental, or veterinary furniture)			
41	940360	Wooden furniture (excluding for offices, kitchens, and bedrooms, and seats)			
42	320611	Pigments and preparations based on titanium dioxide of a kind used to dye fabrics or produce colorant preparations, containing >= 80% by weight of titanium dioxide calculated on the dry weight (excluding preparations of headings 3207, 3208, 3209, 3210, 3212, 3213, and 3215)	Commerce Manual 2065 (B83)	Department of Commerce and Trade and Export Promotion Center	Certification of conformity with a given regulation: required by the importing country, but may be issued in the exporting or the importing country Example: Certificate of conformity for electric products is required.
43	851660	Ovens; cookers, cooking plates, boiling rings, grillers and roasters, electrical, n.e.s.	Collection of Environmental Standard and Related Information (B11)	Ministry of Environment, Government of Nepal	Import prohibition for reasons set out in B1. Example: Imports are prohibited for hazardous substances, including explosives, certain toxic substances covered by the Basel Convention such as aerosol sprays containing CFCs, a range of HCFCs and BFCs, halons, methyl chloroform and carbon tetrachloride.
44	851679	Electro-thermic appliances, for domestic use (excluding hairdressing appliances and hand dryers, space-heating and soil-heating apparatus, water heaters, immersion heaters, smoothing irons, microwave ovens, ovens, cookers, cooking plates, boiling rings, grillers, roasters, coffee makers, tea makers, and toasters)			
45	851712	Telephones for cellular networks mobile telephones or for other wireless networks			

continued on next page

Table A4.3 continued

S.N.	HS Code 6-Digit (2007)	Description	Legislation or Regulation	Details of Regulatory Agency of Nepal	Description of NTM of Nepal
46	852351	Solid-state, non-volatile data storage devices for recording data from an external source (flash memory cards or flash electronic storage cards) (excluding goods of Chapter 37)			
47	852851	Monitors of a kind solely or principally used in an automatic data-processing machine of heading 8471 (excluding with cathode ray tube)			
48	852872	Reception apparatus for television, color, whether or not incorporating radio-broadcast receivers or sound or video recording or reproducing apparatus, designed to incorporate a video display or screen			
49	853529	Automatic circuit breakers, for a voltage exceeding 1,000 volts, n.e.s.			
50	853630	Electrical appliances for protecting electrical circuits, for voltage </=1,000 volts, n.e.s.			
51	853929	Filament lamps, excluding ultraviolet or infrared lamps, n.e.s.			
52	854011	Cathode-ray television picture tubes, including video monitor tubes, color			
53	870323	Motor cars and other motor vehicles principally designed for the transport of persons, including station wagons and racing cars, with spark-ignition internal combustion reciprocating piston engine of a cylinder capacity > 1.500 cm^3 but <= 3.000 cm^3 (excluding vehicles for the transport of persons on snow and other specially designed vehicles of subheading 8703.10)	Collection of Environmental Standard and Related Information (B11, B83)	Ministry of Environment, Government of Nepal	B11: Import prohibition for reasons set out in B1. Example: Imports are prohibited for hazardous substances including explosives, certain toxic substances covered by the Basel Convention such as aerosol sprays containing CFCs, a range of HCFCs and BFCs, halons, methyl chloroform, and carbon tetrachloride. B83: Certification of conformity with a given regulation: required by the importing country, but may be issued in the exporting or the importing country. Example: Certificate of conformity for electric products is required.

BFC = bromofluorocarbon, CFC = chlorofluorocarbon, HCFC = hydrofluorocarbon, HS = Harmonized Commodity Description and Coding System, n.e.s. = not elsewhere specified, NTM = nontariff measure, S.N. = serial number, SPS = sanitary and phytosanitary, TBT = technical barrier to trade.

Source: Asian Development Bank, compiled from information available in MAcMap database.

Table A4.4: Sanitary and Phytosanitary and Technical Barriers to Trade Measures by Sri Lanka on India's Potential Products

S.N.	HS Code 6-digit (2007)	Description	Legislation or Regulation	Details of Regulatory Agency of Sri Lanka	Description of NTM of Sri Lanka
1	040210	Milk powder not exceeding 1.5% fat	Agricultural Produce Agents (Registration) Ordinance (B15)	Department of Agriculture	This ordinance provides for the issuing of licenses to agents dealing with agricultural products to discipline the trading and selling of the aforesaid products. "Agricultural products" are defined as any unmanufactured agricultural, horticultural, and animal produce.
			Regulations amending the Food (Coloring Substances) Regulations, 2006. Published in the Gazette of the Democratic Socialist Republic of Sri Lanka (Extraordinary) No. 1688/28 (A22)	Food Control Administration Unit	These regulations cover the import, labeling and sale of food coloring substances and the use of these substances in food. They specify: flavoring substances that are allowed or prohibited; solvents permitted to be used in flavoring substances; flavor enhancers which may be added to foods subject to observance of good manufacturing practices and where the label clearly carries a declaration as to the particular substance or substances used, and flavor enhancers which shall not be added to any food for infants or young children below 3 years of age
			Food (Preservatives) Regulations, 1990. Published in the Gazette of the Democratic Socialist Republic of Sri Lanka (Extraordinary) No. 615/11 (A22)	Food Control Administration Unit	These regulations establish requirements for preservatives used in food stuff. They specify the following provisions: no food preservative should be used other than a preservative specified in Schedule I; no person shall manufacture, import, sell, store, or distribute any unauthorized food preservative; any food specified in Schedule II may only have in or upon it a preservative specified in the regulations.

continued on next page

Table A4.4 continued

S.N.	HS Code 6-digit (2007)	Description	Legislation or Regulation	Details of Regulatory Agency of Sri Lanka	Description of NTM of Sri Lanka
			Food (Antioxidants) Regulations, 2009. Published in the Gazette of the Democratic Socialist Republic of Sri Lanka (Extraordinary) No. 1617/16 (A22)	Food Control Administration Unit	These regulations prohibit the manufacture, import, sale, storage, distribution, transportation, or advertisement of food containing any antioxidant other than those listed in Schedule I. Any food specified in Column II of Schedule I may have antioxidants specified in proportion corresponding to related Column.
			Food (Preservatives in Milk) Regulations, 1994. Published in the Gazette of the Democratic Socialist Republic of Sri Lanka (Extraordinary) No. 823/16 (A22)	Food Control Administration Unit	These regulations prohibit the use of preservatives in milk. However, under exceptional circumstances, Hydrogen Peroxide of the food quality grade may be used as a preservative in milk and milk collecting centers and/or factories.
			Food (Labeling and Advertising) Regulations, 2005. Published in the Gazette of the Democratic Socialist Republic of Sri Lanka (Extraordinary) No. 1456/22 (A31, B31)	Food Control Administration Unit	These regulations establish detailed labeling requirements for food contained in a package or container. These regulations do not apply to packages of food if the food is of the nature, quality, quantity, origin, or brand requested by the purchaser and is weighed, counted or measured in the presence of the purchaser. They also do not apply to any package containing eggs using transparent blister packaging if that is marked with the date of production and date of expiry of the content.
			Food (Milk Standards) Regulations, 1989. Published in the Gazette of the Democratic Socialist	Food Control Administration Unit	These regulations outline the requirements to be satisfied by milk and milk products to be put on the market. The Regulations lay down respective standards, defining the following products: "Milk Raw

continued on next page

Table A4.4 continued

S.N.	HS Code 6-digit (2007)	Description	Legislation or Regulation	Details of Regulatory Agency of Sri Lanka	Description of NTM of Sri Lanka
			Republic of Sri Lanka (Extraordinary) No. 673/8 (B31, B7)		or Fresh"; "Standardized Milk"; "Toned Milk"; "Skimmed Milk"; "Pasteurized Milk"; "Sterilized Milk"; "Ultra-Heat Treated Milk" and "Flavored Milk." They also provide for compositional and labeling requirements.
			Food (Flavoring Substances and Flavor Enhancers) Regulations 2013. Published in the Gazette of the Democratic Socialist Republic of Sri Lanka (Extraordinary) No. 1795/51 (A22, A31)	Food Control Administration Unit	These regulations aim to control the use of flavoring substances and flavoring enhancers in food items. They specify: flavoring substances that are prohibited (Schedule I); solvents permitted to be used in flavoring substances (Schedule II); flavor enhancers which may be added to foods and flavor enhancers which shall not be added to any food for infants or young children below 3 years of age (Schedule III).
			Food (Sweeteners) Regulations, 2003. Published in the Gazette of the Democratic Socialist Republic of Sri Lanka (Extraordinary) No. 1323/1 (A22, A31)	Food Control Administration Unit	These regulations prohibit the import, storage, distribution, transportation, sale, exposition, or advertisement for sale of any sweetener other than a permitted sweetener for use in any food; the use of any sweetener in food especially prepared for infants or young children; the use of any permitted sweetener exceeding maximum usable doses.
			Food (Melamine in Milk and Milk Products) Regulations, 2010. Published in the Gazette of the Democratic Socialist Republic of Sri Lanka (Extraordinary) No. 1646/18 (A21, A83)	Food Control Administration Unit	No person shall import, manufacture, transport, distribute, or sell any milk or milk products containing melamine in levels exceeding 1.0 mg/kg. Every person importing milk or milk products into the country must produce a Health Certificate from the National Food Safety Authority of the country of origin or the exporting country, as the case may be, which states that the products conforms to the levels specified in these regulations.

continued on next page

Table A4.4 continued

S.N.	HS Code 6-digit (2007)	Description	Legislation or Regulation	Details of Regulatory Agency of Sri Lanka	Description of NTM of Sri Lanka
			Food (Shelf Life of Imported Food Items) Regulations, 2011. Published in the Gazette of the Democratic Socialist Republic of Sri Lanka (Extraordinary) No. 1694/5 (A31, A49, B31)	Food Control Administration Unit	These regulations establish shelf life requirements for imported food products. They specify that all items of food imported into the country shall possess a minimum period of 60% of unexpired shelf life at the point of entry into Sri Lanka. The regulations do not apply to imported fresh fruits, vegetables, and potatoes which have not been peeled or cut. The period of shelf life of imported food shall be determined on the basis of the date of manufacture and the date of expiry as declared by the manufacturer of the product.
			Food (Packaging Materials and Articles) Regulations, 2010. Published in the Gazette of the Democratic Socialist Republic of Sri Lanka (Extraordinary) No. 1660/30 (A22, A31, B31)	Food Control Administration Unit	These regulations specify the requirements to be satisfied to import, manufacture, transport, advertise for sale, sell, package, store, use, or distribute any food packaging material or article. They regulate food packaging material which under normal conditions is injurious to human health; deteriorates the organoleptic characteristics of food, or changes the nature, substance, and quality of food. It shall be certified by the manufacturer that raw material used for the manufacture of the packaging meets the required quality in compliance with international standards.
			Animal Diseases Act (No. 59 of 1992) (A14, A83)	Department of Animal Production and Health	The importation of any animal, animal product, veterinary drug, or veterinary biological products, animal semen, or embryo requires a permit issued by the Department of Animal Production and Health, in the Ministry of Health. To obtain a permit, the importer must produce a certificate from the relevant authority of the country of origin, stating that the product is free from any infective

continued on next page

Table A4.4 continued

S.N.	HS Code 6-digit (2007)	Description	Legislation or Regulation	Details of Regulatory Agency of Sri Lanka	Description of NTM of Sri Lanka
					substance likely to cause disease in animals as well as zoonotic diseases. All animals imported into Sri Lanka are subject to quarantine for a minimum of 30 days.
			Imports (Standardization and Quality Control) Regulations, 2013. Published in the Gazette of the Democratic Socialist Republic of Sri Lanka (Extraordinary) No. 1844/49 (A83, A84, B83, B84)	Sri Lanka Standards Institution	The products listed in these regulations must conform to a Sri Lanka Standard to be imported. Goods are subject to import inspection to ensure their conformity with the relevant standard.
			Food (Control of Import, Labeling and Sale of Genetically Modified Foods) Regulations, 2006. Published in the Gazette of the Democratic Socialist Republic of Sri Lanka (Extraordinary) No. 1456/22 (A14, A15, A31, B14, B15, B31)	Food Control Administration Unit	No person shall import, store, transport, distribute, or sell any genetically modified organism (GMOs) as food for human consumption; any food containing or consisting of genetically modified organisms; any food produced from or containing ingredients produced from genetically modified organisms; without the approval of the Chief Food Authority. Food containing GMOs must be labeled according to the regulations.
2	040210	Milk powder not exceeding 1.5% fat	Food (Irradiation) Regulations, 2005. Published in the Gazette of the Democratic Socialist Republic of Sri Lanka (Extraordinary) No. 1420/5	Food Control Administration Unit	The importation and exportation of irradiated foods shall be done incompliance with the requirements of these regulations and the shipping documents shall be accompanied by: proper labeling documentation; documentation attesting that the Food Irradiation Facility of the country of origin is duly licensed; and a

continued on next page

Table A4.4 continued

S.N.	HS Code 6-digit (2007)	Description	Legislation or Regulation	Details of Regulatory Agency of Sri Lanka	Description of NTM of Sri Lanka
			(A4, A31, A83, A84, B3, B31, B83, B84)		Certificate by the competent authorities of the country of origin, to the effect that the food has been inspected by them.
3	080290	Nuts edible, fresh or dried, whether or not shelled or peeled, n.e.s.	Agricultural Produce Agents (Registration) Ordinance (B15)	Department of Agriculture	This ordinance provides for the issuing of licenses to agents dealing with agricultural products in order to discipline the trading and selling of the aforesaid products. "Agricultural products" are defined as any unmanufactured agricultural, horticultural and animal produce.
4	180690	Chocolate and other preparations containing cocoa, in containers or immediate packings of <= 2 kilograms (excluding in blocks, slabs, or bars and cocoa powder)	Regulations amending the Food (Coloring Substances) Regulations, 2006. Published in the Gazette of the Democratic Socialist Republic of Sri Lanka (Extraordinary) No. 1688/28 (A22)	Food Control Administration Unit	These regulations cover the import, labeling and sale of food coloring substances and the use of these substances in food. They specify: flavoring substances that are allowed or prohibited; solvents permitted to be used in flavoring substances; flavor enhancers which may be added to foods subject to observance of good manufacturing practices and where the label clearly carries a declaration as to the particular substance or substances used, and flavor enhancers which shall not be added to any food for infants or young children below 3 years of age.
			Food (Preservatives) Regulations, 1990. Published in the Gazette of the Democratic Socialist Republic of Sri Lanka (Extraordinary) No. 615/11 (A22)	Food Control Administration Unit	These regulations establish requirements for preservatives used in food stuff. They specify the following provisions: no food preservative should be used other than a preservative specified in Schedule I; no person shall manufacture, import, sell, store, or distribute any unauthorized food preservative; any food specified in Schedule II may only have in or upon it a preservative specified in the regulations.

continued on next page

Table A4.4 continued

S.N.	HS Code 6-digit (2007)	Description	Legislation or Regulation	Details of Regulatory Agency of Sri Lanka	Description of NTM of Sri Lanka
			Food (Antioxidants) Regulations, 2009. Published in the Gazette of the Democratic Socialist Republic of Sri Lanka (Extraordinary) No. 1617/16 (A22)	Food Control Administration Unit	These regulations prohibit the manufacture, import, sale, storage, distribution, transportation, or advertisement of food containing any antioxidant other than those listed in Schedule I. Any food specified in Column II of Schedule I may have antioxidants specified in proportion corresponding to related Column.
			Food (Flavoring Substances and Flavor Enhancers) Regulations 2013. Published in the Gazette of the Democratic Socialist Republic of Sri Lanka (Extraordinary) No. 1795/51 (A22, A31)	Food Control Administration Unit	These regulations aim to control the use of flavoring substances and flavoring enhancers in food items. They specify: flavoring substances that are prohibited (Schedule I); solvents permitted to be used in flavoring substances (Schedule II); flavor enhancers which may be added to foods and flavor enhancers which shall not be added to any food for infants or young children below 3 years of age (Schedule III).
			Food (Sweeteners) Regulations, 2003. Published in the Gazette of the Democratic Socialist Republic of Sri Lanka (Extraordinary) No. 1323/1 (A22, A31)	Food Control Administration Unit	These regulations prohibit the import, storage, distribution, transportation, sale, exposition, or advertisement for sale of any sweetener other than a permitted sweetener for use in any food; the use of any sweetener in food especially prepared for infants or young children; the use of any permitted sweetener exceeding maximum usable doses.
			Food (Labeling and Advertising) Regulations, 2005. Published in the Gazette of the Democratic Socialist Republic of Sri Lanka	Food Control Administration Unit	These regulations establish detailed labeling requirements for food contained in a package or container. These regulations do not apply to packages of food if the food is of the nature, quality, quantity, origin, or brand requested by the purchaser and is weighed, counted, or measured in the presence of the purchaser.

continued on next page

Table A4.4 continued

S.N.	HS Code 6-digit (2007)	Description	Legislation or Regulation	Details of Regulatory Agency of Sri Lanka	Description of NTM of Sri Lanka
			(Extraordinary) No. 1456/22 (A31, B31)		They also do not apply to any package containing eggs using transparent blister packaging if that is marked with the date of production and date of expiry of the content.
			Food (Shelf Life of Imported Food Items) Regulations, 2011. Published in the Gazette of the Democratic Socialist Republic of Sri Lanka (Extraordinary) No. 1694/5 (A31, A49, B31)	Food Control Administration Unit	These regulations establish shelf life requirements for imported food products. They specify that all items of food imported into the country shall possess a minimum period of 60% of unexpired shelf life at the point of entry into Sri Lanka. The regulations do not apply to imported fresh fruits, vegetables, and potatoes which have not been peeled or cut. The period of shelf life of imported food shall be determined on the basis of the date of manufacture and the date of expiry as declared by the manufacturer of the product.
			Food (Packaging Materials and Articles) Regulations, 2010. Published in the Gazette of the Democratic Socialist Republic of Sri Lanka (Extraordinary) No. 1660/30 (A22, A31, B31)	Food Control Administration Unit	These regulations specify the requirements to be satisfied to import, manufacture, transport, advertise for sale, sell, package, store, use, or distribute any food packaging material or article. They regulate food packaging material which under normal conditions is injurious to human health; deteriorates the organoleptic characteristics of food, or changes the nature, substance, and quality of food. It shall be certified by the manufacturer that raw material used for the manufacture of the packaging meets the required quality in compliance with international standards.
			Food (Control of Import, Labeling and Sale of Genetically Modified Foods) Regulations, 2006	Food Control Administration Unit	No person shall import, store, transport, distribute or sell any genetically modified organism (GMOs) as food for human consumption; any food containing or consisting of

continued on next page

Table A4.4 continued

S.N.	HS Code 6-digit (2007)	Description	Legislation or Regulation	Details of Regulatory Agency of Sri Lanka	Description of NTM of Sri Lanka
			Published in the Gazette of the Democratic Socialist Republic of Sri Lanka (Extraordinary) No. 1456/22 (A14, A15, A31, B14, B15, B31)		genetically modified organisms; any food produced from or containing ingredients produced from genetically modified organisms; without the approval of the Chief Food Authority. Food containing GMOs must be labeled according to the regulations.
			Food (Irradiation) Regulations, 2005. Published in the Gazette of the Democratic Socialist Republic of Sri Lanka (Extraordinary) No. 1420/5 (A4, A31, A83, A84, B3, B31, B83, B84)	Food Control Administration Unit	The importation and exportation of irradiated foods shall be done incompliance with the requirements of these regulations and the shipping documents shall be accompanied by: proper labeling documentation; documentation attesting that the Food Irradiation Facility of the country of origin is duly licensed; and a certificate by the competent authorities of the country of origin, to the effect that the food has been inspected by them.
5	190110	Prep of cereals, flour, starch/milk for infant use, put up for retail sale	Food (Standards) Regulations, 1989. Published in the Gazette of the Democratic Socialist Republic of Sri Lanka (Extraordinary) No. 637/18 (B7)	Food Control Administration Unit	These regulations specify identity requirements that food products must satisfy to be put on the market. They lay down respective standards, defining the following food products: "Baking powder"; "Sugar Confectionery"; "Margarine"; "Bakery Shortening"; "Edible Oil of different origin"; "Lard"; "Dripping"; "Cereals"; "Spices, Condiments and Seasonings"; "Cheese"; "Fermented Milk Products"; "Ice creams."
			Agricultural Produce Agents (Registration) Ordinance (B15)	Department of Agriculture	This ordinance provides for the issuing of licenses to agents dealing with agricultural products in order to discipline the trading and selling of the aforesaid products. "Agricultural products" are defined as any unmanufactured agricultural, horticultural, and animal produce

continued on next page

Table A4.4 continued

S.N.	HS Code 6-digit (2007)	Description	Legislation or Regulation	Details of Regulatory Agency of Sri Lanka	Description of NTM of Sri Lanka
			Regulations amending the Food (Coloring Substances) Regulations, 2006. Published in the Gazette of the Democratic Socialist Republic of Sri Lanka (Extraordinary) No. 1688/28 (A22)	Food Control Administration Unit	These regulations cover the import, labeling, and sale of food coloring substances and the use of these substances in food. They specify: flavoring substances that are allowed or prohibited; solvents permitted to be used in flavoring substances; flavor enhancers which may be added to foods subject to observance of good manufacturing practices and where the label clearly carries a declaration as to the particular substance or substances used, and flavor enhancers which shall not be added to any food for infants or young children below 3 years of age.
			Food (Preservatives) Regulations, 1990. Published in the Gazette of the Democratic Socialist Republic of Sri Lanka (Extraordinary) No. 615/11. (A22)	Food Control Administration Unit	These regulations establish requirements for preservatives used in food stuff. They specify the following provisions: no food preservative should be used other than a preservative specified in Schedule I; no person shall manufacture, import, sell, store, or distribute any unauthorized food preservative; any food specified in Schedule II may only have in or upon it a preservative specified in the regulations.
			Food (Antioxidants) Regulations, 2009. Published in the Gazette of the Democratic Socialist Republic of Sri Lanka (Extraordinary) No. 1617/16 (A22)	Food Control Administration Unit	These regulations prohibit the manufacture, import, sale, storage, distribution, transportation, or advertisement of food containing any antioxidant other than those listed in Schedule I. Any food specified in Column II of Schedule I may have antioxidants specified in proportion corresponding to related Column.

continued on next page

Table A4.4 continued

S.N.	HS Code 6-digit (2007)	Description	Legislation or Regulation	Details of Regulatory Agency of Sri Lanka	Description of NTM of Sri Lanka
			Food (Flavoring Substances and Flavor Enhancers) Regulations 2013. Published in the Gazette of the Democratic Socialist Republic of Sri Lanka (Extraordinary) No. 1795/51 (A22, A31)	Food Control Administration Unit	These regulations aim to control the use of flavoring substances and flavoring enhancers in food items. They specify: flavoring substances that are prohibited (Schedule I); solvents permitted to be used in flavoring substances (Schedule II); flavor enhancers which may be added to foods and flavor enhancers which shall not be added to any food for infants or young children below 3 years of age (Schedule III).
			Food (Sweeteners) Regulations, 2003. Published in the Gazette of the Democratic Socialist Republic of Sri Lanka (Extraordinary) No. 1323/1 (A22, A31)	Food Control Administration Unit	These regulations prohibit the import, storage, distribution, transportation, sale, exposition, or advertisement for sale of any sweetener other than a permitted sweetener for use in any food; the use of any sweetener in food especially prepared for infants or young children; the use of any permitted sweetener exceeding maximum usable doses.
			Food (Labeling and Advertising) Regulations, 2005. Published in the Gazette of the Democratic Socialist Republic of Sri Lanka (Extraordinary) No. 1456/22 (A31, B31)	Food Control Administration Unit	These regulations establish detailed labeling requirements for food contained in a package or container. These regulations do not apply to packages of food if the food is of the nature, quality, quantity, origin, or brand requested by the purchaser and is weighed, counted, or measured in the presence of the purchaser. They also do not apply to any package containing eggs using transparent blister packaging if that is marked with the date of production and date of expiry of the content.
			Food (Shelf Life of Imported Food Items) Regulations, 2011. Published in the Gazette of	Food Control Administration Unit	These regulations establish shelf life requirements for imported food products. They specify that all items of food imported into the country shall possess a minimum period of 60% of

continued on next page

Table A4.4 continued

S.N.	HS Code 6-digit (2007)	Description	Legislation or Regulation	Details of Regulatory Agency of Sri Lanka	Description of NTM of Sri Lanka
			the Democratic Socialist Republic of Sri Lanka (Extraordinary) No. 1694/5 (A31, A49, B31)		unexpired shelf life at the point of entry into Sri Lanka. The Regulations do not apply to imported fresh fruits, vegetables, and potatoes which have not been peeled or cut. The period of shelf life of imported food shall be determined on the basis of the date of manufacture and the date of expiry as declared by the manufacturer of the product.
			Food (Packaging Materials and Articles) Regulations, 2010. Published in the Gazette of the Democratic Socialist Republic of Sri Lanka (Extraordinary) No. 1660/30 (A22, A31, B31)	Food Control Administration Unit	These regulations specify the requirements to be satisfied to import, manufacture, transport, advertise for sale, sell, package, store, use or distribute any food packaging material or article. They regulate food packaging material which under normal conditions is injurious to human health; deteriorates the organoleptic characteristics of food, or changes the nature, substance and quality of food. It shall be certified by the manufacturer that raw material used for the manufacture of the packaging meets the required quality in compliance with international standards.
			Food (Control of Import, Labeling and Sale of Genetically Modified Foods) Regulations, 2006. Published in the Gazette of the Democratic Socialist Republic of Sri Lanka (Extraordinary) No. 1456/22 (A14, A15, A31, B14, B15, B31)	Food Control Administration Unit	No person shall import, store, transport, distribute, or sell any genetically modified organism (GMOs) as food for human consumption; any food containing or consisting of genetically modified organisms; any food produced from or containing ingredients produced from genetically modified organisms; without the approval of the Chief Food Authority. Food containing GMOs must be labeled according to the regulations.

continued on next page

Table A4.4 continued

S.N.	HS Code 6-digit (2007)	Description	Legislation or Regulation	Details of Regulatory Agency of Sri Lanka	Description of NTM of Sri Lanka
			Food (Irradiation) Regulations, 2005. Published in the Gazette of the Democratic Socialist Republic of Sri Lanka (Extraordinary) No. 1420/5 (A4, A31, A83, A84, B3, B31, B83, B84)	Food Control Administration Unit	The importation and exportation of irradiated foods shall be done incompliance with the requirements of these regulations and the shipping documents shall be accompanied by: proper labeling documentation; documentation attesting that the Food Irradiation Facility of the country of origin is duly licensed; and a certificate by the competent authorities of the country of origin, to the effect that the food has been inspected by them.
6	210690	Food preparations, n.e.s	Regulations amending the Food (Coloring Substances) Regulations, 2006. Published in the Gazette of the Democratic Socialist Republic of Sri Lanka (Extraordinary) No. 1688/28 (A22)	Food Control Administration Unit	These regulations cover the import, labeling and sale of food coloring substances and the use of these substances in food. They specify: flavoring substances that are allowed or prohibited; solvents permitted to be used in flavoring substances; flavor enhancers which may be added to foods subject to observance of good manufacturing practices and where the label clearly carries a declaration as to the particular substance or substances used, and flavor enhancers which shall not be added to any food for infants or young children below 3 years of age.
			Food (Preservatives) Regulations, 1990. Published in the Gazette of the Democratic Socialist Republic of Sri Lanka (Extraordinary) No. 615/11 (A22)	Food Control Administration Unit	These regulations establish requirements for preservatives used in food stuff. They specify the following provisions: no food preservative should be used other than a preservative specified in Schedule I; no person shall manufacture, import, sell, store, or distribute any unauthorized food preservative; any food specified in Schedule II may only have in or upon it a preservative specified in the regulations.

continued on next page

Table A4.4 continued

S.N.	HS Code 6-digit (2007)	Description	Legislation or Regulation	Details of Regulatory Agency of Sri Lanka	Description of NTM of Sri Lanka
			Food (Antioxidants) Regulations, 2009. Published in the Gazette of the Democratic Socialist Republic of Sri Lanka (Extraordinary) No. 1617/16 (A22)	Food Control Administration Unit	These regulations prohibit the manufacture, import, sale, storage, distribution, transportation, or advertisement of food containing any antioxidant other than those listed in Schedule I. Any food specified in Column II of Schedule I may have antioxidants specified in proportion corresponding to related Column.
			Food (Flavoring Substances and Flavor Enhancers) Regulations 2013. Published in the Gazette of the Democratic Socialist Republic of Sri Lanka (Extraordinary) No. 1795/51 (A22, A31)	Food Control Administration Unit	These regulations aim to control the use of flavoring substances and flavoring enhancers in food items. They specify: flavoring substances that are prohibited (Schedule I); solvents permitted to be used in flavoring substances (Schedule II); flavor enhancers which may be added to foods and flavor enhancers which shall not be added to any food for infants or young children below 3 years of age (Schedule III).
			Food (Sweeteners) Regulations, 2003. Published in the Gazette of the Democratic Socialist Republic of Sri Lanka (Extraordinary) No. 1323/1 (A22, A31)	Food Control Administration Unit	These regulations prohibit the import, storage, distribution, transportation, sale, exposition, or advertisement for sale of any sweetener other than a permitted sweetener for use in any food; the use of any sweetener in food especially prepared for infants or young children; the use of any permitted sweetener exceeding maximum usable doses.
			Food (Labeling and Advertising) Regulations, 2005. Published in the Gazette of the Democratic Socialist Republic of Sri Lanka	Food Control Administration Unit	These regulations establish detailed labeling requirements for food contained in a package or container. These regulations do not apply to packages of food if the food is of the nature, quality, quantity, origin, or brand requested by the purchaser and is weighed, counted, or measured in the presence of the purchaser. They also do not apply to any

continued on next page

Table A4.4 continued

S.N.	HS Code 6-digit (2007)	Description	Legislation or Regulation	Details of Regulatory Agency of Sri Lanka	Description of NTM of Sri Lanka
			(Extraordinary) No. 1456/22 (A31, B31)		package containing eggs using transparent blister packaging if that is marked with the date of production and date of expiry of the content.
			Food (Shelf Life of Imported Food Items) Regulations, 2011. Published in the Gazette of the Democratic Socialist Republic of Sri Lanka (Extraordinary) No. 1694/5 (A31, A49, B31)	Food Control Administration Unit	These regulations establish shelf life requirements for imported food products. They specify that all items of food imported into the country shall possess a minimum period of 60% of unexpired shelf life at the point of entry into Sri Lanka. The regulations do not apply to imported fresh fruits, vegetables, and potatoes which have not been peeled or cut. The period of shelf life of imported food shall be determined on the basis of the date of manufacture and the date of expiry as declared by the manufacturer of the product.
			Food (Packaging Materials and Articles) Regulations, 2010. Published in the Gazette of the Democratic Socialist Republic of Sri Lanka (Extraordinary) No. 1660/30 (A22, A31, B31)	Food Control Administration Unit	These regulations specify the requirements to be satisfied to import, manufacture, transport, advertise for sale, sell, package, store, use, or distribute any food packaging material or article. They regulate food packaging material which under normal conditions is injurious to human health; deteriorates the organoleptic characteristics of food, or changes the nature, substance, and quality of food. It shall be certified by the manufacturer that raw material used for the manufacture of the packaging meets the required quality in compliance with international standards.
			Food (Control of Import, Labeling and Sale of Genetically Modified Foods) Regulations, 2006. Published in the Gazette of	Food Control Administration Unit	No person shall import, store, transport, distribute or sell any genetically modified organism (GMOs) as food for human consumption; any food containing or consisting of genetically modified organisms; any food produced from or

continued on next page

Table A4.4 continued

S.N.	HS Code 6-digit (2007)	Description	Legislation or Regulation	Details of Regulatory Agency of Sri Lanka	Description of NTM of Sri Lanka
			the Democratic Socialist Republic of Sri Lanka (Extraordinary) No. 1456/22 (A14, A15, A31, B14, B15, B31)		containing ingredients produced from genetically modified organisms; without the approval of the Chief Food Authority. Food containing GMOs must be labeled according to the regulations.
			Food (Irradiation) Regulations, 2005. Published in the Gazette of the Democratic Socialist Republic of Sri Lanka (Extraordinary) No. 1420/5 (A4, A31, A83, A84, B3, B31, B83, B84)	Food Control Administration Unit	The importation and exportation of irradiated foods shall be done incompliance with the requirements of these regulations and the shipping documents shall be accompanied by: proper labeling documentation; documentation attesting that the Food Irradiation Facility of the country of origin is duly licensed; and a certificate by the competent authorities of the country of origin, to the effect that the food has been inspected by them.
			Imports (Standardization and Quality Control) Regulations, 2013. Published in the Gazette of the Democratic Socialist Republic of Sri Lanka (Extraordinary) No. 1844/49 (A83, A84, B83, B84)	Sri Lanka Standards Institution	The products listed in these regulations must conform to a Sri Lanka Standard in order to be imported. Goods are subject to import inspection to ensure their conformity with the relevant standard.
7	220710	Undenatured ethyl alcohol, of actual alcoholic strength of >= 80%	Regulations amending the Food (Coloring Substances) Regulations, 2006. Published in the Gazette of the Democratic Socialist Republic of Sri Lanka	Food Control Administration Unit	These regulations cover the import, labeling and sale of food coloring substances and the use of these substances in food. They specify: flavoring substances that are allowed or prohibited; solvents permitted to be used in flavoring substances; flavor enhancers which may be added to foods subject to observance of good

continued on next page

Table A4.4 continued

S.N.	HS Code 6-digit (2007)	Description	Legislation or Regulation	Details of Regulatory Agency of Sri Lanka	Description of NTM of Sri Lanka
			(Extraordinary) No. 1688/28 (A22)		manufacturing practices and where the label clearly carries a declaration as to the particular substance or substances used, and flavor enhancers which shall not be added to any food for infants or young children below 3 years of age.
			Food (Preservatives) Regulations, 1990. Published in the Gazette of the Democratic Socialist Republic of Sri Lanka (Extraordinary) No. 615/11 (A22)	Food Control Administration Unit	These regulations establish requirements for preservatives used in food stuff. They specify the following provisions: no food preservative should be used other than a preservative specified in Schedule I; no person shall manufacture, import, sell, store, or distribute any unauthorized food preservative; any food specified in Schedule II may only have in or upon it a preservative specified in the regulations.
			Food (Antioxidants) Regulations, 2009. Published in the Gazette of the Democratic Socialist Republic of Sri Lanka (Extraordinary) No. 1617/16 (A22)	Food Control Administration Unit	These regulations prohibit the manufacture, import, sale, storage, distribution, transportation, or advertisement of food containing any antioxidant other than those listed in Schedule I. Any food specified in Column II of Schedule I may have antioxidants specified in proportion corresponding to related Column.
			Food (Flavoring Substances and Flavor Enhancers) Regulations 2013. Published in the Gazette of the Democratic Socialist Republic of Sri Lanka (Extraordinary) No. 1795/51 (A22, A31)	Food Control Administration Unit	These regulations aim to control the use of flavoring substances and flavoring enhancers in food items. They specify: flavoring substances that are prohibited (Schedule I); solvents permitted to be used in flavoring substances (Schedule II); flavor enhancers which may be added to foods and flavor enhancers which shall not be added to any food for infants or young children below 3 years of age (Schedule III).

continued on next page

Table A4.4 continued

S.N.	HS Code 6-digit (2007)	Description	Legislation or Regulation	Details of Regulatory Agency of Sri Lanka	Description of NTM of Sri Lanka
			Food (Sweeteners) Regulations, 2003. Published in the Gazette of the Democratic Socialist Republic of Sri Lanka (Extraordinary) No. 1323/1 (A22, A31)	Food Control Administration Unit	These regulations prohibit the import, storage, distribution, transportation, sale, exposition, or advertisement for sale of any sweetener other than a permitted sweetener for use in any food; the use of any sweetener in food especially prepared for infants or young children; the use of any permitted sweetener exceeding maximum usable doses.
			Food (Labeling and Advertising) Regulations, 2005. Published in the Gazette of the Democratic Socialist Republic of Sri Lanka (Extraordinary) No. 1456/22 (A31, B31)	Food Control Administration Unit	These regulations establish detailed labeling requirements for food contained in a package or container. These regulations do not apply to packages of food if the food is of the nature, quality, quantity, origin, or brand requested by the purchaser and is weighed, counted, or measured in the presence of the purchaser. They also do not apply to any package containing eggs using transparent blister packaging if that is marked with the date of production and date of expiry of the content.
			Food (Shelf Life of Imported Food Items) Regulations, 2011. Published in the Gazette of the Democratic Socialist Republic of Sri Lanka (Extraordinary) No. 1694/5 (A31, A49, B31)	Food Control Administration Unit	These regulations establish shelf life requirements for imported food products. They specify that all items of food imported into the country shall possess a minimum period of 60% of unexpired shelf life at the point of entry into Sri Lanka. The regulations do not apply to imported fresh fruits, vegetables, and potatoes which have not been peeled or cut. The period of shelf life of imported food shall be determined on the basis of the date of manufacture and the date of expiry as declared by the manufacturer of the product.
			Food (Packaging Materials and Articles)	Food Control Administration Unit	These regulations specify the requirements to be satisfied to import, manufacture, transport, advertise for sale, sell, package,

continued on next page

Table A4.4 continued

S.N.	HS Code 6-digit (2007)	Description	Legislation or Regulation	Details of Regulatory Agency of Sri Lanka	Description of NTM of Sri Lanka
			Regulations, 2010. Published in the Gazette of the Democratic Socialist Republic of Sri Lanka (Extraordinary) No. 1660/30 (A22, A31, B31)		store, use, or distribute any food packaging material or article. They regulate food packaging material which under normal conditions is injurious to human health; deteriorates the organoleptic characteristics of food, or changes the nature, substance and quality of food. It shall be certified by the manufacturer that raw material used for the manufacture of the packaging meets the required quality in compliance with international standards.
			Food (Control of Import, Labeling and Sale of Genetically Modified Foods) Regulations, 2006. Published in the Gazette of the Democratic Socialist Republic of Sri Lanka (Extraordinary) No. 1456/22 (A14, A15, A31, B14, B15, B31)	Food Control Administration Unit	No person shall import, store, transport, distribute or sell any genetically modified organism (GMOs) as food for human consumption; any food containing or consisting of genetically modified organisms; any food produced from or containing ingredients produced from genetically modified organisms; without the approval of the Chief Food Authority. Food containing GMOs must be labeled according to the regulations.
			Food (Irradiation) Regulations, 2005. Published in the Gazette of the Democratic Socialist Republic of Sri Lanka (Extraordinary) No. 1420/5 (A4, A31, A83, A84, B3, B31, B83, B84)	Food Control Administration Unit	The importation and exportation of irradiated foods shall be done incompliance with the requirements of these regulations and the shipping documents shall be accompanied by: proper labeling documentation; documentation attesting that the Food Irradiation Facility of the country of origin is duly licensed; and a certificate by the competent authorities of the country of origin, to the effect that the food has been inspected by them.
			Special Import License Regulations,	Department of Imports and Export Control	Products listed in Schedule I of these regulations are subject to non-automatic import licensing.

continued on next page

Table A4.4 continued

S.N.	HS Code 6-digit (2007)	Description	Legislation or Regulation	Details of Regulatory Agency of Sri Lanka	Description of NTM of Sri Lanka
			2013. Published in the Gazette of the Democratic Socialist Republic of Sri Lanka (Extraordinary) No. 1813/14 (A14, B14)		Products listed in Schedule IV are prohibited to be imported into Sri Lanka. These regulations apply equally to goods originating in all countries.
8	220830	Whiskies	Regulations amending the Food (Coloring Substances) Regulations, 2006. Published in the Gazette of the Democratic Socialist Republic of Sri Lanka (Extraordinary) No. 1688/28 (A22)	Food Control Administration Unit	These regulations cover the import, labeling and sale of food coloring substances and the use of these substances in food. They specify: flavoring substances that are allowed or prohibited; solvents permitted to be used in flavoring substances; flavor enhancers which may be added to foods subject to observance of good manufacturing practices and where the label clearly carries a declaration as to the particular substance or substances used, and flavor enhancers which shall not be added to any food for infants or young children below 3 years of age.
			Food (Preservatives) Regulations, 1990. Published in the Gazette of the Democratic Socialist Republic of Sri Lanka (Extraordinary) No. 615/11 (A22)	Food Control Administration Unit	These regulations establish requirements for preservatives used in food stuff. They specify the following provisions: no food preservative should be used other than a preservative specified in Schedule I; no person shall manufacture, import, sell, store or distribute any unauthorized food preservative; any food specified in Schedule II may only have in or upon it a preservative specified in the regulations.
			Food (Antioxidants) Regulations, 2009. Published in the Gazette of the Democratic Socialist	Food Control Administration Unit	These regulations prohibit the manufacture, import, sale, storage, distribution, transportation, or advertisement of food containing any antioxidant other than those listed in Schedule I. Any

continued on next page

Table A4.4 continued

S.N.	HS Code 6-digit (2007)	Description	Legislation or Regulation	Details of Regulatory Agency of Sri Lanka	Description of NTM of Sri Lanka
			Republic of Sri Lanka (Extraordinary) No. 1617/16 (A22)		food specified in Column II of Schedule I may have antioxidants specified in proportion corresponding to related Column.
			Food (Labeling and Advertising) Regulations, 2005. Published in the Gazette of the Democratic Socialist Republic of Sri Lanka (Extraordinary) No. 1456/22 (A31, B31)	Food Control Administration Unit	These regulations establish detailed labeling requirements for food contained in a package or container. These regulations do not apply to packages of food if the food is of the nature, quality, quantity, origin, or brand requested by the purchaser and is weighed, counted or measured in the presence of the purchaser. They also do not apply to any package containing eggs using transparent blister packaging if that is marked with the date of production and date of expiry of the content.
			Food (Sweeteners) Regulations, 2003. Published in the Gazette of the Democratic Socialist Republic of Sri Lanka (Extraordinary) No. 1323/1 (A22, A31)	Food Control Administration Unit	These regulations prohibit the import, storage, distribution, transportation, sale, exposition, or advertisement for sale of any sweetener other than a permitted sweetener for use in any food; the use of any sweetener in food especially prepared for infants or young children; the use of any permitted sweetener exceeding maximum usable doses.
			Food (Shelf Life of Imported Food Items) Regulations, 2011. Published in the Gazette of the Democratic Socialist Republic of Sri Lanka (Extraordinary) No. 1694/5 (A31, A49, B31)	Food Control Administration Unit	These regulations establish shelf life requirements for imported food products. They specify that all items of food imported into the country shall possess a minimum period of 60% of unexpired shelf life at the point of entry into Sri Lanka. The regulations do not apply to imported fresh fruits, vegetables, and potatoes which have not been peeled or cut. The period of shelf life of imported food shall be determined on the basis of the date of manufacture and the

continued on next page

Table A4.4 continued

S.N.	HS Code 6-digit (2007)	Description	Legislation or Regulation	Details of Regulatory Agency of Sri Lanka	Description of NTM of Sri Lanka
					date of expiry as declared by the manufacturer of the product.
			Food (Packaging Materials and Articles) Regulations, 2010. Published in the Gazette of the Democratic Socialist Republic of Sri Lanka (Extraordinary) No. 1660/30 (A22, A31, B31)	Food Control Administration Unit	These regulations specify the requirements to be satisfied to import, manufacture, transport, advertise for sale, sell, package, store, use. or distribute any food packaging material or article. They regulate food packaging material which under normal conditions is injurious to human health; deteriorates the organoleptic characteristics of food, or changes the nature, substance and quality of food. It shall be certified by the manufacturer that raw material used for the manufacture of the packaging meets the required quality in compliance with international standards.
			Food (Control of Import, Labeling and Sale of Genetically Modified Foods) Regulations, 2006. Published in the Gazette of the Democratic Socialist Republic of Sri Lanka (Extraordinary) No. 1456/22 (A14, A15, A31, B14, B15, B31)	Food Control Administration Unit	No person shall import, store, transport, distribute, or sell any genetically modified organism (GMOs) as food for human consumption; any food containing or consisting of genetically modified organisms; any food produced from or containing ingredients produced from genetically modified organisms; without the approval of the Chief Food Authority. Food containing GMOs must be labeled according to the regulations.
			Food (Irradiation) Regulations, 2005. Published in the Gazette of the Democratic Socialist Republic of Sri Lanka (Extraordinary) No. 1420/5 (A31, A4, A83,	Food Control Administration Unit	The importation and exportation of irradiated foods shall be done incompliance with the requirements of these regulations and the shipping documents shall be accompanied by: proper labeling documentation; documentation attesting that the Food Irradiation Facility of the country of origin is duly licensed; and a Certificate by the competent

continued on next page

Table A4.4 continued

S.N.	HS Code 6-digit (2007)	Description	Legislation or Regulation	Details of Regulatory Agency of Sri Lanka	Description of NTM of Sri Lanka
			A84, B31, B4, B83, B84)		authorities of the country of origin, to the effect that the food has been inspected by them.
			Food (Flavoring Substances and Flavor Enhancers) Regulations 2013. Published in the Gazette of the Democratic Socialist Republic of Sri Lanka (Extraordinary) No. 1795/51 (A22, A31)	Food Control Administration Unit	These regulations aim to control the use of flavoring substances and flavoring enhancers in food items. They specify: flavoring substances that are prohibited (Schedule I); solvents permitted to be used in flavoring substances (Schedule II); flavor enhancers which may be added to foods and flavor enhancers which shall not be added to any food for infants or young children below 3 years of age (Schedule III).
9	382490	Products, preparations and residual products of the chemical or allied industries, including those consisting of mixtures of natural products, n.e.s. (excluding binders for foundry molds and cores; naphthenic acids, their water-insoluble salts and their esters; non-agglomerated metal carbides mixed together or with metallic binders; prepared additives for cements, mortars, and concretes; nonrefractory mortars, and concretes; sorbitol)	Order under section 23W of the National Environmental Act 1980 (B11)	Central Environmental Authority	This order prohibits the import of the substances specified in the Schedule as being ozone depleting substances. The substances may continue to be used for the limited purpose of servicing equipment or industrial plants which have been installed before 1 January 2000.
			National Environmental (Protection and Quality) Regulations, No. 1 of 2008. Published in the Gazette of the Democratic Socialist Republic of Sri Lanka (Extraordinary) No. 1534/18 (B14, B15)	Central Environmental Authority	These regulations provide for industrial pollution control through environmental protection licensing schemes. Wastes which may cause pollution or cause noise pollution may be discharged, deposited, or emitted only under the authority of an Environmental Protection License issued by the Central Environmental Authority, and in accordance with the standards and criteria specified in Schedule I attached to these regulations. Licenses are also compulsory for any person involved in the management of scheduled waste as specified in Schedule VIII.
			Special Import License Regulations, 2013. Published	Department of Imports and Export Control	Products listed in Schedule I of these regulations are subject to non-automatic import licensing.

continued on next page

Table A4.4 continued

S.N.	HS Code 6-digit (2007)	Description	Legislation or Regulation	Details of Regulatory Agency of Sri Lanka	Description of NTM of Sri Lanka
			in the Gazette of the Democratic Socialist Republic of Sri Lanka (Extraordinary) No. 1813/14 (A14, B14)		Products listed in Schedule IV are prohibited to be imported into Sri Lanka. These regulations apply equally to goods originating in all countries.
10	390720	Polyethers, in primary forms (excluding polyacetals)	National Environmental (Protection and Quality) Regulations, No. 1 of 2008. Published in the Gazette of the Democratic Socialist Republic of Sri Lanka (Extraordinary) No. 1534/18 (B14, B15)	Central Environmental Authority	These regulations provide for industrial pollution control through environmental protection licensing schemes. Wastes which may cause pollution or cause noise pollution may be discharged, deposited, or emitted only under the authority of an Environmental Protection License issued by the Central Environmental Authority, and in accordance with the standards and criteria specified in Schedule I attached to these regulations. Licenses are also compulsory for any person involved in the management of scheduled waste as specified in Schedule VIII.
11	392690	Articles of plastics or of other materials of Nos. 39.01 to 39.14, n.e.s.	Special Import License Regulations, 2013. Published in the Gazette of the Democratic Socialist Republic of Sri Lanka (Extraordinary) No. 1813/14 (A14, B14)	Department of Imports and Export Control	Products listed in Schedule I of these regulations are subject to non-automatic import licensing. Products listed in Schedule IV are prohibited to be imported into Sri Lanka. These regulations apply equally to goods originating in all countries.
12	710239	Diamonds, worked, but not mounted or set (excluding industrial diamonds)	National Gem And Jewelry Authority Act (No. 50 of 1993) (B15)	National Gem and Jewelry Authority	Importing or exporting gems and jewelry requires a permit and can be done only by operators registered with the National Gem and Jewelry Authority (B15).
13	710391	Rubies, sapphires, and emeralds further worked than sewn or rough shaped			
14	840490	Parts of auxiliary plant of headings 8402 or 8403 and condensers for steam or other vapor power units, n.e.s.	National Environmental (Protection and Quality)	Central Environmental Authority	These regulations provide for industrial pollution control through environmental

continued on next page

Table A4.4 *continued*

S.N.	HS Code 6-digit (2007)	Description	Legislation or Regulation	Details of Regulatory Agency of Sri Lanka	Description of NTM of Sri Lanka
15	840999	Parts suitable for use solely or principally with compression-ignition internal combustion piston engines, n.e.s.	Regulations, No. 1 of 2008. Published in the Gazette of the Democratic Socialist Republic of Sri Lanka (Extraordinary) No. 1534/18 (B14, B15)		protection licensing schemes. Wastes which may cause pollution or cause noise pollution may be discharged, deposited, or emitted only under the authority of an Environmental Protection License issued by the Central Environmental Authority, and in accordance with the standards and criteria specified in Schedule I attached to these regulations. Licenses are also compulsory for any person involved in the management of scheduled waste as specified in Schedule VIII.
16	842199	Parts of machinery and apparatus for filtering or purifying liquids or gases, n.e.s.			
17	842619	Transporter or bridge cranes exported			
18	843149	Parts of machinery of headings 8426, 8429, and 8430, n.e.s.			
19	843880	Machinery for the preparation or manufacture of food or drink, n.e.s.			
20	847130	Data processing machines, automatic, portable, weighing <= 10 kilograms, consisting of at least a central processing unit, a keyboard and a display (excluding peripheral units)	Special Import License Regulations, 2013. Published in the Gazette of the Democratic Socialist Republic of Sri Lanka (Extraordinary) No. 1813/14 (A14, B14)	Department of Imports and Export Control	Products listed in Schedule I of these regulations are subject to non-automatic import licensing. Products listed in Schedule IV are prohibited to be imported into Sri Lanka. These regulations apply equally to goods originating in all countries.
21	847150	Processing units for automatic data-processing machines, whether or not containing in the same housing one or two of the following types of unit: storage units, input units, output units (excluding those of headings 8471.41 or 8471.49 and excluding peripheral units)	National Environmental (Protection and Quality) Regulations, No. 1 of 2008. Published in the Gazette of the Democratic Socialist Republic of Sri Lanka (Extraordinary) No. 1534/18 (B14, B15)	Central Environmental Authority	These regulations provide for industrial pollution control through environmental protection licensing schemes. Wastes which may cause pollution or cause noise pollution may be discharged, deposited, or emitted only under the authority of an Environmental Protection License issued by the Central Environmental Authority, and in accordance with the standards and criteria specified in Schedule I attached to these regulations. Licenses are also compulsory for any person involved in the management of scheduled waste as specified in Schedule VIII.

continued on next page

Table A4.4 continued

S.N.	HS Code 6-digit (2007)	Description	Legislation or Regulation	Details of Regulatory Agency of Sri Lanka	Description of NTM of Sri Lanka
22	847432	Machines for mixing mineral substances with bitumen	National Environmental (Protection and Quality) Regulations, No. 1 of 2008. Published in the Gazette of the Democratic Socialist Republic of Sri Lanka (Extraordinary) No. 1534/18 (B14, B15)	Central Environmental Authority	These regulations provide for industrial pollution control through environmental protection licensing schemes. Wastes which may cause pollution or cause noise pollution may be discharged, deposited, or emitted only under the authority of an Environmental Protection License issued by the Central Environmental Authority, and in accordance with the standards and criteria specified in Schedule I attached to these regulations. Licenses are also compulsory for any person involved in the management of scheduled waste as specified in Schedule VIII.
23	848180	Taps, cocks, valves and similar appliances, n.e.s.			
24	850213	Generating sets with compression-ignition internal combustion piston engines—diesel or semidiesel engines—of an output > 375 kVA exported			
25	851712	Telephones for cellular networks mobile telephones "or for other wireless networks"	Telecom-munications Ordinance (No. 67 of 1979)	Department of Imports and Export Control	A permit is needed to import any wireless telegraphy apparatus into Sri Lanka.
			National Environmental (Protection and Quality) Regulations, No. 1 of 2008. Published in the Gazette of the Democratic Socialist Republic of Sri Lanka (Extraordinary) No. 1534/18 (B14, B15)	Central Environmental Authority	These regulations provide for industrial pollution control through environmental protection licensing schemes. Wastes which may cause pollution or cause noise pollution may be discharged, deposited, or emitted only under the authority of an Environmental Protection License issued by the Central Environmental Authority, and in accordance with the standards and criteria specified in Schedule I attached to these regulations. Licenses are also compulsory for any person involved in the management of scheduled waste as specified in Schedule VIII.
			Special Import License Regulations, 2013. Published in the Gazette of	Department of Imports and Export Control	Products listed in Schedule I of these regulations are subject to non-automatic import licensing. Products listed in Schedule IV are prohibited to be imported into Sri Lanka. These regulations

continued on next page

Table A4.4 continued

S.N.	HS Code 6-digit (2007)	Description	Legislation or Regulation	Details of Regulatory Agency of Sri Lanka	Description of NTM of Sri Lanka
			the Democratic Socialist Republic of Sri Lanka (Extraordinary) No. 1813/14 (A14, B14)		apply equally to goods originating in all countries.
26	853400	Printed circuits	National Environmental (Protection and Quality) Regulations, No. 1 of 2008. Published in the Gazette of the Democratic Socialist Republic of Sri Lanka (Extraordinary) No. 1534/18 (B14, B15)	Central Environmental Authority	These regulations provide for industrial pollution control through environmental protection licensing schemes. Wastes which may cause pollution or cause noise pollution may be discharged, deposited, or emitted only under the authority of an Environmental Protection License issued by the Central Environmental Authority, and in accordance with the standards and criteria specified in Schedule I attached to these regulations. Licenses are also compulsory for any person involved in the management of scheduled waste as specified in Schedule VIII.
27	853620	Automatic circuit breakers for a voltage not exceeding 1,000 volts	Special Import License Regulations, 2013. Published in the Gazette of the Democratic Socialist Republic of Sri Lanka (Extraordinary) No. 1813/14 (A14, B14)	Department of Imports and Export Control	Products listed in Schedule I of these regulations are subject to non-automatic import licensing. Products listed in Schedule IV are prohibited to be imported into Sri Lanka. These regulations apply equally to goods originating in all countries.
28	853931	Fluorescent lamps, hot cathode			
			National Environmental (Protection and Quality) Regulations, No. 1 of 2008. Published in the Gazette of the Democratic Socialist Republic of Sri Lanka	Central Environmental Authority	These regulations provide for industrial pollution control through environmental protection licensing schemes. Wastes which may cause pollution or cause noise pollution may be discharged, deposited, or emitted only under the authority of an Environmental Protection License issued by the Central Environmental Authority, and in

continued on next page

Table A4.4 continued

S.N.	HS Code 6-digit (2007)	Description	Legislation or Regulation	Details of Regulatory Agency of Sri Lanka	Description of NTM of Sri Lanka
			(Extraordinary) No. 1534/18 (B14, B15)		accordance with the standards and criteria specified in Schedule I attached to these regulations. Licenses are also compulsory for any person involved in the management of scheduled waste as specified in Schedule VIII.
29	870322	Motor cars and other motor vehicles principally designed for the transport of persons, including station wagons and racing cars, with spark-ignition internal combustion reciprocating piston engine of a cylinder capacity > 1.000 cm³ but <= 1.500 cm³ (excluding vehicles for the transport of persons on snow and other specially designed vehicles of subheading 8703.10)	Motor Traffic (Amendment) Act (No. 08 of 2009) (B14)	Department of Motor Traffic	A permit is needed to import motor vehicles into Sri Lanka
			National Environmental (Protection and Quality) Regulations, No. 1 of 2008. Published in the Gazette of the Democratic Socialist Republic of Sri Lanka (Extraordinary) No. 1534/18 (B14, B15)	Central Environmental Authority	These regulations provide for industrial pollution control through environmental protection licensing schemes. Wastes which may cause pollution or cause noise pollution may be discharged, deposited, or emitted only under the authority of an Environmental Protection License issued by the Central Environmental Authority, and in accordance with the standards and criteria specified in Schedule I attached to these regulations. Licenses are also compulsory for any person involved in the management of scheduled waste as specified in Schedule VIII.
			National Environmental (Air, Fuel and Vehicle Importation Standards) Regulations (No. 01 of 2003) (B7, B83)	Central Environmental Authority	These regulations provide for the allowed vehicular exhaust emission limits for every motor vehicle in use in Sri Lanka, including imported vehicles. No person shall import a motor vehicle that discharges exhaust emissions into the atmosphere in excess of the Vehicular Emission Standards set in Schedule III. Importers must produce a compliance certificate of Vehicular Exhaust Emission Standards for every motor vehicle imported, issued by a manufacturer or a vehicle emission testing center authorized by the Government of the exporting country

continued on next page

Table A4.4 continued

S.N.	HS Code 6-digit (2007)	Description	Legislation or Regulation	Details of Regulatory Agency of Sri Lanka	Description of NTM of Sri Lanka
30	870323	Motor cars and other motor vehicles principally designed for the transport of persons, including station wagons and racing cars, with spark-ignition internal combustion reciprocating piston engine of a cylinder capacity > 1.500 cm³ but <= 3.000 cm³ (excluding vehicles for the transport of persons on snow and other specially designed vehicles of subheading 8703.10)	Motor Traffic (Amendment) Act (No. 08 of 2009) (B14)	Department of Motor Traffic	A permit is needed to import motor vehicles into Sri Lanka.
			National Environmental (Protection and Quality) Regulations, No. 1 of 2008. Published in the Gazette of the Democratic Socialist Republic of Sri Lanka (Extraordinary) No. 1534/18 (B14, B15)	Central Environmental Authority	These regulations provide for industrial pollution control through environmental protection licensing schemes. Wastes which may cause pollution or cause noise pollution may be discharged, deposited, or emitted only under the authority of an Environmental Protection License issued by the Central Environmental Authority, and in accordance with the standards and criteria specified in Schedule I attached to these regulations. Licenses are also compulsory for any person involved in the management of scheduled waste as specified in Schedule VIII.
			National Environmental (Air, Fuel and Vehicle Importation Standards) Regulations (No. 01 of 2003) (B7, B83)	Central Environmental Authority	These regulations provide for the allowed vehicular exhaust emission limits for every motor vehicle in use in Sri Lanka, including imported vehicles. No person shall import a motor vehicle that discharges exhaust emissions into the atmosphere in excess of the Vehicular Emission Standards set in Schedule III. Importers must produce a compliance certificate of Vehicular Exhaust Emission Standards for every motor vehicle imported, issued by a manufacturer or a vehicle emission testing center authorized by the Government of the exporting country.
31	870332	Motor cars and other motor vehicles principally designed for the transport of persons, including station wagons and racing cars, with compression-ignition internal combustion piston engines of a cylinder	Special Import License Regulations, 2013. Published in the Gazette of the Democratic Socialist	Department of Imports and Export Control	Products listed in Schedule I of these regulations are subject to non-automatic import licensing. Products listed in Schedule IV are prohibited to be imported into Sri Lanka. These regulations apply equally to goods originating in all countries.

continued on next page

Table A4.4 continued

S.N.	HS Code 6-digit (2007)	Description	Legislation or Regulation	Details of Regulatory Agency of Sri Lanka	Description of NTM of Sri Lanka
		capacity > 1.500 cm³ but <= 2.500 cm³ (excluding vehicles for the transport of persons on snow and other specially designed vehicles of subheading 8703.10)	Republic of Sri Lanka (Extraordinary) No. 1813/14 (A14, B14)		
32	870333	Motor cars and other motor vehicles principally designed for the transport of persons, including station wagons and racing cars, with compression-ignition internal combustion piston engines of a cylinder capacity > 2.500 cm³ (excluding vehicles for the transport of persons on snow and other specially designed vehicles of subheading 8703,10)			
33	870870	Wheels including parts and accessories for motor vehicles	National Environmental (Protection and Quality) Regulations, No. 1 of 2008. Published in the Gazette of the Democratic Socialist Republic of Sri Lanka (Extraordinary) No. 1534/18 (B14, B15)	Central Environmental Authority	These regulations provide for industrial pollution control through environmental protection licensing schemes. Wastes which may cause pollution or cause noise pollution may be discharged, deposited, or emitted only under the authority of an Environmental Protection License issued by the Central Environmental Authority, and in accordance with the standards and criteria specified in Schedule I attached to these regulations. Licenses are also compulsory for any person involved in the management of scheduled waste as specified in Schedule VIII.
			Special Import License Regulations, 2013. Published in the Gazette of the Democratic Socialist Republic of Sri Lanka (Extraordinary) No. 1813/14 (A14, B14)	Department of Imports and Export Control	Products listed in Schedule I of these regulations are subject to non-automatic import licensing. Products listed in Schedule IV are prohibited to be imported into Sri Lanka. These regulations apply equally to goods originating in all countries.

continued on next page

Table A4.4 continued

S.N.	HS Code 6-digit (2007)	Description	Legislation or Regulation	Details of Regulatory Agency of Sri Lanka	Description of NTM of Sri Lanka
34	901890	Instruments and appliances used in medical, surgical, dental, or veterinary sciences, n.e.s.	National Environmental (Protection and Quality) Regulations, No. 1 of 2008. Published in the Gazette of the Democratic Socialist Republic of Sri Lanka (Extraordinary) No. 1534/18 (B14, B15)	Central Environmental Authority	These regulations provide for industrial pollution control through environmental protection licensing schemes. Wastes which may cause pollution or cause noise pollution may be discharged, deposited, or emitted only under the authority of an Environmental Protection License issued by the Central Environmental Authority, and in accordance with the standards and criteria specified in Schedule I attached to these regulations. Licenses are also compulsory for any person involved in the management of scheduled waste as specified in Schedule VIII.

HS = Harmonized Commodity Description and Coding System, n.e.s. = not elsewhere specified, NTM = nontariff measure, S.N. = serial number.

Source: Asian Development Bank, compiled from information available in MAcMap database.

Appendix 5
Stakeholders Interviewed for Sanitary and Phytosanitary and Technical Barriers to Trade India Diagnostic Study

Stakeholders from New Delhi Field Survey

Name of Stakeholder	Designation	Affiliation	In Person or Via Telephone
Anil Jauhri	Chief executive officer	National Accreditation Board for Certification Bodies	In person
Anil Kumar	Advisor, Standards	Food Safety and Standards Authority of India	In person
J. R. Chaudhary	Scientist-F	Bureau of Indian Standards	In person
Murali Kallummal	Professor	Center for World Trade Organization Studies	In person
Parmod Siwach	Assistant director (Technician)	Export Inspection Council of India	In person
Ram Singh	Professor	Indian Institute of Foreign Trade	In person
V. K. Vidyarthi	General manager	Agricultural and Processed Food Products Export Development Authority	In person
Pratik Navle	Researcher, India Trade Portal	Indian Export Organization	In person

Source: Asian Development Bank field survey, New Delhi.

Stakeholders from Mumbai Field Survey

Name of Stakeholder	Designation	Affiliation	In Person or via Telephone	Engaged in
Abhay Chaudhari	Country managing director	Praj Industry, Pune	Telephone (9890400589)	Merchant exporter
Anil Vijitkar	--	Andheri, Mumbai	Telephone (9820222481)	Exporter
Ganesh Karandikar	Deputy manager	ATC Global Logistics Pvt. Ltd., Belapur – Navi Mumbai	In person	Customs clearance work
Jose	Technocraft	Andheri, Mumbai	In person	Exporter
Nilesh Desai	--	Kirloskar Pneumatic Co. Ltd., Pune	Telephone (9850810456)	Exports to Thailand
Paresh C. Shah	Customs House Agent	RPS Logistic, Chembur, Mumbai	In person	Exports of chemicals to Bangladesh
Sandeep Patil	Manager, Export Division	Parle Agro Pvt. Ltd., Andheri, Mumbai	In person	Exports to Gulf countries, Canada, and some South Asian countries (except South Asia Subregional Economic Cooperation countries)
Shikhar Biswas	Deputy general manager	Mahindra and Mahindra Ltd., Kandivali, Mumbai	In person	Exports tractors and other vehicles to Bangladesh, Nepal, and Sri Lanka
Soni Hazari	Group owner	Shosova Group Chennai	Telephone	Exports food products to Sri Lanka
T. P. Balakrishnan	Export manager	Jyoti Steel Industries, Bandra – Mumbai	In person	Exports steel items (semi-finished) to South Asian Association for Regional Cooperation, South America, Latin America, and some Southeast countries
Sandip Parab	Representative	Unique Shipping Service (Logistics with a difference)	In person	Clearance and forwarding business
Deepak Kumar	Chairman	Deepak Fertilisers and Petrochemicals Corporation Ltd., Mumbai	Telephone (9930320579)	Exports fertilizers to Sri Lanka
Prakash Kumar	Group owner	Parakh Agro Industries Ltd., Pune	Telephone	Exports fast moving consumer goods (FMCG)
Harshad Chheda	Customs House Agent	Aarti Industries	In person	Exports to South Asia and East Asia
Ravi	Manager	Stelmach Ltd	In person	Exports to Bangladesh

S.N. = serial number.
Source: Asian Development Bank field survey, Mumbai.

References

ADB. 2008. *Quantification of South Asian Trade Benefits*. Asian Development Bank.

Banga, R. 2016. India's Global Value Chains: Integrating LDCs. Commonwealth Trade Express. No. 4. Commonwealth Secretariat. London. http://dx.doi.org/10.14217/5jlsjckjvvmx-en.

Bangladesh Food Safety. 2017. Contaminants, Toxins, and Harmful Residues. Regulations). http://www.bfsa.gov.bd/index.php/law-justice.

———. 2017B. Labeling Regulations. http://www.bfsa.gov.bd/index.php/law-justice.

Bangladesh Food Safety Authority. 2017. *Extraordinary Gazette of Bangladesh*. 9 May 2017. http://www.bfsa.gov.bd/index.php/law-justice.

Bangladesh Motor Vehicles Ordinance. 1983. http://www.brta.gov.bd/newsite/en/motor-vehicle-ordinance-1983-modified-upto-29th-november-1990-ordinance-no-lv-of-1983/.

Bangladesh Standards and Testing Institution (BSTI) Ordinance. 1985. http://bsti.portal.gov.bd/sites/default/files/files/bsti.portal.gov.bd/page/0cdb608c_c6e3_42b8_9271_610e5bfbf7c9/1.%20The%20Bangladesh%20Standards%20and%20Testing%20Institution%20Ordinance,%201985%20(Ordinance%20No.%20xxxvii%20of%201985)(2).pdf.

Central Motor Vehicles Rules of India. 1989. http://www.tn.gov.in/sta/Cmvr1989.pdf.

Center for WTO Studies. 2012. *Trade Policies and Institutions*. http://wtocentre.iift.ac.in/FA/INDIA.pdf.

Cosmetic Device and Drug Act. 1980. *Extraordinary Gazette, Democratic Socialist Republic of Sri Lanka.* 2 December 1985. http://apps.who.int/medicinedocs/documents/s17094e/s17094e.pdf.

CUTS International and Center for the Analysis of Regional Integration. 2012. *International Qualitative analysis of a potential Free Trade Agreement between the European Union and India.*

Das, K. 2008. *Addressing SPS Challenges in India.* Working Paper. Center for WTO Studies.

De, P. 2016. *Measuring NTM Restrictiveness in South Asia. South Asian Network on Economic Modeling.*

Drug (Control) Ordinance. 1982. *Extraordinary Gazette, People's Republic of Bangladesh.* 12 June 1982. http://www.mohfw.gov.bd/index.php?option=com_docman&task=doc _download&gid=11491&lang=en.

Food Safety and Standards Act, 2006, No. 34 of 2006. Ministry of Health and Family Welfare, Government of India. https://fssai.gov.in/cms/food-safety-and-standards -act-2006.php

Food (Labeling and Advertising) Regulations. 2005. *Extraordinary Gazette, Democratic Socialist Republic of Sri Lanka.* 19 January 2005. http://203.94.76.60/FOODWEB/files/ regulations/current/food_(labelling_and_advertising)_regulations_2005.pdf.

Food Safety and Standards (Contaminants, Toxins and Residues) Regulations. 2011. http:// fssai.gov.in/dam/jcr:755c6420-a74b-44f4-9301-4ddd289b23fc/Contaminants _Regulations.pdf.

Food Safety and Standards (Food Products Standards and Food Additives) Regulations. 2011. http://fssai.gov.in/dam/jcr:99067191-c774-4c81-b9c8-708b9e72b770/Food _Additives_Regulations.pdf.

Food Safety and Standards (Import) Regulation. 2017. http://fssai.gov.in/dam/jcr:2eae2ab1 -96fe-4968-8c9b-6533991ef9ca/Food_Import_Regulations.pdf.

Food Safety and Standards (Laboratory and Sample Analysis) Regulations. 2011. http:// fssai.gov.in/dam/jcr:c66a53f5-b799-4177-865b-01d74145495a/Lab_Sample _Regulations.pdf.

Food Safety and Standards (Packaging and Labeling) Regulations. 2011. http://fssai.gov .in/dam/jcr:2d48f646-d9f9-4bc1-af03-493f29cc45a9/Packaging_Labelling _Regulations.pdf.

Henson, S. J. 2012. *Impact of Sanitary and Phytosanitary Measures on Developing Countries.* Report of Department of Agricultural and Food Economics of University of Reading.

International Trade Center (ITC), Physikalisch – Technische Bundesanstalt (PTB), and Federation of Nepalese Chambers of Commerce and Industry (FNCCI). 2016. *Managing Quality in Nepal: A Directory of Services for SMEs.* 2016. http://www.intracen. org/publication/Managing-Quality-in-Nepal-A-directory-of-services-for-SMEs1/.

ISEC. 2015. *Non-Tariff Barriers under Free Trade Agreement – A Study on India and Sri Lanka.* Institute for Social and Economic Change.

Jairath, M. S., and P. Purohit. 2013. Food Safety Regulatory Compliance in India: A Challenge to Enhance Agri-Businesses. *Indian Journal of Agriculture Economics.* 68 (3).

Kallummal, M. 2012. *SPS Measures and Possible Market Access Implications for Agricultural Trade in the Doha Round: An Analysis of Systemic Issues.* ARTNeT Working Paper. No. 116. July. Bangkok. ESCAP.

———. 2016. *SPS Agreement India's Legal and Institutional Capacity.* Center for WTO Studies. New Delhi.

Kaul, R. 2016. *WTO Agreement on the Application of Sanitary and Phytosanitary Measures and the Indian Experience.*

Ministry of Surface Transport (Transport Wing) 1996. *Extraordinary Gazette of India.* 18 October 1996. http://tis.nhai.gov.in/Admin/pdf/2301201732PM04_9567.pdf.

Maldives Food and Drug Authority. 2017. *National Food Safety Policy, 2017–2026.* Ministry of Health. http://www.health.gov.mv/Uploads/Downloads//Informations/Informations(69).pdf.

Mukherji, N. I., and K. Iyengar. 2013. *Deepening Economic Cooperation between India and Sri Lanka.* Asian Development Bank.

Nanda, N. 2012. *Agricultural Trade in South Asia: Barriers and Prospects.* SAWTEE Working Paper No. 03/12.

New National Drug Policy. 2005. *Extraordinary Gazette, People's Republic of Bangladesh.* Ministry of Health and Family Welfare, Government of People's Republic of Bangladesh. 5 May 2005. http://apps.who.int/medicinedocs/documents/s17825en/s17825en.pdf.

Ojha, P. 2013. *Addressing the Challenges of Non-Tariff Barriers in South Asia.*

Prasai, S. 2015. *Mapping Barriers in South Asia.* Asian Foundation.

Raihan, S. 2012. *Non-Tariff Barriers Facing South Asia: Case of Bangladesh.*

Raihan, S., M. A. Khan, and S. Quoreshi. 2014. *NTMs in South Asia: Assessment and Analysis.* SAARC–TPN.

Reddy, S.B.S. 2006. *Policy Brief on SPS and TBT Measures–India's Concerns.* Regional Trade Policy Course. Hong Kong, China.

Singh, H. 2016. *Trade Policy Reforms in India since 1991.* Brooking India.

Special Import License Regulations. 2013. *Extraordinary Gazette, Democratic Socialist Republic of Sri Lanka.* 5 June 2013. http://www.imexport.gov.lk/web/images/PDF_upload/Gazettes/english/1813-14_e.pdf.

UNCTAD. 2012. International Classification of Non-Tariff Measures.

UN Comtrade. 2016. *World Integrated Trade Solutions.*

Weerahewa. 2009. *Impact of Trade Facilitation Measures and Regional Trade Agreements on Food and Agricultural Trade in South Asia.* Asia-Pacific Research and Training Network on Trade Working Paper Series, No. 69.

Yang, H. 2017. *Food Safety in India: Status and Challenges.* Tata Cornell Institute. https://agriknowledge.org/downloads/th83kz33c.

Websites:

Bangladesh Food Safety Authority. http://www.bfsa.gov.bd/.

Bangladesh Standards and Testing Institution. http://bsti.portal.gov.bd/.

Bhutan Agriculture and Food Regulatory Authority (BAFRA). http://www.bafra.gov.bt/.

Bhutan Standards Bureau (BSB). http://www.bsb.gov.bt/.

Bureau of Indian Standards. http://www.bis.gov.in/.

Export Inspection Council of India. http://www.eicindia.gov.in/.

Government Information Center, Democratic Republic of Sri Lanka. http://www.gic.gov.lk/gic/index.php?lang=en.

www.ingramcontent.com/pod-product-compliance
Lightning Source LLC
Chambersburg PA
CBHW050042220326
41599CB00045B/7259